Spanish-Language Newspapers in New Mexico, 1834–1958

Spanish-Language Newspapers in New Mexico, 1834–1958

A. Gabriel Meléndez

The University of Arizona Press
Tucson

The University of Arizona Press

First University of Arizona Press paperbound printing 2005

∞ This book is printed on acid-free, archival-quality paper.
Manufactured in the United States of America

10 09 08 07 06 05 6 5 4 3 2 1

ISBN 0-8165-2472-6
Library of Congress Control Number 2004111783

Originally published as *So All Is Not Lost: The Poetics of Print in Nuevomexicano Communities, 1834–1958,* by the University of New Mexico Press, Albuquerque, N.M.

Para Cristina:
sin ella, los caminos
a ninguna parte conducen.
Para Alejandro,
y para Cheo, que viene a estarse un tiempo con nosotros:
para que sepan de las obras
de sus antepasados en
caminos que nos trajeron hasta aquí.
Finalmente, para que no todo permanezca relegado al olvido.

For Cristina:
Without her, roads lead nowhere.
For Alejandro,
and for Cheo, who is coming to stay with us a while:
so that they may
know of the work of
their antepasados *upon the roads that have*
brought us all here.
Finally, so all does not remain lost.

Contents

List of Illustrations

Acknowledgments

The impetus for this book comes from both the intellect and the heart. A number of guides and confidants have nurtured these twin dimensions of my work along the road to publication. I count as my good fortune the several mentors and many colleagues who have entered my life at various points and whose influence and boundless generosity have enriched my mental, intellectual, and spiritual journey. Those who encouraged me at an earlier time are Mario Cavallari, Ronald Coleman, Eduardo Elías, Tamara Holzaphel, Angel González, Clark Knowlton, Enrique Lamadrid Sr., Estella Martínez, María Sandoval, Elizabeth Siekhaus, Luis Torres, Sabine Ulibarrí, Marta Weigle, Enrique R. Lamadrid, and Tomás Ybarra-Frausto. Their support has guarded against the threat that this work might wither, and their counsel has infused it with the substance and consequence of intellectual and scholarly inquiry.

I am indebted to Anselmo Arellano for pointing the way with his pioneering work in nineteenth century New Mexican newspapers and for his generosity in sharing his encyclopedic knowledge of *Nuevomexicano* history with me. Thanks to my colleague, Phillip Gonzales, at the University of New Mexico, for his thorough critique of an early version of my monograph. Genaro Padilla and Erlinda Gonzales-Berry, editors of the *Pasó Por Aquí Series*, have offered inspiration, support, and encouragement at each stage of my research and writing. I wish to thank María Teresa Marquez not only for her friendship and steadfast support, but also for bringing Chicano and Chicana scholars together through CHICLE, and by that most modern "circuit of communication," the internet.

Several grants and fellowships have allowed me to pursue my archival research over the last five years. Among the institutional support I have received, the academic year (1991-92) I spent as a Rockefeller Humanities Fellow at the Southwest Hispanic Research Institute at the University of New Mexico stands as a high point. My thanks go to José Rivera, then director of SHRI, and to his staff for making my residency both productive and enjoyable. Institutional assistance has also come from Tobías Durán and the Center for Regional Studies at University of New Mexico and from Nicolás Kanellos and the *Recovering the U.S. Literary Heritage Project* at the University of Houston. Grants from these programs made it possible to employ Eva Gallegos, Patricia Sánchez-Flavian, and Vicky Longoria as research assistants. Their work saved me countless hours in the indexing and cataloguing of materials extracted from newspaper microfilm collections. I am grateful for the conversations and exchanges I have had with my faculty associates at Southwest Hispanic Research Institute. Among this group, the occasional inquiries as to the progress of my work has been of inestimable value, for these have prompted me forward even as I would have much rather tarried a while more. I am in debt to my colleagues in the department of American Studies: Vera Norwood, Charles Biebel, Jane Caputi, Ruth Salvaggio, Jane Young, Gerald Davis, and James Treat. I thank each of them for the honesty and the passion they exhibit in their work and for respecting the requirements of my intellectual pursuits. A note of thanks to Felix Gutiérrez, Clara Lomas, and Ramón Gutiérrez for taking time to read my study in manuscript form. Their criticism and commentary provided me incisive feedback that dispelled the weariness which comes from the isolation of writing and research. I want to express my great appreciation to my editor, Andrea Otañez at UNM Press, for going the first and last mile to prepare this manuscript for publication.

At its earliest source, the intellect and the heart that drive my work are infused by memory and the need to account for certain aspects of the personal and collective experience of my community not chronicled elsewhere. My gratitude, thus extends to my mother, Adela Valdez Meléndez, and my father, Manuel Santos Meléndez (both deceased), first for holding their family together against all that would undo it, and second, for having left me an enduring presence of the *periodiquero* generation in the form of a copy of José Fernández's 1911 biography of Casimiro Barela, *Cuarenta años de legislador, o la vida de Casimiro Barela.* Substantiating the value of this text as a cultural representation of a generation of New Mexicans has also been about connecting its significance to the praise my father often directed to members of that generation: *Tenían el don de la palabra.* [They possessed the gift of the word.] My thanks extends as well to Lucy M. Lucero, Elba C. de Baca. John Phillip Sosa, Herminia Chacón González, Walter Archuleta, and Pedro Ribera-Ortega for sharing their memories and personal papers with me. As the guardians of family histories their vivid recollections add flesh to the gift of the word as it was manifest in the works and deeds of their own forebears. Months and years of research have made these connections real and substantial for me, and I trust I have made their importance clear for my readers as well. My own family has been a key element in completing this book. My thanks to Cristina and Alejandro for their love and optimism; my thanks to the members of my extended family for the expressions of support over the years. I hope my work has done justice in according a place to the cultural production left by the subjects of my study and adds to the growing scholarship on *Nuevomexicano* culture studies and letters.

Spanish-Language Newspapers in New Mexico, 1834–1958

Introduction

I began this study of Spanish-language journalism as an archival recovery project to glean literary texts from Spanish-language newspapers published by Mexican Americans in New Mexico during the late territorial and early statehood period. It was to be a simple matter of unearthing texts, lifting them out of the vagaries of their time and their production to present them anew. But that intent soon gave way as my work turned to explaining the desire of Mexican Americans during this time to use their presses to voice sociohistorical concerns and to represent themselves as a determinant group of communities in Nuevo México—a particularly resilient corner of the Chicano homeland. After weeks and months of surveying newspapers published a century ago, I realized that the texts I encountered were not simply literary gems to be gouged out of prosaic tracks of news and information of incidental value to Chicano cultural historians. To examine these texts in isolation severed them from the discourse that supplies them with their ultimate meaning.

Each time the blank space of an item clipped from a newspaper appeared, I was reminded of the effects of dislodging the stone, as the blank form threatened to pull me through its frame into a chasm of silent space. Thus my expectation was left wanting: What text had been lifted, by whom, and why? What factors explain its publication in the first place?

Having been brought up in northern New Mexico, I knew that many of the missing texts had gone to the readers of these newspapers and that they were treasured and shared. Cut from newspapers were *poemas*, *canciones*, *corridos*, *oraciones*, and other textual reliquiae that form the touchstones of a system of shared cultural belief and signification in *nativo* communities. Often the texts were abraded of newsprint as they passed from hand to hand and from one generation to the next. At other times they were consigned to memory in the manner described to me by one *anciano:*

> I grabbed on to these stories because in those days my father . . . he used to get newspapers, you see. He took *El Faro*, he took [papers] from Juárez, he took [papers] from around here . . . *El Nuevo Mexicano*. Each time a story appeared, I cut it out and saved it, cut it out and saved it. . . . And my mind would save it and seems they are not forgotten. We'll see.[1]

When I set off to find out about *Nuevomexicano* editors and writers in the sanctioned literary and cultural histories of the Southwest, I discovered that, other than a few brief and labored acknowledgments of the work of Padre Antonio José Martínez and his Taos press, their work had not been chronicled. There were no surveys, indexes, biographical profiles, not even a timeline attesting to the chronology and duration of Spanish-language newspapers founded by a generation of *periodiqueros* [newspaper journalists]. The entire matter of Spanish-language publication having been consigned to archival dungeons has insured the erasure of a good measure of Mexican-American social history in the nineteenth century. The excision of this textual and cultural production leaves only the negative space of historical misrepresentation, cultural disfigurement, and dislocation from which the bare-boned sociocultural history of Chicanos in *Nuevo México* emerges. As this became clear to me, the scope of my project grew to include the matter of documenting the sequential record of Spanish-language publication beginning with the arrival of the first press in the region in 1834.

Overwhelmed by the volume materials in these newspapers, I have struggled with the need to provide interpretative and analytical readings of the writings they contain while bringing forth bibliobiographical detail about authors, editors, and the readers of these texts. For it seems to me that knowing who authored the piece, who published it, who read it and with what end in mind is as important as knowing the content of a given text. Genaro Padilla sees this challenge as central to the full understanding of nineteenth-century writings by Mexican Americans. Describing such efforts as the "first-phase recovery of a rich literary discourse" (1993, xi), Padilla argues for the need to reconcile each stage of the research process to fully demonstrate the importance of such writings.

While my work has also become a matter of describing the multifaceted aspects of print discourse within the Mexican-American community of a hundred years ago, I am aware of the number of sources that inform that discourse. The shear volume of *Mexicano* print discourse in the Southwest requires differentiation by region and time period, for it is obvious that in an area as large as the Southwest, Spanish-language print discourse developed at different times, at different places, and with differing purpose. There is the case of the *Tejano* press, whose roots in the Spanish viceroyalty of Nuevo Santander eventually spread with the issuance of the Nacogdoches papers,

La Gaceta and *El Mexicano* in 1813 (Gutiérrez 1978, 32). The first press in California, owned and operated by Agustín Zamorano, began publication in Monterey in 1834. Its appearance inspired other *californios* to use the press as a tool of literacy, and there is record of papers being published up and down the state throughout the second half of the nineteenth century: *La Crónica* (San Francisco, 1855), *El Clamor Público* (Los Angeles, 1855), and *La Gaceta* (Santa Barbara, 1879) (Gutiérrez, Leal). Likewise, Mexican newspapers in border towns like Ciudad Juárez, Nuevo Laredo, and Matamoros form the dialogical counterpart to Spanish-language publication in the Southwest. *Canjes* [newspaper exchanges] in northern Mexico provided timely transfers of cultural capital to Spanish-language papers "on this side of the Bravo" in formative years. To these developments, swathed in distinct sociohistorical contexts, should be added the work of Mexican exiled publishers early in this century. Particularly important in this regard is the work of Ignacio Lozano, who established *La Prensa* in San Antonio in 1913 and *La Opinión* in Los Angeles in 1926 (Kanellos).

I have elected to center a discussion of print discourse in New Mexico and adjacent areas not only because I am *un chicano del norte*, but because the distinctive characteristics of this discourse are so marked that they demand specific treatment. The New Mexican case is characterized by a localized pattern of development that precedes, and for a variety of reasons, survives the blow of the American conquest. From its beginning in Santa Fe the *Nuevomexicano* press extended its influence to neighboring regions, linking itself to parallel developments in northern Mexico, West Texas, southern Arizona, and southern Colorado. Critically important is that within this production one finds major efforts to forge a cultural and literary movement to contest the dehistorization of the *Mexicano* culture in the Southwest, a feature which marks it as a precursive movement in Mexican-American letters and intellectual formation. And while that movement may not correspond point for point to the ideological panoply of contemporary Chicano socioliterary production, it nonetheless is surprisingly similar at its core, where it evinces all the dynamism of a mass movement meant to assert a powerful validation of Mexican-American cultural practices.

The Poetics of Print Among *Nuevomexicanos*

The acquisition of the press by Padre Martínez and others in New Mexico in 1834 pushed what had been essentially a residual oral and manuscript culture (Ong 1989) toward the development of a complex system of communication based on the production and distribution of multiple copies of written material. The hallmark of a "culture of print" is precisely that it involves individuals beside the author in the production of printed materials (Ong 1989). Print discourse as it emerges from the journalistic activity of New Mexico's

Spanish-speaking populace is framed by its intellectual/cultural purpose. It is this interrelated sphere of activity, involving the producers of print (authors, editors, correspondents, printers) and a community of readers, that is of interest to me, since it is clear that a culture of print is animated by the consonance of thought and the orchestration of initiatives, which in Robert Darnton's view forms the "communications circuit" of print discourse.

In regions that Walter Ong describes as "preserving massive residual orality" (Ong 1989)—an apt characterization of New Mexico in the nineteenth century—the viewpoint of the group often resides with its bards, its orators, its *ancianos*. In them one finds those agents of culture authorized by tradition to speak in the name of the group. Prior to the introduction of the press, *Nuevomexicanos* relied heavily on these cultural guardians to transmit and validate their society's cultural epistemology. Known variously to the community as *bardos, trobadores, oradores* (bards, troubadours, orators), they expressed a distilled knowledge of the past through speech forms grounded in a tradition of oral poetics, oratory, and rhetoric.

Nuevomexicano newspapers induced a shift from an oral/manuscript paradigm toward general literacy, and information exchange through print. The shift from orality to print involved the emergence of other agents of cultural expression. Cultural voicing widened to include written composition, a development that is not without its consequences, for as Ong notes, "This gives thought different contours from those of orally sustained thought" (Ong 1989, 96). Likewise, authority to voice the experience of the group extended itself to include individuals educated and trained as journalists. Partaking of *el don de la palabra impresa* (the gift of the printed word) molded native editors into an identifiable cultural force. As literates (biliterates in reality), *los periodiqueros* channeled the ethnopoetics of their region into print discourse for the first time. The backdrop of orality, what Ong calls "residual orality," echoes in the work of *los periodiqueros,* who relied heavily on the modes of expression of their *antepasados.*

Popular and literary journalism in the Southwest was the result of the unprecedented transformation of the region, a key point being that print culture in Mexican-origin communities in the Southwest remained an expression of opposition to Anglo-American political, social, and cultural hegemony in the Southwest after 1848. And the volume of that resistance is impressive. From 1880 to 1935 more than 190 newspapers were founded in over thirty communities in New Mexico, Colorado, Arizona, and Texas.

By numbers alone, the establishment of newspapers under the guidance of native-born editors constitutes irrefutable evidence that print culture shaped and influenced *Mexicano* communities in important ways. When viewed as textual artifacts, these early newspapers resemble historical tracts, and they remain visually responsive texts in the manner that the broadside or the posted notice communicates the urgency of its publication. Unlike modern day counterparts, whose raison d'être is to log the daily record of events in the life of a particular community or region, there is an immediacy in Spanish-language papers that speaks of the urgency of their purpose and intent.

The multiple functions of *Mexicano* newspaper presses resulted in the production of "culture bearing" documentation wherein are found cultural projections of every kind in prose, poetry, and the editorial essay. Newspapers became the principal means for *Nuevomexicanos* to tap the wellspring of their Indo-Hispano literary and expressive sensibility and share it publicly via the printed word. Newspaper publication stimulated public debate and gave voice to the overriding concerns of the period. In essence, newspaper publication released the creative impulse of *Mexicano* thought in the U.S. Southwest.

The impact of this journalism is important on a number of cultural and historical levels that have not figured in discussions of the period. For one thing, it opens up a space for a generation of *Mexicanos* to enter the professions through *periodismo cultural.* Drawing strength from intellectual activity and social activism, the movement posited language as a principal tool in the struggle for cultural survival. Spanish was promoted in a public forum. Its literary and artistic use was displayed in the publication of local and regional authors, along with the writers and thinkers of the broader Spanish-speaking world.

Spanish-language newspaper publication in the Southwest represents a gradual, though never absolute, transition from oral to print culture. Newspaper publication progressed sequentially from the initial introduction of the printing press to the point where the widespread use of the press among *Mexicanos* qualifies as a discursive culture, subordinate but resilient to the effects of internal colonialism (Barrera, 1979), social antagonism, and historical erasure. The movement is marked by notions of ascendancy, confidence, and self-evidential displays of educational attainment.

The cultural program of most newspapers was consigned to two major objectives. First, Mexican-American editors worked toward the development of an autonomous literary tradition among *nativos:* a corpus of writings they self-styled as *una literatura nacional* (a national literature). A form of cultural regionalism, *una literatura nacional* became a way to voice the reality of Mexican Americans within the framework of the U.S. body politic. A naive position, perhaps, but one that by its very proposition challenged the miosis and ethnocentrism of monolithic Anglo hegemonic cultural perspectives in the nineteenth century. Second, this generation called for the publication of *nativo* history to correct misrepresentations propagated by writers from outside of that community. That history, they argued, should stand against Anglo-American ideations of the region. That this work should suggest itself to this generation of cultural activists is not, in and of itself, extraordinary. What is novel is that this generation did not relinquish its cultural ambitions easily. To the contrary, it began to offer self-reflexive commentary and a critical assessment on how to arrive at intellectually liberating sites of opposition and contestation. These formulations of cultural emancipation should be seen as the precursive period of intellectual and social activism that predate the Chicano movement of the 1960s.

The new understanding of a genesis for Chicano letters aside, *Chicano/a* theorists continue to hold to various positions regarding the ideological foundations of Chicano literature and the poetics of its formation. Among the most assertive critical postulations is the interpretive analysis provided by Ramón Saldívar, who considers the ideological parentage of contemporary Chicano narratives to be rooted in the folk-based oral performance of the border ballad or *corrido.* In Saldívar's view, the *corrido* is a "residual cultural force" that becomes transfigured in the work of subsequent generations of Mexican-American writers (Saldívar 1990, 41).

If one focuses attention on the genealogy and transmission of "resistance literature," new theoretical considerations must likewise follow, if only because *periodiqueros* attended with great respect to the publication of compositions by local *trovadores* and *corridistas.* In many instances, the editors of important publications maintained a standing in the verbal arts as *corridistas* or *bardos* and offered their own compositions for publication. All of which lends credence to Ong's supposition that performance-based narrative traditions "develop on the edge of orality" (Ong 1989), that is, in conjunction with the broadside and other author-composed texts. In *Mexicano* communities in the nineteenth century one finds the oral rendition of *cuentos, corridos,* and *dichos* enmeshed in a much larger set of inter- and metatextual relationships located at the interstices of print culture as represented by Spanish-language newspaper publication. This being so, one must then ask to what degree did the publication of what had been performance-based *corridos* and other narrative-compositions assist, aid, or otherwise prolong the vitality of these texts, thus creating subsequent renditions, and by extension, reinforcing *Mexicano* cultural and political identity across generations?

It is my contention that the call for poetic and artistic autonomy among *Mexicanos* in the United States took residence and was proclaimed stridently in New Mexico nearly a century ago. That such acts have not been acknowledged in our own time underscores Francisco Lomelí's assertion that "like the tip of the iceberg, the year 1965 represents a larger and unknown body of artistic activity that had been ignored—one of the best kept secrets of the Southwest for 120 years" (Lomelí 1984, 105).

In Light of Cultural and Social Excision

In addressing the absence that characterizes much of nineteenth-century Mexican-American social and cultural history, I distinguish between willful and accidental acts of occlusion. In some instances the fragility of newsprint itself is to be blamed, in others it is the will to exclude the past of the conquered by the conqueror that is responsible for such omission. The actions of the pen-knife wielding harvester of *versos* of a century ago is certainly distinct from the force of Anglo-American hegemony directed at erasing and undoing the work of a *nativo* press. Where one act mares the record, the other obliterates it.

Cultural hegemony has the additional effect of producing parallel versions of literary history as well. Anglo-American writings receive official acknowledgment while those of Hispanic writers are subjected to historical erasure (Lomelí 1987, 16). If the purpose and program of most Spanish-language newspapers is fixed by cultural conflict, the agency of their editors is set toward attaining standing in the politically and socially antagonistic climate resulting from the U.S. takeover of the Southwest. Such development suggests that journalism actuates a literary and cultural movement precisely at a moment of deep political, economic, and cultural concern over the future of *Nuevomexicano* communities.

Anglo-Americans seemed self-assured in the notion that within a generation or so, Mexican cultural forms would yield and give way to their own. One Anglo-American observer in New Mexico all too wistfully proclaimed in 1899, a "still sharper contrast—the real American incursion, with its railroads, its barbed-wire fences, and its public schools. And the Greaser is passing. It is now quite in order to write his obituary" (*Atlantic Monthly* 1899, 753).

The damaging effects of this maneuvering was evident within a few short years after the arrival of the *Americanos,* and the subject was broached repeatedly in countless essays and other writings in columns of Spanish-language newspapers across the territory. *Nuevomexicano* editors time and time again denounced policies meant to exclude them from public life.

Despite assumptions that Hispano cultural forms would disappear from the scene, *Nuevomexicanos* continued to hold their own in matters cultural and political, a condition that brought forth such observations as "but their final assimilation was slowed because their numerical superiority in New Mexico encouraged the continued use of Spanish and the old customs. Had this small number of Hispanos been scattered out over the United States, assimilation would have been rapid" (Stratton 1969, 126). Regardless of this take, the numerical superiority of *Nuevomexicanos* in the region is not the sole explanation for their retention of ethnic identity and the integrity of cultural forms late into the twentieth century. One overlooked factor is the role of Spanish-language newspaper publication.

In trying to examine the impact of print as a cultural medium my study is guided by two major themes, which I have structured as (Part I) "A *Nuevomexicano* Culture of Print," and (Part II) "Neo-Mexicano Culture in Print." Part I concerns itself with describing the formative elements that give material structure to Spanish-language print discourse in *Mexicano* communities. I begin with a chapter devoted to "*Mexicanos* in the Early History of the Press," which documents the desire of *Nuevomexicanos* to acquire and use the press to advance a number of social and educational agendas during the Mexican and American Territorial periods. Chapter 2 provides an analysis of the contravention and transitionality that characterized life for Mexican Americans in the Southwest in the decades following the signing of the Treaty of Guadalupe-Hidalgo in 1848. The chapter details the educational formation of a generation born under American rule and traces the emergence of a cadre of journalists working in *Mexicano* communities. Chapter 3 centers on the activities of La Prensa Asociada Hispano-Americana (the Spanish-American Associated Press), the organizational manifestation, the structure, if you will, by which print culture is deployed in *Nuevomexicano* communities.

In Part II "Neo-Mexicano Culture in Print," I move to examine a number of texts of history, culture, and literature produced by the *periodiquero* generation. My analysis presupposes the high aspirations of Mexican Americans of this generation who worked to bequeath testimony of the time and the reality they lived for future generations, an idea best expressed by one *nativo* editor as "para que no todo quede relegado al olvido" (so all is not lost) and which served as the original book title.

Chapter 4 takes up a discussion of a number of historical narratives produced by cultural insiders and published in the Spanish-language press after 1880, while chapter 5 deals with the call by editors for the creation of a body of literature (*una literatura nacional*) for the purpose of bringing *Mexicano* culture into the discourse of national life. The last chapter of my study takes up matters of continuity and discontinuity, and of the constriction of Spanish-language publication in the post-statehood period in New Mexico and considers the ways the dominant cultural group has contained the forms of self-representation developed by Mexican Americans in earlier periods of their history.

I am privileged to work in an area of scholarly endeavor rich in a superb inventory of literary and sociocultural writings whose significance, I believe, will ultimately remap, reconfigure, and rechart Chicano intellectual tradition at the intersection of socioaesthetic desire and paradigmatic representation.

Part I
A *Nuevomexicano* Culture of Print

Sociopolitical factors weigh heavily on attempts to make sense of the territorial period in the Southwest. The advent of Spanish-language journalism during this time is no less tied to practical developments in education, literacy, and the politics of territorial society. The rise to public life of New Mexico's *periodiqueros* (journalists), and their work of establishing a "culture of print" in communities where it had never existed before, came about over several decades. It is not surprising that decades which preceded the dynamic growth in periodical activity of the 1890s were those in which *Nuevomexicanos* worked feverishly to gain access to formal education and acquire mechanical presses (though not always in this order). Despite these visible gains, Anglo-American "structures of power" continued to subordinate regional cultures in the nineteenth century and in doing so they threatened the survival of a Mexicano way of life in the Southwest.

Part I of this study describes the social transformation that creates, and is created, as a "culture of print" is deployed in *Nuevomexicano* communities beginning in the 1830s. Inasmuch as "official" histories have not addressed this reality, readers will find here the life histories of a number of individuals who made key contributions to a *Nuevomexicano* culture of print. This life and times approach offers a way to understand the nature of the communicative acts this generation engaged in and information about the communicators of those acts within the context of a social economy that shaped the meaning of their words and deeds. This bibliographic foreground unearths recognizable and sympathetic individuals out of the murk of previously unrecorded history and illuminates the experiences of a generation that strove to acquire "the tools of literacy." Likewise, print culture in *Mexicano* communities was often mirrored in the lives of *Nuevomexicano* literates, for upon the interpersonal relationships of *periodiqueros*—and through their socialization, education, and entrepreneurship—rested a grid of interlocking discursive activity that formed the professional acumen of this generation. Uniting this generation is a shared sense of adversity that is as much the result of material dispossession as it is the consequence of Anglo political hegemony. A circumstance that lessened "the full potentialities of literacy" (Goody 1968, 11), or in this case, the full impact of print among the Spanish-speaking of the Southwest.

1

Mexicanos in the History of the Early Press in the Southwest

A las cuentas conclucion,
Puse en preces que esmeran
Mis intentos que quisieran,
Haber dado por perfeccion
Pero les falta estencion
Yo quisiera tener tiempo
Mas mis tareas ¡Lo siento!
Me embarazan la atencion.

[This closing of accounts
I place in careful supplication
my intention and wish
(would have been) to perfect them
as I see they are in need of prolongation
I wish I had time
but my duties, I must confess
hinder the attention they require.][1]

Cuaderno de cuentas por el presbítero Antonio José Martínez,
Impreso en la oficina del mismo a cargo de Jesús María Baca.
Taos, Nuevo Méjico año de 1836 [Primer on Arithmetic by the
Presbytery Antonio José Martínez, printed at His direction and in
His offices by Jesús María Baca. Taos, New Mexico, 1836].

The verses above appear on the eleventh and final page of *Cuaderno de Cuentas,* a primer on arithmetic that Padre Antonio José Martínez directed Jesús María Baca to publish in 1836. Scant, indeed, were the tools of literacy available to *Mexicanos* and native Indians in the Southwest. Between Taos, New Mexico, and Monterey, California, only two presses operated during the whole of the Mexican period. The verses, like the primer's "prácticas fáciles á instruirse [easy to learn drills]," aim at the same objective: to bring learning to the untutored masses of a vast region, especially to those "jóvenes aplicados a esta facultad [young people with the desire to learn]."[2]

Book historians, particularly those concerned with the "material embodiments" of printed texts such as books, broadsides, periodicals, and primers, are generally of the opinion that such items "cannot be understood apart from the society that creates them" (Davidson 1989, 20). Underlying this assumption is the notion that the production of texts, and their route to "material embodiment," may signify a good deal about ideas inscribed within these texts. Said another way, the ultimate signification of texts cannot be divorced from the practicalities of the social economy that printed and published those texts. These considerations are particularly relevant in attempting to account for the development of print culture and the diffusion of knowledge in excluded populations, where regional, ethnic, or gender differences have been determined and shaped by an uneven social development. For as Cathy Davidson puts it, "technological innovation can have dramatically different impact on different social groups or classes or in different regions of the nation" (15).

Similarly Ronald Zboray's observation that "any account of a given system of literacy must consider the reciprocal relation between literacy and culture" (1989, 142) compels an historiographic assessment of the sociopolitical factors impinging upon the development of print discourse in *Mexicano* communities in the Southwest beginning in the first third of the nineteenth century. The matter is complicated by the need to view the acquisition of the tools of literacy (printing, books, etc.) against escalating social tensions that developed at mid-century between Mexico and United States.

Nuevomexicanos (New Mexicans) became Mexican Americans by political default in 1848. But even prior to becoming a conquered people they desired the benefits that the establishment of the press in their particular corner of the wòrld might bring them. Before the conquering armies of the United States visited them, poverty, isolation, and lack of educational opportunities had slowed *Nuevomexicano* social, cultural, and historical development. But the desire to communicate with each other about social, literary, and political matters seems never to have been completely lost to them. In the early decades of the nineteenth century, *Nuevomexicanos* contemplated, gauged, and speculated on the value of the press and the possibilities afforded by this technology to encode and disseminate their ideas. For in the absence of print, the greater part of that discourse was carried on through the exchange of manuscripts and through oral performance narrative.

The mechanical printing press, and the possibility it provided for producing multiple copies of written materials, was unknown in New Mexico prior to the 1830s, although the need for print technology had already been registered by more than one leader there. In fact, New Mexico's ecclesiastical and political leadership took steps to acquire a press in the decade prior to the war between Mexico and the United States. The first mechanical press in the region arrived in Santa Fe in August 1834. These early actions to bring print to New Mexico occurred despite unfavorable material conditions and cultural isolation. Situated at the northernmost reaches of the Mexican frontier, New Mexico had since the time of its founding been a sparsely populated frontier that produced little wealth despite the bounty of its natural resources and arable lands.

From time to time *Nuevomexicanos* had been painfully reminded of the deplorable material condition of the region, and in their writings *Nuevomexicanos* recognized the economic and educational difficulties plaguing the territory. For example, Pedro Bautista Pino had traveled to Spain in 1812 to represent the province of New Mexico in the newly formed Spanish *Cortes,* his aim being to bring attention to conditions in the province and to obtain aid for New Mexico from a newly reorganized government. In a concise report, Pino laid out the problems affecting New Mexico, pointing to the lack of schools, teachers, and the means to prepare *Nuevomexicanos* for entering the professions. Pino's report calls attention to the historical neglect of the Spanish colonial administration of New Mexico:

> The province of New Mexico does not have among its public institutions any of those found in other provinces of Spain. So backward is it in this matter that the names of such institutions are not even known. The benefit of primary letters is given only to the children of those who are able to contribute to the salary of the school teacher. Even in the capital it has been impossible to engage a teacher and to furnish education to everyone. Of course there are no colleges of any kind. This condition gives rise to the discouragement of many people who notice the latent scientific ability of the children in the province. For a period of more than two hundred years since the conquest, the province has made no provision for any of them in any of the literary careers, or as a priest, something which is ordinarily done in other provinces of America. (*Noticias históricas* 1849, 61)[3]

At the time of Pedro Pino's diplomatic mission, Spain was itself a nation beset by the civil strife brought on by Napoleon's invasion of the peninsula four years earlier. At best, Pedro Pino may have managed to stir in the minds of representatives of the *Cortes* at Cadiz a distant and ephemeral memory of a lost colony in the Americas. These men could offer little more than a sympathetic ear to a bygone concern of Spain's imperial past. The outlook painted by Pino did not improve after Mexico gained its independence from Spain. In June 1832 a comprehensive survey and assessment of the province of New Mexico was dispatched to Mexico City by Licenciado Antonio Barriero, an official of the Mexican government, who had been sent to New Mexico to act as legal advisor to the provincial authorities in Santa Fe. Barriero's "Ojeada sobre Nuevo México" (An Overview of New Mexico) recounts the bleak conditions in New Mexico regarding education, learning, and the availability of instructional materials for use among the general populace. Like Padre Martínez of Taos, Barriero was a student of enlightenment ideas. In a section of the "Ojeada" titled "Freedom of the Press," Barriero dwells on the virtues of the press:

> Liberty of the press is the vehicle which communicates enlightenment to all classes of society, especially to the lowest class of people. This precious gift, granted to us by the wisdom of the great legislators of our Republic, is the firmest support of liberal institutions; for more than by physical strength, these institutions are conserved by moral vigor, which results from the enlightenment of the citizens.

Returning to his observations of New Mexico, Barriero laments:

> But this inestimable good is as if dead for this Territory, as not a press is known, nor do papers circulate which would spread abroad that public spirit which is the soul of republican liberty. The scarcity of books, particularly of those elementary ones which contribute so largely in disseminating ideas, is another obstacle opposed to enlightenment and another, no less, is the enormous distance at which this place lies, and the lack of communication which it obtains with the interior of the Republic. (*Noticias históricas* 1849, 62)[4]

Barriero was not alone in seeking the benefits of the press and to see it as an instrument to lift the moral and intellectual life of the citizens of the province. Shortly thereafter he entered into partnership with Padre Antonio José Martínez and Ramón Abreú, two prominent *Nuevomexicanos* who shared a similar desire to establish the press. Although the exact dealings these three entertained in their acquisition of a printing plant are still a matter of speculation, there is no doubt that it was through their efforts the first printing press came to New Mexico over the Santa Fe Trail (Wagner 1937).

That press arrived in Santa Fe in the summer of 1834 at the same time that moves to establish a press in other Mexican territories were also underway. In California, Agustín V. Zamorano, an influential citizen of Monterey, acquired a press similar to the one in New Mexico. The press arrived in Monterey via clipper ship. Within days Zamorano was issuing various texts on the press. Writing on the establishment of the early press in California, Luis Leal notes the various documents published:

> While we suspect that newspapers in Spanish existed in Alta California before 1848, we have no notice of them. . . . We know that the first document printed in 1834 was the *Provincial Regulations for the Government of Alta California*, and the first book, in 1835, was the *Manifesto to the Mexican Republic* by General José Figueroa. It is also possible that a newspaper may have been issued on Agustín Zamorano's presses in Monterey where Figueroa's *Manifesto* was published.[5]

The *Californio* and *Nuevomexicano* situations are comparable not only for what Wagner holds as "more than [the] bare coincidence" (1937) of presses having reached both areas in the same year, but also for what might be called the enclavement of print culture these lone presses represent. For in each case print is surrounded by scarcity and is forced to rely on a preindustrial social infrastructure to exist. Not surprisingly, this early stage of print culture in *Mexicano* communities, "bound to economics and consumption of print" (Brown 1983, 301)—as all such development is—operated within the limitations imposed by the lack of other print technologies (better presses, lower paper costs, distribution systems, etc.) The social economy of both regions demanded multifunctionality and flexibility in the use of the press.

In New Mexico the press was a much sought after resource that functioned in various purposes and causes. The Barriero, Martínez, and Abreú press was quickly put in service on several fronts. Historian Henry Wagner points to evidence that suggests that Ramón Abreú was first among the partners to use the printing press. According to Wagner, a June 25, 1834, broadside printed in Santa Fe confirms that Abreú had begun the publication of a newspaper under the name *El Crepúsculo de la Libertad.* Antonio Barriero continued to publish *El Crepúsculo de la Libertad* through the fall of 1834 with the aim of generating public support for his reelection to a second term as *diputado* from New Mexico to the Mexican Congress. By November 1835 Padre Antonio José Martinez had the press and was publishing *El Crepúsculo* at Taos (Wagner 1937).

Even though all three men held an interest and partnership in the New Mexico press, the purchase and establishment of it is generally accorded to Padre Martínez, a testimony to the influence Martínez effected in all spheres of life in New Mexico in the middle of the nineteenth century. While it is generally accepted that Padre Martínez had the press moved to Taos as early as 1834, there is no proof of his exclusive ownership of the printing press until the year of the Chimayó Rebellion in 1837. On this matter, Wagner is inconclusive, saying, "It seems likely then that Abreú was instrumental in having it [the press] brought to New Mexico or had obtained it afterward. In August 1837 he and his brother, Santiago, were both assassinated and there is some evidence to the effect that the press was then bought by Father Antonio

José Martínez" (1937, 3, 12). Wagner's reproof of the dissolution of the partnership, "it is not always safe to draw such an inference regarding business transactions carried on between Mexicans" (3, 12) sheds no light here, although he may have been suggesting that Martínez bought Abreú's share of the press at the time of his death. No mention is made of Barriero's interest in the press, if indeed he still had one at this date.

The Martínez Press and the Ideology of Literacy

A progressive thinker and an adherent of nineteenth-century liberalism, Padre Antonio José Martínez (1793–1867) has been rightly seen as "New Mexico's most significant educator in the nineteenth century and also one of it most important publishers" (Mares 1988, 37). Driven by a commitment "to better the condition of his faithful, and of the country in general" (Sánchez [1903] 1978, 38), Martínez not only established the first college "for the education of youth of both sexes" at his home in Taos in 1826, but also made the most extensive and constructive use of the press in the years following its arrival in New Mexico. Born at the village of Abiquiú, Martínez trained for the priesthood in Durango, Mexico, from 1817 to 1823, the years that saw the culmination of the struggle for independence in Mexico. He returned to New Mexico, "imbued with liberal political philosophy and great admiration for the late Padre Hidalgo" (Mares 1988, 23). Martínez's theological and political development place him in the company of leading social thinkers in the nineteenth century and mark him as subscribing to a particular brand of liberal optimism that saw education and literacy as "something of a panacea for curing the world's ills" (Mares 1988, 44). Consequently a steadfast belief in the "efficacy of literacy" as the means to improve society became the moral imperative of his work. The popular axiom that "literacy leads to freedom, literacy *constitutes* freedom" (Salvino 1989, 140), would certainly have appealed to Martínez, more so given the dismal condition of letters and learning in preindustrial New Mexico. Education, literacy, freedom, and progress became conflated ideals that fueled Padre Martínez's activism and lent power to his resolve to "disseminate [education] among all classes of society" (Sánchez [1903] 1978, 38).

According to his biographer, Pedro Sánchez, Martínez bought a press, "the first one seen in the province," with his own savings in 1835. Martínez was moved to action, "seeing the need for a press to make up for the scarcity of books for his students" (Sánchez [1903] 1978, 63). Martínez began his work as publisher by "print[ing] a first reader which contained the rudiments of letters and the alphabet, syllabication, vocabulary, likewise he published a multitude of prayer and grammar books, he had printed books on rhetoric, logic, physics, arithmetic, etc. He distributed these free of charge throughout the territory; always keeping those books necessary for the use of his students" (ibid., 63).

Martínez resumed publication at Taos of *El Crepúsculo de la Libertad*, a paper Sánchez describes as "a sharp weapon used to cut down the excesses of public officials" (ibid., 63). In December 1835, shortly after moving the press to Taos, he issued *Cuaderno de Ortografía*, the first book published in New Mexico. Subsequently, Martínez directed the publication of numerous other books, manuals, and pamphlets on orthography, arithmetic, legal procedure, and religious instruction.

Throughout the middle decades of the century, Martínez worked closely with Jesús María Baca, a printer who had returned with Martínez from Durango, and with whose help and talent he waged "a war against the most despicable and worst of dependencies: *Mental Slavery*" (ibid., 84). Jesús María Baca's distinctive style as a printer identifies a great many of the early imprints done on the Martínez press (Wagner, 1937, 7). Within this collaboration Martínez assumes the mantle of intellectual architect who directs Baca in the use of the press, but it is important to keep in mind that whatever impact Martínez had on educational and political matters results from the central role that Baca, the printer, brought to the partnership.

As much a result of who owned the press as the social needs present in the community, the Taos press would be used in a number of endeavors. According to Wagner, Martínez appended a partial list of the works he had published to date in his 1839 *Discurso Político* [Discourse on Politics] (*see* Wagner 1937, 6: 12).

Among the early Martínez-Baca imprints are the priest's memoirs. The life-narrative appeared in 1838 with the title, *Relación de Méritos del Presbítero Antonio José Martínez* (An Account of the Merits of the Presbytery Antonio José Martínez). The worked, signed simply "El Historiador," is generally assumed to have been authored by Martínez.

A few of the early Martínez-Baca imprints have survived, but the extent and actual number of texts produced is not known. The printing plant itself later passed into other hands. In 1844, the press was moved once again to Santa Fe and was used the following year to issue *La Verdad*, an official newspaper of the Mexican government. One of the few *Nuevomexicano* recollections of the early development of print culture during the middle years of the century is found in the memoirs of the Civil War veteran Rafaél Chacón. He writes:

> Since Father Martínez in 1835 had for a short time published in Taos, *El Crepúsculo* [the Dawn], which was the first newspaper in New Mexico, nothing had been done to establish journalism in this region. The only papers known came from the South, and these were few, and only men of means were able to take them. The need of some publication of a local character being thus felt in New Mexico, in 1845 there appeared at Santa Fe *La Verdad*

> [The Truth], but it was suspended shortly afterward for lack of support. A little while afterward a proposition was taken to publish another paper, which was to be known as *El Payo de Nuevo México* [The New Mexico Rube]. This paper never even came out and the only thing that it ever published was its prospectus, of which I still preserve a copy. *La Verdad* suspended publication in May of 1845, and the prospectus of *El Payo* came out on the twenty-first of July 1845, from the government press under the charge of Jesús María Baca (Meketa 1986, 60).

As can be seen in Chacón's description, printing and publishing in the middle decades of the nineteenth century in New Mexico were activities characterized by scarcity and disjuncture. These difficulties continued until the eve of the American invasion. Padre Antonio José Martínez's catechisms, primers, and other works represent the only points of light penetrating the shadow of material poverty shrouding New Mexico.

To this history of scarce printing would soon be added abeyance in the wake of political change. Padre Martínez's efforts to keep publishing alive would be cut short dramatically with the arrival of General Stephen Watts Kearny's Army of the West in Santa Fe, in August 1846. In an action fraught with symbolism, Kearny employed the Martínez press, the only one in Santa Fe, and ordered the publication of the Kearny Code, the general's mandate installing military law over New Mexico and the recently conquered *Nuevomexicanos.*

In one of the first studies on the history of publishing in New Mexico, Wagner privileges the conquering general with a beneficent attitude and transforms what for *Nuevomexicanos* could only have been an act of suppression into the momentous installation of the "American press" in New Mexico:

> The American press may be said to have started definitively with a notice published by Kearny September 22, 1846. The most important publication at this period, the "Kearny code," is dated October 7. These were both printed with the Taos type and no doubt on the old Martínez press, and the type at least continued to be used until the Santa Fé *Republican* was started (Wagner 1937, 12).

In truth Kearny's action aborted communication by print for *Nuevomexicanos* that had begun with the Martínez press. More important, the American administration of the Southwest would fundamentally alter the future development and direction of printing and publication in the region.

Print culture in New Mexico prior to American rule was clearly limited to whatever impact a single press might have among a populace generally accustomed to communicating through manuscripts and oral discourse. The Martínez press, nonetheless, introduced print culture to *Nuevomexicanos* and established its functionality and potential in important ways. The coming of the *Americanos* also brought *Nuevomexicanos* in contact with the accoutrements of a communications revolution built on print technologies that were operative in the United States. The deployment of such technology in eastern states, as one print historian remarks, had fueled "the explosion of printed matter in the early nineteenth century" (Brown 1983, 300). In contrast to scarcity and disjuncture of publishing in the Southwest, print culture on the eastern seaboard was supported by the technological advances of the Industrial Revolution. Continual advancements and refinements in this area, would, in time, lower prices for presses and printing products, in turn accelerating a deeper and wider use of print technologies in the Southwest.

The story of Hispanic literary and popular journalism in the latter half of the nineteenth century, then, is rooted in the paradox of improving material conditions and the coerced transformation of *Nuevomexicano* society under the pressure of a politically and economically dominant Anglo-American social structure. During the last third of the nineteenth century an unprecedented number of *Nuevomexicanos* came into possession and ownership of printing presses being imported to the Southwest. As *Nuevomexicanos* gained greater use of this technology, they gave voice and expression to concerns rooted in the conflict and open racial hostility directed at them. *Nuevomexicanos*, it is clear, used "Yankee ingenuity" to counter Anglo-American attempts at a cultural conquest of the region.

The Press in New Mexico After the American Conquest

The signing of the Treaty of Guadalupe-Hidalgo in February 1848 officially ended the war between Mexico and the United States. Former Mexican citizens still residing in those territories taken from Mexico now faced an uncertain future and the political and cultural autonomy they enjoyed prior to the American conquest was placed in doubt. While in theory the Treaty of Guadalupe-Hidalgo guaranteed protection of their language, culture, and properties, in practice, *Mexicanos* would be dispossessed at every turn. For *Nuevomexicanos,* the inevitability of this new political order had been made apparent by the defeat of the popular rebellion lead by *Nuevomexicanos* in the Taos, Río Arriba, and Mora areas in the winter of 1847. The suppression of this outbreak was clear evidence of the futility of armed resistance to American rule. *Nuevomexicanos* were now forced to acknowledge that they were no longer in charge of their own political future and faced an uncertain destiny. *Nuevomexicanos* quickly began to examine the possibilities inherent in the dicta of a new social order.

Relying on the guarantees made by the Treaty of Guadalupe-Hidalgo, *Nuevomexicanos* reasoned that while they no longer held the reigns of power in their homeland, the stipulations of the treaty did provide a means to defend their birthright and secure the protection of their language, religion, culture, and properties. The Treaty of Guadalupe-Hidalgo, in the minds of *Nuevomexicanos,* was the supreme authority in their struggle to assert their cultural and civil rights. When J. D. Sena, a prominent citizen of Santa Fe, submitted a communiqué titled "Twenty-Four Reasons: Why Native New Mexicans—these being the Mexicans as they are called—Should vote for the Constitution and Become a State" to Santa Fe's *El Nuevo Mexicano,* his defense of full participation for *Nuevomexicanos* in the social compact resulting from the U.S. conquest of the Southwest was drawn directly from the provisions of the Treaty of Guadalupe-Hidalgo. Sena declares as his first point:

> 1. Because the time is here to demand of the government the complete fulfillment of its promises to incorporate us to the fraternity of States of the Federal Union and admit us into the enjoyment of being true citizens of the United States as stipulated in the Treaty of Guadalupe-Hidalgo, which was the greatest inducement that could have been offered to us [so that we might] embrace the rights of citizens of the United States and renounce those [rights] as citizens of the Republic of Mexico.[6]

It is important to note that Sena's item appears in print forty-two years after the treaty's ratification. It confirms the fact that *Nuevomexicanos'* concern regarding its implementation had not waned even after several decades of territorial rule.

In the civic and cultural arena, *Nuevomexicanos* did exert a measure of influence and power. Anglo Americans entering the territory in the wake of American occupation quickly realized that in most aspects of life in New Mexico, *Nuevomexicanos* were a force to reckon with. Faced with the numerical superiority of the *Mexicanos* in the region and with an entire cultural complex that set precedent and usage in language, law, religion, property, and custom, they came to understand that the wholesale dispossession of *Mexicanos* in New Mexico could not be expected to follow that which had occurred in the decade prior in Texas and California. In those areas the Mexican population was quickly overwhelmed by Anglo-American immigration and influence. The situation in New Mexico called for adjustment, modification, and compromise with the native peoples of the region. As a result, Anglo Americans tended to curb their presumption to the spoils of their conquest and, at least during the era in which *Nuevomexicanos* comprised the majority of the population, Anglo Americans were obliged to acknowledge and to an extent engage in the particular cultural practices of the region.

Materially, the press benefited from the U.S. takeover of the western territories as manufactured goods and technology imported from middle-western cities like St. Louis and Independence, Missouri, became available. Although goods and merchandise still needed to be freighted long distances across the Santa Fe Trail, Anglo-American merchants, investors, and brokers were now in a position to move freely into the territory to sell their wares or hock their services without the regulations imposed by the Mexican government.

In the decade following the signing of the Treaty of Guadalupe-Hidalgo the number of presses in New Mexico slowly increased. Anglo-American editors and publishers entered the region in greater numbers and began to establish newspapers at Santa Fe, Taos, Las Vegas, and Albuquerque. Because of the political and cultural estrangement produced by martial law and, in no small measure, owing to the loss of the one press in the region that was previously at the service of the Spanish-speaking population, *Nuevomexicano* periodical activity abated during the same period. However, *Nuevomexicanos* continued to influence the development of the press and print discourse in New Mexico in two key ways. First, Anglo-American editors and publishers quickly came to understand that the predominance of the Spanish language among the majority of the citizens of the territory meant that the "American" press would need to respond to this linguistic reality by publishing materials in Spanish, and second, *Nuevomexicanos* played important roles as associate editors, translators, and printers for many early newspapers.

Newspaper historian Porter Stratton observes that most newspapers after 1848 were either partially or totally printed in Spanish. Although Anglo-Americans may have viewed this as a "problem," from its inception the "American press" in New Mexico was a quintessential bilingual phenomenon:

> Journalism in New Mexico in this era presented the unique problem of a predominantly Anglo-American press serving a population overwhelmingly Spanish-American. The first paper edited by an Anglo-American, the *Santa Fe Republican*, set the pattern for most of the early papers by dividing its pages between the two languages. Although there were some efforts to break away from this by printing a paper in each language in areas of heavy Spanish-American population, most territorial editors followed the bilingual practice (Stratton 1969, 12).

In this manner, *Nuevomexicanos*, as the majority readership of these newspapers, shaped much of the scope and nature of early Anglo-American periodical activity.

Partnerships between *Nuevomexicanos* and Anglo Americans favored the latter group since *Nuevomexicanos* were engaged principally to provide language and translating skills to these newspapers, while Anglo publishers controlled ownership and editorial policy. These arrangements were quite common, encouraged as they were by the bilingual and bicultural reality of the communities in which these newspapers operated. The relatively small number of autonomous *Nuevomexicano* presses during this period is explained by the continued lack of educational opportunities available to *Nuevomexicanos* and to the difficulty aspiring journalists would have encountered in attempting to raise the capital to buy presses of their own. As Potter Stratton observed, "Despite the heavy usage of the Spanish language in newspapers, only about 12 per cent (ten out of eighty) of the journalists were Spanish-Americans. Apparently other Spanish-Americans were employed only to translate the English-language copy into Spanish" (ibid., 12–13).

The Emergence of Spanish-language Journalism in New Mexico

From 1848 to 1879 *Nuevomexicanos* managed to establish only a handful of Spanish-language newspapers over which they exerted complete editorial authority. However, important work in printing and publication among *Nuevomexicanos* continued in those years as *Nuevomexicanos* began to position themselves to enter the professions. Santa Fe historian Benjamín M. Read reported that by the late 1860s, Urbano Chacón had published a newspaper called *El Explorador* in Trinidad, Colorado, and by the first years of the next decade was publishing a weekly in Taos, New Mexico, called *El Espejo*. Chacón's newspapers clearly inspired others to follow suit, and as an editor, Chacón was guiding the work of younger *Nuevomexicanos* in journalism. Enrique H. Salazar, for example, one of the founders of *La Voz del Pueblo* in Santa Fe, later credited Urbano Chacón with giving him his start in journalism by providing him an apprenticeship at *El Espejo.* Chacón himself remained a force in this emergent journalism until his untimely death in 1888.

By the late 1870s *Nuevomexicano* journalists were harkening back to early concerns over the lack of educational advancement in the region, a situation made all the more patent by a general discontent and disillusionment among the populace with New Mexico's status as a territory. Adhering to the conviction that "literacy and education are the avenue to social and economic advancement" (Salvino 1989, 140), *Nuevomexicanos* encouraged the use of the press as the vehicle to liberate the mind and spirit in the face of what they viewed as educational neglect.

At Las Vegas, several *Nuevomexicanos* began issuing *El Anunciador de Nuevo Méjico.* This weekly began publication on October 12, 1871, and continued to be published until January 1879. Although only one issue of the paper survives into the present and very little is known otherwise about the publication or its publishers, *El Anunciador* appears at the outset of a sustained period of journalism in which *Nuevomexicanos* held editorial and economic control over an increasing number of periodicals. The disposition of *Nuevomexicanos* wishing to increase their influence in the pubic sphere accounts for the high expectations that accompanied the appearance of new publications in these years. *El Anunciador*, for example, contains the prospectus for *La Estrella de Mora*, a paper which, in the words of its editor, would speak "for the society in which we live, especially for the nativos of this territory." The prospectus of *La Estrella de Mora* sounds a familiar note intoned with the same urgency that guided Padre Martínez and others earlier in the century to consider the press as an instrument to educate the native populace. Severino Trujillo, the author of the prospectus, declares:

> For sometime now, I have carefully observed and examined the circumstances that encircle our homeland, which, without doubt, lags far behind other nations, in regards to a culture of knowledge and the development of the mental abilities of mankind. From whence stems the ominous destitution that has spread like a contagious gangrene that has infected every social class.[7]

Here, as with Barriero and Martínez before, the doctrine of literacy, or what Trujillo calls "the development of the mental abilities of mankind," is elevated to a moral imperative and the first priority of the press. Trujillo thus outlines his mission to provide a means to educate and inform the masses of his fellow citizens:

> Such is the case, that our homeland lies in misery. This misery originates and emanates directly from the lack of instruction of the masses of the people who are not aware of the need that we all have for some manner of public instruction which will enlighten our ideas and which will operate on the development of our spirit. Which will lead us by the hand—shall we say—to a higher degree of prosperity, [one] that will place us at the same level as the rest of the civilized nations on the surface of the Earth.[8]

The Trujillo text is telling, not only in the manner of its appearance, that is, as a prospectus evincing the intensification of journalistic activity among *Nuevomexicanos* in the late 1870s, but also for the inferences Trujillo's words signal in pointing to the factors that mitigate against the press and the education of the masses. From a contemporary vantage point the prospectus provides evidence of the situation where "the implementation of new printing technologies is not necessarily a first cause but can often itself be seen as a response to preexisting political processes and social needs (real or perceived)" (Davidson 1989,18). The "real" and "perceived" political and social maladies in the New Mexican case are poverty, isolation, social enclavement, and Anglo antagonism to *Mexicano* culture. These are the culprits Trujillo gingerly refers to as "the circumstances that encircle our homeland," and whose injury to *Nuevomexicano* society Trujillo characterized as "a contagious gangrene that has infected every social class."

It is important to remember that *Mexicanos* in this period continued to inhabit a viable regional community that, as social historian Sarah Deutsch points out, "played host to the incoming Anglos" (1987, 7). This explains, in part, the fact that *Nuevomexicano* discursive agency, via new newspaper enterprises, continued to grow and expand in subsequent decades. Even as *Nuevomexicanos* "found themselves *partially incorporated* into an increasingly powerful national international capitalist economy controlled by an alien culture" (ibid., 7), this not fully consolidated social order continued to be marked by "evidence of initiative, enterprise and autonomy" (ibid., 7) on the part of *Nuevomexicanos.*

Not surprisingly, the greatest outpouring of *Nuevomexicano* periodical activity occurred in the decades following the arrival of the railroad in 1879, for as historian Ronald J. Zboray points out, rail development and dispersal of print technology were wedded activities at mid-century:

> Because the West and South lagged far behind the North in economic development, the rails, and indeed, the roads and waterways, served as avenues through which ideas, responses, and approaches of the more mature capitalism of the North penetrated into the interior of the country to compete with regional cultures (1986, 478).

Paradoxically, Yankee incursions in the West also translated into greater access to Yankee print technologies in the region. Porter Stratton reported in his study of the territorial press that approximately sixteen bilingual newspapers were published in the territory, along with some thirteen newspapers published entirely in Spanish in the decade of the 1880s. This proliferation of journalistic enterprise would, however, prove to be the prologue to the true flowering of *Nuevomexicano* periodical activity in the decade of the 1890s. Potter Stratton adds:

> However, by the '90s a larger number of native New Mexicans were literate in the Spanish language, having been educated in that tongue in an increasing number of Catholic schools. As a result, thirty-five Spanish language and eleven bilingual papers were published in the '90s—a decade of reduced journalistic efforts in the territory. (Stratton 1969, 36)

In the thirty years since the American conquest, *Nuevomexicanos* had developed a powerful culture of print with the capacity to communicate with the majority of the citizenry in the Southwest. Its efficacy left English-lan-

Fig. 1. Advertisment for printing jobs featuring the mechanical press "Challenge" used at *La Voz del Pueblo. La Voz del Pueblo,* Santa Fe, New Mexico, 1889.

Toda Clase de Obras Finas.

PARA MAS INFORMACION

Dirijanse a la Oficina de

LA VOZ DEL PUEBLO

AVENIDA DE PALACIO,

SANTA FÉ, NUEVO MÉJICO.

guage publications the role of serving an English-speaking elite. Stratton, whose primary focus is on chronicling publication by Anglo-American journalists, characterizes the period as one of "reduced journalistic efforts in the territory."

The trend started by *El Anunciador* and other papers to establish *Nuevomexicano*-controlled newspapers throughout the territory continued unabated through the decade of the 1890s and through the years leading to statehood in 1912. By 1900 *Nuevomexicano* newspapers had been founded in every important settlement along the Rio Grande corridor. Soon this line of newspapers reached beyond the territorial borders of New Mexico to include El Paso, Texas, in the south and the Trinidad area of southern Colorado to the north. In New Mexico, four cities in particular, Las Cruces, Albuquerque, Santa Fe, and Las Vegas, became the hubs of a journalistic network that extended into other areas of the Southwest.

Nuevomexicanos at Las Cruces had managed to support several Spanish-language periodicals during the decade of the 1880s. The most important and long-running of these was *El Tiempo*, which had been established in 1882 and continued to be published under that title until 1911. Further north at Albuquerque *La Bandera Americana* began publication in 1895 as did *El Nuevo Mundo* two years later in 1897. Santa Fe, long acknowledged as the birthplace of journalism in New Mexico, had seen the establishment of *El Boletín Popular* under the direction of José Segura in 1885; *El Nuevo Mexicano*, the Spanish-language edition of the *Santa Fe New Mexican*, began publication in 1890. Also established in Santa Fe in 1888 was the best known of *Nuevomexicano* newspapers, *La Voz del Pueblo*, a paper which was later moved sixty miles northeast of Santa Fe to Las Vegas, New Mexico. The *Mexicano* community of Las Vegas had been served by *La Revista Católica* since 1875. This paper, under the direction of Italian Jesuits, could boast of publication on the first cylinder model mechanical press in the area. Its impact on the predominantly Catholic Spanish-speaking *Mexicano* community in the Las Vegas vicinity was immediate. *Nuevomexicanos* themselves, influenced by the work of the Jesuits, pursued with unbridled vigor other journalistic endeavors in Las Vegas in the 1890s. *La Voz del Pueblo* resumed publication after its relocation to Las Vegas in the summer of 1890. Two other newspapers followed: *El Sol de Mayo*, a paper founded by Las Vegas resident Manuel C. de Baca, appeared in 1891, and *El Independiente*, the second of Enrique H. Salazar's publications, was issued in 1894.

Canjes: The Dialogic Exchange of Border Papers

By the first decade of the twentieth century, as newspaper activity expanded to include the whole of the Rio Grande corridor, Spanish-language journalism showed signs of having garnered greater prestige as a result of careful and professional work. Ensuing publications improved in appearance and content as *Nuevomexicano* editors strove to better inform and represent their community. Stratton notes that "by 1912 territorial Spanish-language weeklies had reached a peak, attaining greater number and a higher quality than in all prior decades" (1969, 60). In the thirty-two year period marked by the coming of the railroad in 1879 and New Mexico's admission to statehood in 1912 more than ninety Spanish-language newspapers were published in New Mexico alone.

The scope of Spanish publication across the whole of the Southwest suggests that a more accurate characterization of this publishing phenomena would define it not solely as the enclavement of print but as introducing and sustaining print culture as a major feature in *Mexicano* communities. The widening exposure to printed materials and the deployment of periodical after periodical in the region changed reading and writing habits in *Mexicano* communities and created the kind of "self-intensifying spiral of growth in production, distribution, and consumption of print" that likened it to the hallmark of print culture in New England at the beginning of the nineteenth century. This culture of print was buoyed by a "communications circuit," operating in the manner which Robert Darnton ascribes to the production of books. Darnton's commentary to the effect that communications circuits "operate in consistent patterns" (1989, 47) is worth noting here, for such patterns are readily observable in *Mexicano* and *Nuevomexicano* communities in the 1890s where print culture acted as a system of dialogic exchange. In Darnton's words, this system functions "so the circuit runs full cycle. It transmits messages, transforming them in route, as they pass from thought to writing to printed characters and back to thought again" (1989, 30).

This "communications circuit" would eventually mold itself around the activities of La Prensa Asociada Hispano-Americana, or the Spanish-American Associated Press, an organization that brought together editors from every important Spanish-language newspaper in Arizona, Colorado, New Mexico, and West Texas. Such work established a network of *canjes* or newspaper exchanges, which provided a mechanism for the informal syndication of materials published on both sides of the border.

The first organizational meetings of La Prensa Asociada Hispano-Americana were held in late 1891 in Las Vegas, New Mexico. In the ensuing months of 1892 the association met regularly at Las Vegas, Santa Fe, Albuquerque, Las Cruces, and El Paso, Texas. La Prensa Asociada Hispano-Americana would continue to grow throughout the decade, making it the first and only such organization among the Spanish-speaking in the Southwest.

The synergism fostered by La Prensa Asociada seemed to confirm the growing sense of confidence and enthusiasm among *Nuevomexicanos,* who began to see themselves of agents of change and progress in their community. This was an especially powerful development when viewed against poverty, isolation, and the lack of technology that had been so prevalent in the years prior to the arrival of the railroad.

In acquiring print technology and the tools of literacy, and in bringing organizational structure and discursive coherence to a culture of print, *Nuevomexicanos* exhibited tremendous adaptability with respect to technological and political change after 1848. This tendency toward accommodation has been characterized by Deutsch as the "strategies of power and community survival." These strategies represented nonacquiescent forms of agency that permitted *Nuevomexicanos* to habituate themselves to external political exigencies while managing to perpetuate their language and cultural practices. "Selective acculturation," Deutsch reasons, permitted *Nuevomexicanos* to maintain a "remarkable degree of control over the development of their own culture" (1987, 39). But this feature does not appear in the post-statehood years as Deutsch suggests, rather it had been a part of *Nuevomexicano* cultural strategy since the arrival of *los Americanos.*

To fully appreciate *Nuevomexicano* agency in matters of culture, print, and literacy, it is important to consider how the "communications circuit" used by local journalists functioned, on the one hand, as counterhegemonic discourse that subverted assaults on *Mexicano* culture, and on the other, as a way to channel the power of literacy to change society. Deutsch considers that such development was self-selected by *Nuevomexicanos* whose actions minimized the deleterious effects often associated with the imposition of technology on traditional cultures. For as Deutsch puts it, "The new technology and industrial objects that Hispanics adopted did not represent fundamental cultural changes" (1987, 39).

Severino Trujillo's description of the press as "la necesidad que todos tenemos de un medio de instrucción pública [the need we all have of a means of public instruction]" reminds us that the business of promoting culture and language was bound up in the idea that "literacy carried important currency" (Salvino 1989, 146).

Book historians are not alone in expressing their skepticism toward an unbounded belief that the "supreme efficacy of literacy" (Salvino 1989, 141) will eradicate the moral, social, and political malaise of any society. As the New Mexican case clearly demonstrates the success of such social problem-solving remained dependent on the degree to which "the possessors of that advanced literacy can negotiate society's power structures" (Davidson 1989, 13). This does not diminish whatsoever the importance of the *periodiquero* (journalist's) movement, even as the road it charted to "lead [*Nuevomexicanos*] by the hand" leaned toward the utopian.

The chapters that follow describe the formation of *Neo-Mexicano* print discourse and in doing so lend particular attention to print in its, "relation[s] with other systems, economic, social, political, in the surrounding environment" (Darnton, 30). They assess the role of the press as a source of a socioaesthetic desire and paradigmatic representation for *Mexicanos* who were forced to habituate to new social codes or face social death. In support of the theory that an "interactive model of print culture" developed in *Mexicano* communities after Guadalupe-Hidalgo, chapter 2 begins with an examination of the mechanisms for formal education available to *Mexicanos* in the borderlands and argues that this question becomes a critical determinant in the formation of the *periodiquero* movement, a phenomenon that cannot be understood without considering the social and educational transformation of a corner of the world long practiced in oral traditions.

2

A Generation in Transition

Upon learning of the *Americano* takeover, Padre Martínez is said to have remarked to his students, "You came to this college for the purpose of studying for the priesthood. In this regard I have done everything possible so you might obtain your desired goal. However, now that the government has changed, it might be necessary to change ideas" (Sánchez [1903] 1978, 68). The decades following the installation of American rule in New Mexico were an unsettled and uneasy time for the region's *nativos* (the native Spanish-speaking people). Martínez's admonitions had an immediate effect; his seminarians "consecrated themselves to the study of civil law and the English language" (ibid., 68). Social and technological change would required far greater adjustment, for the tragic residuum of conquest was not a simple, nor easily dispensable matter. Social conventions, economic and political allegiances that made ready sense before 1848, shattered and fell away, leaving in the wake consternation, ambiguity, and uncertainty about the future. In the face of the trauma produced by the American takeover, New Mexico's *nativos,* if they wished to survive as a cultural group, needed to shake off the stultifying effects of their conquest. They proceeded to do this with a resolve Genaro Padilla describes as "reconstructing life anew within the rupture, transforming rupture into the expanding—and expansive—space of intercultural possibility" (1993, 15). The evolution of *Nuevomexicano* social economy after 1848 would be complicated and protracted. The onus of legitimizing *Nuevomexicano* society under American rule fell to the generations coming into public life in the years following the arrival of the *Americanos.*

Nuevomexicanos coming of age after 1848 would find it particularly painful to habituate themselves to the radical transformation of their society, not because they were adverse to change, but because that transformation called for the nullification of their own cultural and social practices. This dynamic had not fully revealed itself to Padre Martínez or his seminarians who in their naiveté "to do what needed to be done" had not entertained the idea that *los extranjeros* (recent immigrants) were not particularly interested in whether *Mexicanos* studied at all. In the years that followed it would become apparent that the *Nuevomexicano* homeland hung in the balance, and if *Nuevomexicanos* were to survive, they would need to restore a sense of order and social purpose for themselves and their posterity to counter the destabilizing social, political, and economic maneuvers that had been set loose upon them by the politics of conquest. *Nuevomexicanos* were caught in the dialectic of how best to reformulate cultural agency and realize self-actualization in a post-1848 world circumscribed by what Padilla characterizes as "a matrix of social constraints" (ibid. xi).

By the late 1880s and 1890s *Nuevomexicanos* born into American rule entered public life. This generation was the first to receive the benefits of a formal education, a good measure of which was imparted in the Spanish language. In addition, this generation experienced drastic changes ushered into the region by the arrival of the railroad and the breakdown of the geographic isolation that had characterized the Southwest in the past.

The arrival of the railroad in New Mexico in 1879 is generally viewed as the beginning of modernity in the region. Anglo-American historians would later write that it was the single most important event that brought "the region into the fold of the Union." The arrival of the railroad brought with it greater access to presses and printing, but it also ushered in a massive wave of immigration of Anglo Americans who came into direct competition with native populations.

Witnessing Social Change: The Life of J. M. H. Alarid

> Nourish me now, not when I'm dead.
>
> —Jesús María Hilario Alarid, Galisteo, New Mexico, 1888

The life of the village teacher Jesús María Hilario Alarid (1834–1917) is linked to a dialogism by which the oral traditions of the region were enveloped in an emergent print discourse in the *Mexicano* community in the second half of the nineteenth century. Alarid's prestige as a *bardo*, a poet of the people, did not diminish as the print culture of newspapers and journalism took hold in New Mexico. Rather, it seem that Alarid's status in village society grew as his knowledge of native practices, matrixed through his facility with the spoken word, found its way into print. Alarid's talents had been nurtured in the oral traditions and in time the titles of *bardo* (bard) and *maestro* (teacher) were conferred upon him by his friends and neighbors. In village society these forms of address were reserved for the most respected individuals of the community. As the village teacher at Galisteo, Alarid taught the lower grades (reading and writing) and served as an intermediary between village society and the outside world. His privileged position of *mae-*

stro lent significance to his pronouncements (oral and written) on education, politics, religion, and the condition of *Nuevomexicano* society under the force of *Americano* law and political power.

Alarid, like his contemporary Rafaél Chacón (1833–1925), witnessed the commonplace political change and military strife of his day, and like Chacón, he served his adoptive country during the Civil War years as one of a number of *Nuevomexicanos* who rendered service at the Battle of Valverde. Alarid and Chacón continued to move across a cultural landscape made familiar by the retention of language, customs, and familial-social relations, but they both experienced the acute Americanization of public life in New Mexico.[1]

In their early training, education, and psychological development, members of Alarid's generation remained profoundly tied to an earlier version of life in New Mexico and to its unadulterated Spanish-Mexican cultural milieu. For Genaro Padilla this formation locates a sense of self for these men in "the ecology of a Hispano cultural habitat" (Padilla 1993). But Alarid, Chacón, and others of their generation would inherit the dialectic of "expanding possibility" in the field of letters amid increasing competition for the representation of their culture in the public forums of society.

Beginning in the late 1880s, Alarid became closely identified with Spanish-language journalism. Jesús María Hilario, who often signed J. M. H. Alarid, was born at Galisteo, a village located in the vicinity of Santa Fe, the New Mexican capital. His father, Jesús María Alarid, Sr., was *secretario del departamento* during the Mexican period. The elder Alarid, nicknamed "El Chiquito," had also been among Governor Albino Pérez's party when it was set upon by the insurgents of the Chimayó rebellion of 1837. Salpointe in his account of the rebellion notes of the elder Alarid, "On the same day, Jesús María Alarid, secretary of the department, and Santiago Abreú, formerly governor ad interim, were killed on the Mesa a few miles south of Agua Fria" ([1898] 1967, 167).

The tragic circumstances of Alarid's father's death presaged in more than one way the tenor of the era. In 1841, external aggressors threatened New Mexico. In that year Anglo-Texans bent on expansion into New Mexico launched the infamous Texan-Santa Fe Expedition. The expedition, in the guise of a trading mission, soon came to the attention of Mexican officials in Santa Fe who routed and jailed this Anglo-Texan party of expansionists and profiteers.[2] The Texan-Santa Fe affair proved to be an initial conflict in an era of increasing U.S. expansionism into New Mexico and other Mexican territories. These events made a strong impression on young Alarid. By the time he was a young man these events, including the circumstance of the rebellion in which his father had been killed, had been consecrated in the way of poem-songs and dramatizations that were part of the *tientas,* or recitations, of the local troubadours. These performances encoded the historiographic detail of these events into popular forms that circulated across the whole of the region. Jesús María H. Alarid himself grew to add a good number of these poetic forms to his own repertoire of narrative poems and songs, many of which would later be published in local newspapers.

Little is known of Alarid's formal education. Historian Anselmo Arellano reports that Alarid practiced law as a young man, but notes that the practice was "limited principally in the courts of the *alcaldes*" (1976, 36). Such information suggests that Alarid was self-taught and self-authorized in his profession. His literacy and knowledge of the legal system sufficiently qualified him to teach and the record bears out that Alarid became one of the first native-born teachers in the community schools of the rural villages of New Mexico.

His poetry and other writings reveal Alarid to be a man of above average intelligence. His competency was derived from formal study, but also from his ability to use oratorical and performative skills rooted in traditional *Nuevomexicano* poetics. Known for his verbal artistry, Alarid was often invited to speak at social affairs and to deliver eulogies. His status in *Neo-Mexicano* communities was further enhanced by his reputation as an accomplished musician and musical director. Around 1890 Alarid founded *La banda lírica,* a twenty-five piece string orchestra that played regularly at community and civic events in and around Las Vegas, New Mexico. In addition Alarid was teacher and preceptor at the community school at Galisteo, New Mexico,[3] and taught for a time at the village school at Raton, a mining town situated just south of the Colorado-New Mexico border.

Jesús María H. Alarid contributed to the *Nuevomexicano* journalism in several ways. It is probable that he worked on the staff of *El Anunciador de Nuevo Méjico* in the 1870s. Beginning in the 1890s he frequently traveled to outlying communities in northeastern New Mexico where his orchestra performed at baptisms, weddings, and other village celebrations. On these occasions he frequently sent communiqués detailing his travels to newspapers such as *El Independiente* (Las Vegas), *El Boletín Popular* (Santa Fe), and the bilingual *Santa Fe Gazette.* His letters and other submissions to these papers provide personal descriptions and firsthand accounts of the manners and customs that prevailed in the *Mexicano* communities of his day.

In a letter to a Las Vegas newspaper in February 1895, Alarid tells of a visit he made with his orchestra to the fledgling ranching communities of Watrous and Wagon Mound, situated at the eastern edge of Mora County. Jesús María's commentary registers his close affiliation with the people of these communities and his identification with the tribulations in their lives: "At Wagon Mound, our fellow countrymen put on a little dance which the best families attended, it was so full of glee that even an aging man like I, felt the urge to dance. Today has been most enjoyable because Mass fortunately was celebrated by the able priest Reverend P. Rivera. My orchestra played solemn marches and hymns during Mass to accompany the devotion of the people."[4] Apparent in this same text is Alarid's penchant for expressing *sentimiento,* or what might be called the shared experience of community in its tragic as well as celebratory moments. In the text of his letter, Alarid records how the joy of the communal celebration of a baptism quickly turned to sorrow with the news of the death of one of the village's respected elders:

> After Mass there were several baptisms which were celebrated with pomp and circumstance; among these, that of the baby Romualdo, the gift of Señora Roibal. The godparents were our good-natured young friend Don Serapio Romero, and his wife Señora Juanita B. de Romero. From the church a group marched accompanying the infant, but, as not all in life is joy, upon arriving at the house [where the baptism was to be held] we were given news of the death of our friend and honest citizen, the honorable Felipe Delgado—may he rest in peace—here ended our joyous celebration which turned to pain as the sorrow of the grieving family was brought to mind.[5]

The appearance of print in a given society is often associated with the sweeping away of an oral culture's traditional forms. But, if as Rhy Issac suggests, "Oral cultures are dominated by mnemonic formulas that enable their traditions to be remembered and thus to survive" (1983, 233), it is reasonable to assume that these traditions will not easily be dislodged as printed forms emerge. Such thinking must give way to situating print within the wider range of human intercourse that includes the communicative world of orality and script. Robert Darnton holds to the view that "influences ran both ways when oral traditions came into contact with printed text" (1989, 47). The mechanization of the word by the extensive use of the printing press did not immediately disrupt traditional modes of cultural expression in *Mexicano* communities of the Southwest; to the contrary it expanded their possibilities. Alarid's case is representative of the coexistence of print and the verbal traditions in *Nuevomexicano* communities in the years after the coming of the railroad.

During the most active years of Spanish-language journalism, Alarid, whose verbal artistry had been formed in traditional oral genres of *décimas, corridos,* and *cuandos* as well as ritual elegies and testimonials, was a constant contributor to Las Vegas and Santa Fe area newspapers. Jesús María H. Alarid continued to cultivate the traditional forms employed by the *bardo,* an individual held in great esteem by *Nuevomexicanos* for his capacity to bring distinction to the craft of the poet-balladeer. The consummate poet in the mind of *Nuevomexicanos* embodied the performative talents of the troubadour and the mental agility and improvisational wit of the extemporaneous orator. In this regard, Alarid was heir to a tradition of public oratory and poetic improvisation long practiced in *Nuevomexicano* communities. The tradition of the troubadour matching his wit against that of other *poetas* was still alive in Alarid's day. Genaro Padilla describes how the poet-troubadour perpetuated the cultural integrity of *Nuevomexicano* communities. Padilla explains:

> *Trovos*, duels matching repartee and the verbal improvisation of formally complex *cuandos* commemorating important historical events, buffalo hunts, commendatory verse acknowledgments of loved ones, or verse *memorias* of deceased relatives were performed by well-known *poetas*. But villagers were by no means passive auditors witnessing the performance of famed *poetas*. On the contrary, they passed immediate judgment on the ability with which these *trovadores* [troubadours] performed a series of rhetorical feats. Verbal extemporizing was part theater, part intellectual competition between *poetas* and villagers, and part schooling in rhetoric for children who were absorbing the sociolinguistic conventions of their community (1993, 169).

To the requirements above must be added a talent to externalize *sentimiento*. A defining characteristic in *Nuevomexicano* verbal art, *sentimiento* brings into play a wide range of expressive modalities only part of which correspond to the meaning encased in the English word *sentiment*. *Sentimiento* at once represents the competency of the speaker to communicate both his disposition of mind (rationale) and his point of view (opinion) while disclosing an intimate view of self within communitarian life experience. At times of great joy or sorrow within the community, *sentimiento* is revealed in the externalization of deeply felt emotions, feelings, and passions. Thus *sentimiento* remained a particularly apt vehicle for relating the distillation of past experience to the present unfolding life-drama of community. For, as Ong has seen, "The word in its natural, oral habitat is part of the real, existential present. Spoken utterance is addressed by a real, living person to another real, living person or real living persons, at a specific time in a real setting which includes much more than mere words" (1982, 101).

Sentimiento is thus equally present when Alarid expresses a sociopolitical viewpoint as an *estadista* (advocate of statehood) or when he takes up the sacred and communal duty of the *bardo* upon whose authority the emotions of baptisms, wakes, and other commemorations within the village are externalized and shared.

Many of Alarid's submissions to local papers respond to the social consternation facing *Nuevomexicanos* of his generation. In June 1895 Alarid, who was residing in Trinidad, Colorado, sent some verses to be published in *El Independiente* in Las Vegas. The verses are in the form of a *décima*, a traditional verse form consisting of four strophes of ten verses each. The main body of the poem is prefaced by a *planta*, that is, an octosyllabic quatrain that introduces the subject at hand. In the traditional verse improvisation in New Mexico and other parts of the Spanish-speaking world, the poet's command of verse, meter, and rhyme is tested in his or her ability to make each verse of the *planta* become the final verse of each succeeding strophe. On this particular occasion Alarid chose to entertain the readers of *El Independiente* by producing a jovial and humorous sketch in verse of a friend who is accidentally trampled by on oncoming *ferrocarril*, or locomotive. Despite the fatal consequences of the friend's unexpected and tragic end, the event is treated with irony and humor because it had been the habit of the deceased to call out in a loud voice, "-Ay [sic] viene el ferrocarril! [There comes the train!]." The *planta* begins,

> -Ay viene el ferrocarril!
> Estos versos el cantaba
> ¿Quien pudiera presumir
> Que ese ferrocarril lo matara?
>
> ["There comes the train,"
> Are the verses he would sing
> But who would have guessed
> That it would be he, killed by that very train?][6]

This particular *décima* reveals something of the manner in which *Nuevomexicanos* used poetry and oral improvisation to entertain themselves. In the case of "-Ay viene el ferrocarril!," a composition written to be printed in a local newspaper, Alarid obviously hoped to elicit the same amusement among a community of readers as he would have among a group of listeners gathered at a *trovo.* Alarid, like others of his generation, gravitated toward the oral register for inspiration and form, but clearly the subject at hand in this and other verse compositions is the new social and cultural reality that was reconfiguring the collective experience of *Mexicanos* throughout the region. Played for all its effect as humor, the recurring lament of "-Ay viene el ferrocarril!" remains charged with an irony that reminds the reader/listener of the conundrum of social change.

If the politics of conquest had ruptured *Nuevomexicano* social economy, New Mexico's status as a territory continued to destabilize it. Jesús María H. Alarid expressed his *sentimiento* regarding this predicament in a series of pronouncements on the condition and status of *Nuevomexicanos* submitted to local newspapers. These texts take as their subject the all-consuming and unending struggle *nativos* were waging to attain full participation in the governance of their society. The Treaty of Guadalupe-Hidalgo at the end of the Mexican American War had laid out the promise for *Nuevomexicanos* of full participation in all aspects of American life. But to most *Nuevomexicanos* the lofty ideals of democracy and freedom, professed at every opportunity by Anglo Americans, rang hollow. Alarid's observations on the question of statehood for New Mexico, written as a communiqué titled, "Al pueblo Neo-Mexicano," appeared in print for the first time in Santa Fe's *El Boletín Popular* in 1888. As the debate continued, it was reprinted a full seven years later in *El Independiente* of Las Vegas.

A proposal to make New Mexico a state had first been introduced in the territorial legislature some twenty-three years prior to the first printing of Alarid's communiqué. At the time Alarid was serving as secretary of the legislature. "Hablé en favor [I spoke in favor]," he reports, and looking back he recalls that the members of both chambers of the legislature had taken a solemn vow, "as they said there, even to give up their lives," in favor of statehood. Recalling the strength of that resolve Alarid goes on to tersely add that a great many of the members of that session had died and "are buried." It is within the context of the years of convoluted debate that Alarid's frank disclosure, "nourish me now, not when I am dead," assumes greater significance.

The text of "Al Pueblo Neo-Mexicano," calls into question the often repeated charge made by territorial officials that *Nuevomexicanos* were not ready to govern themselves. Alarid begged the question: When will New Mexico be ready to govern itself? His caustic response is loosely styled after the fashion of a *cuando*, a verse form in which the word "cuando," or "when," is used to begin each verse:

> ¿Cuándo estará? ¿Cuándo vengan otros ó lleguen grande número de población americana (como dicen y esperan algunos americanos) para tener entre ellos la mayoría para elegir el boleto del estado? ¿Cuándo se vea el cumplimento de la profesía que dice: "Otra raza vendrá y pondrá sus leyes sobre los moradores del país?" [When will it be ready? When others come, or when a great number among the American population arrives (as they say and as some *Americanos* expect) so that they can form a majority among themselves so as to elect the ballot of the state? Or (will it be only) with the fulfillment of the prophecy: "Another people will come and place their laws upon the inhabitants of the land?"][7]

Alarid's 1889 poem "El idioma español" has been cited by contemporary literary historians of nineteenth-century Hispanic texts as a clear and forthright distillation in lyrical form of a *Nuevomexicano* defense of language and cultural rights. Alarid held to the view that the cultural survival of his people rested largely on maintaining the ethnolinguistic identity imparted to them by their common language. No other topic engendered more passion and discussion among *Nuevomexicanos.* Even at this early date when Alarid's "El idioma español" made its appearance and Spanish was spoken by a majority of *nativos*, the threat to the language's survival was real. As Anglo Americans clamored for its proscription in public instruction and called for limiting its use in the affairs of government, Alarid responded with displeasure and indignation. In the opening verses of "El idioma español" he writes,

Hermoso idioma español	[Lovely Spanish
¿Qué te quieren proscribir?	What? They want to banish you?
Yo creo que no hay razón	I believe there is no reason
Qué tú dejes de existir.	For you not to exist.]

While Alarid defends the need to retain Spanish, he remains open to and even encourages bilingualism as a viable and sustainable linguistic option:

Cuando el mejicano entienda	[When the Mexican understands
Bien el idioma materno	The maternal tongue
Muy fácil será que aprenda	It will be easy for him to learn
El idioma del gobierno	the language of the Government
Rogaremos al eterno	We beseech the heavens
Que nos dé sabiduría	Grant us understanding
Y que se nos llegue el día	And [grant] us the day when
De poder hablar inglés	We are able to speak English
Pues señores justo es	Gentlemen, it is only just
Que lo aprendamos hablar	That we learn to speak it
Y siempre darle lugar	And always reserve a place
Al idioma nacional	For the language of the nation
Es justo y es racional	It is just and reasonable
Pero les hago un recuerdo	But, I wish to remind you
Para a San Pablo adorar	That paying homage to Saint Paul
No desadoren a San Pedro.	Does not disgrace Saint Peter.][8]

No doubt the subscribers of Spanish weeklies, nodded in agreement as they read Alarid's submissions, for not only was *sentimiento* now externalized, but print provided a means to widely disseminate it among the masses of *nativos* in a way not possible before. Throughout his lifetime Alarid was recognized as *bardo* and *maestro*. In his old age, when he lost his eyesight and was forced to retire, *La Bandera Americana* of Albuquerque would often relay communiqués from Galisteo informing readers of the circumstances of Alarid's life: ". . . he is retiring from active politics and will dedicate his time to maintaining the friendship of everyone, especially of those noble hearts who throughout his misfortune have not forgotten him and have offered him solace and material assistance. . . . Professor Alarid lives quietly with his lovely wife in the village of Galisteo, where he was teaching when he was beset by the dreaded sickness that caused his blindness."[9] And it seems Alarid was not forgotten; his obituary in 1918 reads, "Professor Alarid was prominent throughout his life in the state of New Mexico and in Colorado as an educator, public speaker, and musician; he was a principal at various times, a magnetic orator, and an artist in the realm of music."[10]

Structures of Domination

By the time the first railway lines reached New Mexico in 1879, New Mexico had been a territory of the United States for over thirty years and the full impact of Anglo-American presence was being felt throughout the Southwest. In the decades that followed, Anglo Americans moved to consolidate their power in the economic, social, and political arenas in New Mexico. Anglo Americans imposed new systems of trade, commerce, and politics on the region. *Nuevomexicanos* reacted to these developments with apprehension. The politics of exclusion practiced by recent immigrants threatened to limit *Nuevomexicano* participation in the mainstream of public life, was particularly repugnant to native residents. Most injurious, however, was the realization that such things should occur in what they considered to be their homeland.

The U.S. takeover of the Southwest produced a skewed and fractured political reality for the native inhabitants of the region. The material conditions of the territory seemed to improve, especially among certain social classes. The introduction of manufactured goods and of new technologies led many *Nuevomexicanos* to believe that the U.S. takeover would bring about beneficial and desirable change. The movement of peoples and ideas from the eastern seaboard seemed to corroborate the popular conception that all peoples and all classes in the acquired territories would share in the unprecedented change and prosperity. The possibilities inherent in this point of contact with Anglo-American society gave rise to new expectations among a generation of young *Nuevomexicanos* born toward the middle of the century. But racism, notions of cultural superiority, and class distinctions clouded much of this contact.

Despite the clear aim among Anglo Americans to dispossess and displace *Nuevomexicanos*, these ambitions were often thwarted by *Nuevomexicanos*, who resisted such aggressive posturing at every opportunity. The work of *los periodiqueros* provides evidence that *Nuevomexicanos* were not the passive, docile people they were made out to be in the eastern press. To the contrary they rapidly armed themselves with the press and began to refute the ill-spirited view of them propagated by Anglo-American immigrants to the region.

Couched in the trappings of Manifest Destiny, Anglo-American historians, anthropologists, and others uniformly promoted their own achievements while excising those of the *Nuevomexicano* community from accounts of the American Southwest. In the realm of civic leadership and achievement Anglo-American historians tended to promote the biographies of other Anglo-Americans. Rarely, and most often only in instances where political expediency demanded it, did the lives of native New Mexicans figure in these histories. Such omissions served to aggrandize the achievement of the Anglo-American community at the expense of *nativos*.

In matters of educational attainment and intellectual merit the effects of Anglo-American domination was most acute and damaging. Anglo Americans transposed literary and historiographic paradigms to New Mexico that had had time to mature on the eastern seaboard and concluded that by comparison *Nuevomexicanos* had nothing to offer. Their ideas were built upon the ideology that the *Mexicano* was racially inferior and, by extension, intellectually deficient. Anglo-American scholars, writers, and essayists uniformly proceeded to diffuse this discourse of derision. In most instances, political containment in the Southwest was preceded by intense negativism and racism directed at *Nuevomexicanos* and other non-Anglo communities. Anglo-American journalists and writers visiting the Southwest for the first time supplied eastern readers with an endless stream of articles that exoticized the natives of the region or typecast them in countless harangues and diatribes that belittled the cultural and social institutions they had developed. As Sarah Deutsch points out, this discourse of domination saw *Nuevomexicano* resistance to Americanization as cultural intransigence: "Hispanics were seen as isolated, static, inflexible, paternalistic, and passive" (1984, 5). Such characterizations were used to rationalize and justify the right of Anglo Americans to expand their social and cultural provenance to other peoples who stood in the way of their push westward. Proving the moral, social, and cultural inferiority of *Nuevomexicanos* became the subtext to a vast majority of writings on New Mexico.

This intense negativism fostered the belief that the cultural practices of *Nuevomexicanos* were equally useless and therefore had no place in the histories of the region. Even as the century waned this attitude prevailed among Anglo-American observers. In 1899, for example, *The Atlantic Monthly* published a chapter-length article that carried the loathsome title "The Greaser." The author of the article unabashedly asserted that Anglo Americans were superior to the *Mexicano* inhabitants of New Mexico: , "Some one—I think it was Herbert Spencer—has declared that the unmistakable mark of a high race of men is individualization, differentiation, heterogeneity, and variation from type. If that be a test we need not hesitate to say of the Greaser that he stands very low on the scale; for, to lapse into a Western mode of speech, he is all alike. Choose one, and you have a pattern from which all his brethren could be drawn, with only slight modifications in the items of beard and adipose" (753). The author of the piece concludes that *Nuevomexicanos* are ignorant, poverty-ridden, backward, and less enterprising than the Indians of the region. The air of superiority and self-righteousness that spurs the author in his conclusions produced such summations as, "One who is dominated by the modern American spirit would be likely to predicate the downfall of the Greaser, upon one fact, that he is lacking in 'enterprise.' Nothing could be more truly said of him than that he is not 'progressive' (ibid., 1899, 755). The prevalence of this view suggests that Anglo Americans of the period were not interested in nurturing the educational and intellectual progress of a people they most often viewed as their moral inferiors. It is clear that whatever progress and attainment *Nuevomexicanos* made during the territorial period resulted from their own initiatives.

New Mexico's territorial laws impacted every aspect of life for its inhabitants and tended on the whole to exacerbate the racial and cultural divisions among *Nuevomexicanos*, Native Americans, and Anglo Americans. This arrangement favored the Anglo-American political overseers of the territory appointed in Washington. Despite countless petitions seeking the admission of the territory as a state of the Union, New Mexico would remain an internal colony of the United States for over sixty years. In the interim a network of political appointments made in Washington controlled the governance of territorial affairs. Anglo-American political appointees back in New Mexico consorted openly and allied themselves to special interests and economic rings. The most notorious, the Santa Fe Ring, lead by Thomas B. Catron, brought together Anglo-American lawyers, bankers, land speculators, and venture capitalists. The ring's members exerted tremendous influence and power, thus gaining control over the major resources of the region. Native leadership, quite expectedly, found itself ostracized and powerless. Echoing the sentiments voiced by Jesús María Hilario Alarid, *La Voz de Pueblo* of Las Vegas called this new political arrangement "pupilaje territorial [territorial wardship]" and demanded representation for New Mexicans at all levels of government. An 1889 editorial reads: "We should keep in mind that it is diminution for our people to be governed by upstarts and strangers when we have among us good and competent men to fill all positions from the first to the last of them."[11] The exclusion decried by *La Voz del Pueblo* had the additional affect of discouraging *Nuevomexicano* participation in public life by downplaying *nativo* achievement uniformly.

It is in this context that *Nuevomexicanos* grappled to achieve social parity with Anglo Americans after 1880. In their attempt to compete, *Nuevomexicanos* began to muster their own resources in the hope of creating greater educational opportunities for their community. Their aspirations were aligned with the efforts of the Catholic church to establish parochial education in the territory.

Education, Biliteracy, and the World Beyond the Village

> (B)orn were the academies, the institutes, and the public schools, and since then—in the Catholic and secular institutions—our young people could be seen. Eager for knowledge, they would leave their remote villages to go to those institutions where they

> earnestly drank of the blessed and sweet waters of precious fountains, which, in short time, would shortly bear fruit in [the form of] the bright intellect of the *Neo-Mexicanos*.
>
> —José Escobar, *Las Dos Repúblicas,* Denver, Colorado, 1896.

The story of New Mexico's *periodiqueros* and their success in creating a native tradition in journalism is also the story of the establishment and development of New Mexico's first schools and the dramatic changes in education that followed. There is no doubt but that the newly arriving Catholic clergy entering the territory from the east decisively impacted the first generation of *Nuevomexicanos* to come of age after 1848. The "new literacy" derived from formal study now began to redefine the role of literates within a predominantly oral community. Three institutions in particular, St. Michael's College in Santa Fe, Lorreto Academy, and the Jesuit College at Las Vegas, had the greatest effect in educating a generation of young men and women who would provide leadership to the *Nuevomexicano* community.

Arriving soon after the American takeover, the first archbishop of Santa Fe, Jean Baptiste Lamy, acted to establish parochial schools in the most populated towns in New Mexico. Lamy aimed to create a feeder network of schools that would serve to encourage vocations to the priesthood among native New Mexicans. To this end, Lamy recruited a group of Italian Jesuits in 1867 for the purpose of organizing a seminary in New Mexico.

Earlier, however, Lamy had established a school for boys in Santa Fe in 1851. The school's primary mission was to teach English. Two years later, Lamy brought the Sisters of Loretto from Baltimore to supervise the establishment of a school for girls in Santa Fe. The school they established was *La Academia de Nuestra Señora de la Luz,* or the Academy of Our Lady of Light, which would later become Loretto Academy. The work of the Sisters of Loretto in subsequent years extended to other towns in the region. Over the next two decades the Sisters of Loretto established schools at Taos (1863), Mora (1864), Las Vegas (1869), Las Cruces (1870), and Bernalillo (1875). In these communities the nuns' primary role and mission became to establish schools and curriculum to meet the needs of rural areas.

Nearly all of New Mexico's *periodiqueros* and the generation that was to become its literati were trained at private institutions of higher education. Lamy next recruited the Christian Brothers to establish a school for young men in Santa Fe. That school, El Colegio de San Miguel, later known as St. Michael's College, opened its doors in November 1859. St. Michael's quickly became the flagship of Catholic education in New Mexico. *Nuevomexicanos,* who were quite aware of the dearth of educational opportunity that had characterized New Mexico since its earliest days, mustered their resources in order to gain access to these new schools. *Nuevomexicano* families sent their children in large numbers to the new schools.

The *rico* class was obviously in the best position to pay for the education of their children, but children of the poorer classes also attended these institutions. A few *ricos* had means enough to discriminate in the choice of schools their children would attend, and did so whenever possible. Presbyterian missionary Mrs. Thomas Harwood reported in 1874 that attempts to establish Protestant schools in New Mexico were often frustrated by the missionaries' inability to satisfy the requirements of certain *rico* families who demanded more than rudimentary schools.

> Our Mission school at this place (La Junta) is the most advanced of any in the territory and it might be made a great success with sufficient means to erect suitable buildings. The Mexicans go a great deal on outward show and style and until we can have fine buildings we shall not be patronized much by the wealthy. They generally send their children to the States to be educated. (Harwood [1908] 1983, 253)

Indeed after 1860 some *Nuevomexicano* families sent their sons and daughters to universities and institutions of higher learning in the "States." By the 1880s *Mexicano* graduates of Catholic institutions such as St. Louis University and Notre Dame were returning to the Southwest and entering the professions. Many more *Nuevomexicanos*, however, would be trained and educated at local institutions. Anselmo Arellano reports that St. Michael's College had 250 day students and 30 boarders at the end of the first year. By 1866 the college provided two classes free of charge to those students unable to pay (1990, 115). An 1894 advertisement in *El Independiente* of Las Vegas noted of the school and its curriculum, "This institution under the direction of the Christian Brothers Schools was established in 1859. Its program of study includes courses in elementary and business English; French, Spanish, and German lessons; phonology and typographical writing; the study of chemistry, study of minerals and instrumental music."[12]

The Jesuit Imprint

> Salve Gasparri. Vínculo fraterno,
> Perpetuamente enlace en su destino
> Al Nuevo México y á la Italia bella.
>
> [Praise to Gasparri
> —Fraternal link, eternal tie,
> (linking) the destiny of New Mexico to lovely Italy.]
>
> —Eleuterio Baca, Las Vegas, New Mexico, 1882, "A Padre Donato María Gasparri: Facellido el 18 de diciembre de 1882"

The arrival of the Jesuits in New Mexico in 1867 signaled a renewed effort by Archbishop Lamy to cull vocations to the priesthood from the native population by establishing institutions of higher learning in New Mexican communities outside of Santa Fe. The Reverend Donato M. Gasparri, an Italian Jesuit, journeyed from Europe in 1867 to head the Jesuit missions in New Mexico. Gasparri organized what came to be known as the New Mexico-Colorado Mission and was at its head during its early years. Gasparri also established the Catholic press in New Mexico and was the first editor of *La Revista Católica.*

Gasparri initially planned to establish a college at Albuquerque, and first considered installing his printing press there. Both a site for the school and a printing press brought by cart from the "States" had been acquired when flooding of the Río Grande in May 1874 threatened to undo Gasparri's plans. He was forced to reassess Albuquerque as a suitable site for the permanent location of the Jesuit College. Beyond the fear of future flooding along the Río Grande, Gasparri also had become convinced that Las Vegas in northeastern New Mexico was outpacing Albuquerque's growth and was experiencing an unprecedented economic boom. As a result, Gasparri relocated the press and his mission to that city soon after the floods of May 1874 subsided. Plans to open a Jesuit College at Las Vegas began in June 1877. The college was opened at "Old Town" Las Vegas in a house donated for the purpose by Don Francisco López, a resident of the upper plaza (Vollmar 1939).

That *Nuevomexicanos* wanted a second college in the territory is shown by the immediate support they lent to the Jesuits. Local enthusiasm for education grew in anticipation. The Jesuit fathers reported early after their arrival in Las Vegas that there simply were not enough schools in the territory to meet the demand for education. The prospectus for Las Vegas College stipulated that the school would be open for day scholars and boarders regardless of religious affiliation. Its course of study, stated the school's prospectus, would accommodate the special needs of students:

> Only such matters will be taught as are deemed to meet the special requirements of our Territory, and will be adapted to the capacity and gradual proficiency of pupils. Consequently, Reading and Writing, and elementary lessons in English and Spanish Grammar, in History, Geography, Arithmetic and Book-keeping will be part of the regular course.—A few applications for the study of Latin having been received, that language together with French, Italian and music of piano or organ, will be left to the option of parents. (Vollmar 1939, 15)

The cost to boarders of the college was set at two hundred dollars a year. Day scholars were required to pay a fee of one to three dollars a month and arrangements could be made to waive the costs of tuition in cases of hardship. Perhaps because these were Italian Jesuits they felt little compulsion to disturb the language practices of the *Nuevomexicanos* and while they may not have altogether embraced local religious culture, here too they seemed to be more tolerant than Anglo-American clergy. In the classroom they were pragmatic enough to acknowledge the need to provide instruction in Spanish, and *Nuevomexicanos* seemed to sense an enduring bond with the Italian clergy based on spiritual and cultural affinities.

The majority of students in the first year were drawn from Las Vegas and neighboring ranching communities. The school catalog at the end of the first term listed 132 students. Of these, 25 were boarders and 4 were half-boarders. As the school's reputation grew, students came to study from Colorado and from distant cities such as Chihuahua, Durango, and Mexico City. Interestingly, in addition to the Spanish-speaking students, the Jesuits reported that by 1884 "the day scholars at the College included all the Jewish boys of Las Vegas" (ibid., 129).

Once established in Las Vegas, the Jesuits were quick to respond to the peculiar educational needs of the typical *Nuevomexicano* student. They noted that the major obstacle to learning was the poverty of the territory, which made it difficult to retain students long enough to complete the entire course of study. The first Anglo-American Jesuit to teach at Las Vegas College notes as much in a letter dated March 29, 1888, "Think of the consolation we derive from our work when we know that the highest ambition of the boys whom we try to educate is to become a *ranchero* or a clerk. One boy last year—to give an instance—took music lessons. At the end of the year he left all his music behind, giving as a reason that he would not need it any longer, as he was going to work on a ranch" (ibid., 22).

The Jesuits ran the college at Las Vegas for eleven years, during which time improvements included the construction of a new school building in East Las Vegas. The curriculum continued to evolve and the students at the college began to show educational attainment that could finally be considered college level. Despite their school's rocky start, the Jesuits at Las Vegas never lost sight of the aim to raise the educational attainment of their students. Jesuit historian, Edward Vollmar writes that the years between 1882 and 1885 saw the greatest improvements at Las Vegas. "The period saw the expansion of the College, the fulfillment of the long cherished plans. Then, too, the school was rapidly becoming recognized as an institution of higher learning worthy of competing with those 'back East' " (ibid., 22).

The students at the College of Las Vegas represented a cross-section of society and children of *rico* and *pobre* families attended classes. Having little access to cash, *Nuevomexicanos* made special arrangements with the Jesuits to exchange goods or services for the tuition of their children. In some in-

Fig. 2. Unidentified members of the class of 1881 of Jesuit College at Las Vegas. Donnelly Collection, New Mexico Highlands University. Courtesy of Las Vegas Committee for Historic Preservation.

stances this arrangement seems to have incurred the displeasure of some members of the order. According to one, "The college was finished and in running order for the second year. But the worries of the Superiors had just begun. They found the greatest difficulties in keeping it open, because they received so little money for the boys' tuition. The Mexicans hated to part with their 'dinero' and much preferred to pay for the tuition with 'oves et boves et pecora campi' (ibid., 1939, 37).

By 1882 the Jesuits were providing a rigorous course of study based on training in the classics. As Vollmar suggests, "The long tradition of classical education certainly had its influence on the planning of the course of studies for the colleges of the New Mexico-Colorado Mission. Some of the members of the mission had attended the College of Nobles in Naples, and all had the classical course that forms part of the training of every Jesuit" (Ibid., 1939, 21).

Memorializing Acts of Daily Life: Eleuterio Baca

The Jesuit imprint on the educational and spiritual formation of a generation lasted well beyond the relatively short existence of the college at Las Vegas. Time and again *los periodiqueros* would draw on their early training, weaving allusions to classical and world literature into their writings, as in the following verse-tribute by Eleuterio Baca to the school's founder, Donato Gasparri,

De virtud y saber portento miro,
Obra de Dios!—Si yo seguir pudiera
Nadando por el aire de la esfera
A tu bella alma en su feliz retiro!
Tus gloriosos ejemplos cuanto admiro,
O los prodigios de tu celo santo.

[I marvel at the virtue and knowledge in this work of God,
If only I could swim across the
spheres and follow
the beauty of your soul to
its safe retreat.
How I marvel at the deeds,
the wonders of your works of saintly fervor.][13]

Typically, as in the case of Eleuterio Baca, *Nuevomexicano* youth of the period received their early education at private schools and then went on to study in the territory's parochial schools. As a boy in Santa Fe, Baca studied with the Christian Brothers then continued his formal instruction with members of the order for another two terms (1865–66) at an extension school that had been established by this time at Mora, New Mexico. His mentors saw promise in the young man and later urged him to advance his studies at St. Louis University, another Catholic institution.

Eleuterio's ancestors had been among the first families that settled the area under the Las Vegas Grandes land grant in 1836. By the latter half of the nineteenth century the Bacas were well represented among the merchants, ranchers, and civic leaders in the Las Vegas area. Eleuterio's father, Juan María Baca and his wife, Dolores Sandoval Baca, placed a high value on education and providing for their children's education. Eleuterio and a younger brother Francisco N. de Baca were both sent to study in the "States" and both took their degrees from St. Louis University.

At St. Louis University, Eleuterio was among the few "foreign" students at the institution. His letters to family, many written in English, indicate that he was completely conversant and literate in his adopted language. A letter to his brother Benito in September 1871 tells of other *Nuevomexicanos* residing in St. Louis at the time and of the cross-cultural position they occupy in that city: "Mrs. Otero and family are all enjoying perfect health; she regrets that I did not bring Juanito with me, and so it is your business to do so when you come to the States again so that she may teach him the manners of a country which at a not distant day he will be forced to adopt."[14]

While a student Baca showed an inclination toward the study of letters and joined the Philalethic Society, an organization dedicated to excellence in

Fig. 3. Eleuterio Baca. Read, *Historia Ilustrada de Nuevo México* (73).

public speaking and to the cultivation of the literary arts. The school's yearbook, the *Jubilee,* notes of the Philalethic Society, "She has, almost from the foundation of the University, been the recognized literary organization of the institution, the speakers for all public occasions have almost invariably been chosen from her members, and the men who have achieved distinction for themselves and their school in Oratory or Literature made their first appearances in Philalethic Hall."[15] Baca served the organization as its vice president during the 1891 school year.

After returning to New Mexico, Baca taught school in several rural communities in New Mexico and West Texas. In 1890 he returned to Las Vegas, the city that would remain his home, and became the associate editor of *La Voz del Pueblo,* which had only recently been moved to Las Vegas. Baca maintained a lifelong association with Enrique H. Salazar, the proprietor and editor-in-chief of *La Voz,* and when no longer employed in the offices of *La Voz,* he remained a friend and a frequent contributor to *La Voz* and later to the second of Salazar's papers, *El Independiente*.

Baca's university training won him unbridled respect and admiration among his fellow *Nuevomexicanos*. It also reified his achievement and gave social status to the position and aspirations of literates formed in the "new literacy" of the age. In 1891 *La Voz del Pueblo* noted, "Don Eleuterio Baca, a faithful and noble disciple of Calderón and Lope de Vega, first among the *Nuevomexicano* poets, was in the city this week, [he was] down from his residence in Sapelló."[16]

Baca's poetry, like that of Jesús María Hilario Alarid, is linked to the tradition of the poet-troubadour. Occupying an honored place within the community, Baca was entrusted with the expression of the collective *sentimiento* of his community. In paying tribute to the virtues and meritorious deeds of his neighbors and friends, Baca returned favors to his community. Baca's occasional verse may strike the contemporary reader as pithy and oversentimentalized, but these poems reveal a great deal about the social signification of memorializing and explain the eagerness of his neighbors and friends to have him write occasional poems and commendatory verse to accompany and record the momentous transitions in the life cycle. The baptism of Eleuterio's godchild, Nemesia, in December 1894 elicited, "A Nemesia Sandoval [To Nemesia Sandoval]," an *octavilla* based on a classic eight-verse strophe. The death of his mentor and the first director of the Jesuit College moved Baca to pen an elegy he titled, "A Padre Donato María Gasparri: Fallecido el 18 de diciembre de 1882 [To Father Donato María Gasparri: Died on the 18th of December of 1892]." The desire to memorialize the life of his second wife occasioned "En Memoria de Cleofitas S. de Baca Tributo de su esposo Eleuterio Baca [In Memory of Cleofitas S. de Baca: A Tribute from her husband Eleuterio Baca]." The birthday celebration of one of Baca's pupils brought about "Poesía en la Ocasión de Un Cumpleaños [Poetry on the Occasion of a Birthday]," a work in the *cancionero* or narrative-song tradition of the region. These poems show the influence of a lettered tradition, but their stylization is clearly meant to serve the requirements of recitation and publication for a local community. They are in effect mnemonic markers for community rituals, that is, for the externalization of a collective consciousness in life situations (at a wake, baptismal font, fiesta in the patio of the house), the function and purpose of which was redoubled through their appearance in the local paper.

As "professional remembrencer" (Goody 1968, 31), Baca is charged with memorializing the life of his community. Baca's patterned poems have metatextual meaning: They make clear the relevance of past lives to an ever-unfolding sociocultural present. Baca drew on his formal training in letters to accord to his poetry the conventions of meter, rhyme, and measure. Eleuterio observed the classical forms of Hispanic poetry, yet, notwithstanding this concession to formalism, Baca's poems follow the long-established tradition in the oral register of New Mexican life. For example, the obituary Baca penned for his brother Francisco and which was published in *El Independiente*, ends with the obligatory release of *sentimiento*, which wells up in the *despedida*, or last farewell, to his deceased brother:

—Quizás de mi muerte el dia	[Perhaps the day I die
Habrá una alma generosa	A generous soul will
que riegue llanto en mi loza	Bathe my grave with tears
Como yo en tu tumba fría	As I [do upon] your frozen tomb
En tanto que el alma mía,	And so my soul
Con toda sinceridad,	Sincerely moved
A impulsos de la verdad,	by the [sad] fate
Que nos ha unido a los dos	That unites us
Te envía su último Adios	[My soul] sends out to the immense
Por la inmensa Eternidad!	Universe its last farewell to you.][17]

New Mexico at the turn of the century continued to have a predominantly Spanish-speaking populace and a politically powerful Anglo minority. The demographic distribution of the population created a need for capable translators to mediate written materials between English and Spanish. This need moved Baca later in his life to turn his creative aspirations more and more toward translation and renderings of literary and scholarly works in both languages. In 1910 he translated Benjamín M. Read's *Historia Ilustrada de Nuevo México* to English.

The Jesuits, who were particularly adept at fostering the humanities and the study of letters, organized the Philharmonic and Dramatic Association, and the Literary Society at the College of Las Vegas. Both of these organizations fostered extracurricular activities that redoubled the course of study in the humanities. One father noted that the effects of such work began to take hold in student activities soon after their introduction: "The students had given their first dramatic performance at the Distribution of Prizes in 1881. The Mexicans loved to act and dramatics soon became one of their favorite pastimes" (Vollmar 1939, 41).

The most durable journalistic achievement of the Jesuits at Las Vegas was the establishment of the Jesuit newspaper *La Revista Católica. La Revista* offered *Nuevomexicano* youth and the *Mexicano* community of Las Vegas and the rest of New Mexico unheard possibilities for voicing positions on secular and religious issues.[18] For the first time, journalism became a realistic aspiration for the region's youth.

That some of the most prominent voices of the *Nuevomexicano* literati had been students of the College of Las Vegas is proof Eleuterio Baca and others of his generation were well served by their education. Eusebio Chacón, a practicing attorney in Trinidad. Ezequiel C. de Baca, editor of *La Voz de*

Pueblo; Antonio Lucero, associate editor of *La Voz*; and Camilo Padilla, a popular and successful publisher in Santa Fe, would all pass through the halls of the Jesuit College of Las Vegas.

Ritual Displays of Learning: Severino Trujillo

> Our ruin is unavoidable if the frightful confusion that threatens us remains unopposed.
>
> —Severino Trujillo, Mora, New Mexico, 1894

Severino Trujillo, the author of the 1879 prospectus for *La Estrella de Mora*, was born in the mountain village of Guadalupita (Mora County) and had the rare opportunity among members of his generation to travel and study in Europe. While this may seem a minor accomplishment, to *Nuevomexicanos* of his day, and especially in light of the poverty and geographic isolation that continued to hold fast in the mountain valleys of northern New Mexico, indeed to Severino himself, it must have occasioned the sensation of a weary traveler coming over a rise in the road and seeing a great city lying ahead.

The details of Trujillo's life not only adds to the knowledge of *Neo-Mexicano* literates formed in the "new literacy" imparted by schools and lyceum, but clues us to the workings of print discourse in *Nuevomexicano* communities. If one traces Trujillo's personal and professional associations they point to an interlocking grid of discursive activity that bound together important segments of the *nativo* society. Trujillo's ecclesiastical, political, and communitarian socialization provided him the authority to voice *sentimiento.* His accreditation in village society was augmented by his apprenticeship under Lamy's French clergy, by his stay in a French seminary, and later by his association with Casimiro Barela and *Nuevomexicano* literates in the Trinidad area.

Severino Trujillo began his early education at the Christian Brothers School in Mora, which had been established in 1865. As would have been the case with most children of his day, Severino received his religious and moral education from the parish priest and nuns in residence at Mora. At the time the priest assigned to the village was the French prelate Father John B. Guerín, or as he was known to the parishioners of Santa Gertrudis Church, "el padre Juan." Guerín was the third parish priest in residence at Mora after American rule. He, along with a large number of French prelates, had been recruited to do missionary work in New Mexico by Jean B. Lamy, the first archbishop of Santa Fe. Guerín was ordained in December 1854. After his assignment to New Mexico he served as parish priest at Mora until his death on June 10, 1885 (Salpointe [1898] 1967, 27).

Guerín's predecessor in Mora was Jean Bautiste Salpointe—later to become the second archbishop of New Mexico. Salpointe, in fact, had invited the Christian Brothers to establish a school in the Mora township. It was an institution that served the Mora community for some nineteen years, seeing the graduation of countless numbers of the valley's children. Severino Trujillo came under the tutelage of Padre Guerín and served as his assistant, aiding the priest in his duties and rounds to the outlying missions of the parish. Guerín's influence, and that of his predecessor, Salpointe, in the education and moral upbringing of the youth of area had a lasting impact. Salpointe, for example, had shaped the early development of Casimiro Barela, who went on to have a distinguished career in the Colorado legislature. Barela's service as senator from Las Animas County for some forty years earned him the title of "father of the Colorado Senate." Barela also founded two important Spanish-language newspapers, *El Progreso*, established in Trinidad in 1890, and *Las Dos Repúblicas,* a paper founded in Denver in 1896 (Fernández 1911, 42).

Severino Trujillo and Casimiro Barela both became protégés of Jean Bautiste Salpointe. As a protégé, and an assistant to the parish priest, Barela was groomed in an apprenticeship in the classic sense. Like the urchin of the picaresque novel, this relationship was one based on service to the master, who in turn provided room, board, and instruction to the young man. Barela's biographer describes just such an exchange:

> Young Casimiro went to Father Salpointe's aid to render services in the cleaning and domestic chores of the house, to help as an altar boy in the sacrifice of the Mass, and to accompany the priest while making the rounds of his ministry. In return for the services he provided to the priest, he would have board, clothes, food, and the instruction that the priest would impart to him.[19]

It is in this vein that Trujillo also received his early education, when young Severino assumed Barela's duties as the priest's assistant. Guerín in turn induced Severino to study Latin and Greek in preparation for the priesthood. Through the priest's offices Trujillo traveled to Paris in 1872 to enter the Seminary of St. Suplice as a seminarian. He remained there until completing his studies in 1876. Electing not to enter the priesthood, he returned to the Mora area the year of his graduation, whereupon he was appointed to local political office. Shortly after his return to Mora County he penned his prospectus for *La Estrella de Mora.*

In 1884, Severino moved to Trinidad, Colorado, to assist his long-time friend Casimiro Barela, court secretary for Las Animas County. In Trinidad, Trujillo helped to launch the Asociación de Mutuo Adelantamiento, a mutual aid society dedicated to the advancement of southern Colorado's Mexican-origin community.

Throughout the 1880s Trujillo alternately resided in Trinidad and in Mora, New Mexico. He became active in county and territorial politics in New

Mexico and in 1887 sought election to the territorial legislature under the banner of El Partido del Pueblo Unido, the People's party ticket, a third-party initiative to county politics dominated by the major parties. In 1889 he was selected to serve as Mora County representative to the constitutional convention of 1890.

Severino Trujillo distanced himself from the political arena, and sometime after 1897 moved to eastern Mora County, where he established a private school at the ranching community of Wagon Mound. Trujillo made use of his credentials in recruiting students to his new school. A note in Santa Fe's *El Boletín Popular* reported that Trujillo had credentials from "the best universities in Europe" and that his private school afforded *Nuevomexicano* youth "the rare opportunity to study with a teacher of his caliber." Trujillo, according to the historian Benjamín Read, was still teaching classes at his school in Wagon Mound as late as 1911 (Read 1911, 542).

The world Severino Trujillo had been born into was increasingly fissuring along the lines of race and ethnicity. Given that "Anglos attacked every aspect of Hispanic culture, from language to food" (Deutsch, 1984, 37), it is not surprising that religious differences inflamed social divisions. Systemic shifts in religiocultural orientation underway in Trujillo's lifetime festered into social antagonism and discursive reprisal. Trujillo, like others of his generation, took up strong positions in this ideological battle for the hearts and minds of *nativos. Nuevomexicanos,* who were seen by incoming Protestants as "victims of their own heritage—their Catholicism, their environment and their own elite" (ibid., 5), quite naturally responded with counterreprisals. The religious schism of the period requires research for its own sake, but it is important to note that in an atmosphere charged by questions of religion and dogma, *Nuevomexicanos* felt a strong compulsion to reprove their attackers, even in situations not overtly germane to the debate.

Severino Trujillo, for example, voiced his allegiance to his Catholic benefactors in a speech he delivered in honor of the visit of Archbishop Chapelle to Trujillo's birthplace, Guadalupita, in Mora County in August 1892. After a note of welcome, Trujillo launched into a scathing attack on Protestantism and what he characterizes as "las sectas heréticas [the heretical sects]," saying, "We see all the schools of philosophy, all the heretical sects—outside of the Church and its authority—go astray, contradict themselves, doubt and despair of finding the truth."[20] Much of Trujillo's speech continues in the same fashion, and while the rigidity of his position offers little room for compromise, the example suggests that this type of contestation was commonplace and that it was rapidly becoming part of print discourse. This oral performance forms part of what Rhys Issac terms the "ritual displays of the authority of learning" (Issac 1983), and in this case shows that even in the most remote of New Mexican villages, "por entre las sinuosidades de estas montañas rocallosas que aqui se levantan, [through these winding rocky

Fig. 4. Severino Trujillo. Read, *Historia Ilustrada de Nuevo Mexico* (542).

mountains that rise up here],"[21] the world of print and book-learning had affected the lives of typical *Nuevomexicano* villagers. Using his book learning to good effect, Trujillo's words connected the theological debate with elements in the natural world sure to resonate with meaning for his *vecinos* (neighbors). In pointing, (no doubt) west to the nearby Sangre de Cristo Mountains, "cuyas cimas cubiertas de nieve [whose peaks are covered with snow]," Trujillo evoked a powerful metaphor when he reminded his listeners (the archbishop included) that the mountain snows are "símbolo de la candidez de sus habitantes [the symbol of the candor of (the mountain) residents]," faithful Catholics all.

Trujillo's speech at the tiny village of Guadalupita would never again be reinvested with the same intensity that the oral recitation must have lent it, but it would reappear again as an article in *La Revista Católica* with the title "La Iglesia Católica [The Catholic Church]." *La Revista Católica* circulated widely among Spanish-speaking people in the Southwest, and whether Trujillo was aware of it or not, his message, *spoken* to fellow parishioners, though he deems them "porción no insignificante de la parroquia de Mora [not an insignificant portion of the Mora Parish]," was transformed in ways its author may not have fully understood when it became a *published* text that reached thousands of readers across the Southwest. With this, Trujillo's treatment of local concerns became enmeshed into wider regional discourses, and the text of Trujillo's speech, like his work as journalist, teacher, and literate, formed part of a larger and intractable ideological struggle that pitted Anglo against *nativo* and ultimately drew *Nuevomexicanos* into heated debate with other *Nuevomexicanos* on questions of religion, culture, and political power.

Neo-Mexicanismo and Cultural Ascendancy

The dichotomy produced by the distress of conquest and a subsequent repositioning around new sociocultural circumstances for *Nuevomexicanos* after 1848 would become the principle concern of an emerging generation of journalists and writers. It would in many ways define and become their mission. A concrescence of educational and technological advancements led *Nuevomexicano* youth in the last two decades of the nineteenth century to consider that they were at the outset of a literary, cultural, and political ascendancy greater than any in their history. That ascendancy was made possible above all by the emergence of a significant and unprecedented number among that generation who were educated at institutions of higher learning in New Mexico and in the "States." Second, this generation came into ever greater possession of the mechanical printing press, and last but perhaps most important, they were infused with a sense of mission and urgency fostered by the social, racial, and political contentions of their age.

This emergent class of journalists represented the aspirations of a wide segment of the *Nuevomexicano* community after 1880. As journalists, writers, and editors these "new professionals" were poised to push beyond the limitations drawn by time, poverty, isolation, racial discrimination, and conquest in New Mexico. Educated in the classics, inspired by the power of the press, seasoned in the copy room, they were driven by the imperative to raise their voices in opposition to the suppression of their culture and language, and as they did so, this generation began to assert its civic, cultural, and human rights as never before. They also began to realize and sense that cultural and political ascendancy was not only desirable, but achievable as well. The ascendancy they struggled to promote and propagate argued for the creation of institutions and vehicles of cultural empowerment heretofore unseen in New Mexico.

This generation's aspirations rested on the belief that the popular press would bring enlightenment and education to the populace and document *Nuevomexicano* achievement in the writing of history and literature by native authors. Such promise was described as *una literatura nacional* (a national literature). *Nuevomexicanos* conceived of this corpus of literature as one that would accurately reflect the *Nuevomexicano* experience. These things, they believed, would contribute to the standing of their community in the affairs of state and government, assuring that the interests of the native population of the territory would not take a back seat to those of outsiders. Their agenda was a bold and significant one that issued a call to all *Nuevomexicanos* to seize control of their social and cultural destiny. Their ideas were as novel for their time as they are for ours.

Nuevomexicanos, in particular this generation of *periodiqueros,* who had found in education an opportunity to voice ideas in the public forums of society, argued vehemently for a radical adjustment to the social compact that tied them to the United States. In no uncertain terms they advocated for the retention of their language and cultural practices. A startling feature of their movement was that *Nuevomexicanos* saw no inconsistency with their desire for civic and political absorption into the body politic of the United States. *Nuevomexicanos,* at least at the outset of contact with *los Americanos,* were generally optimistic and viewed the changes being ushered into their homeland as both a challenge and opportunity. As Alarid's poem "El idioma español" shows, *nativos* realized the advantage and the need to become bilingual and rapidly began to learn and use English, the language of their adoptive country. The introduction of manufactured goods and of new technologies left the impression in the minds of many *Nuevomexicanos* that the U.S. takeover would bring about desirable material changes.

The possibilities inherent in this point of contact with Anglo-American society gave rise to new expectations among an emerging generation of *Nuevomexicanos* born toward the middle of the century. Tied to these developments, questions of group identity also began to coalesce for *Nuevomexicanos.*

An obvious way to gauge group identity and consciousness shared by *Nuevomexicanos* is to examine the ethnic and racial labels they used to identify themselves and others. *Nuevomexicanos* routinely referred to the Anglo Americans as *anglos, anglo-sajónes, sajónes, americanos,* or *extranjeros.* The latter designation of foreigner was used in opposition to *nativo,* or native, a term reflecting the strong ancestral identification of *Nuevomexicanos* with their homeland.

The assumption is that "Spanish-American," has been the self-identifier of choice for the Spanish-speaking in New Mexico. Spanish-language newspapers reveal evidence to the contrary. The term *Spanish-American* is a rather late invention that gained widespread acceptance only after 1900, entering the vocabulary of *Nuevomexicanos* as a response to the question of the statehood[22] and the cultural and ethnic ideation of the post-statehood era. The preferred designations in Spanish-language newspapers before this time are *mexicano, nuevomexicano,* and *hispanoamericano.* The latter term, often translated as "Spanish American" in English newspapers, had a much different meaning for the Spanish-speaking. It was used not only in New Mexico but across the Southwest and northern Mexico. *Hispanoamericano* and its diminutive *Hispano,* connoted a transnational solidarity among and between *Mexicanos* on both sides of the Bravo, much like the present day use of *latinoamericano* or *latino.*

The degree to which the feeling of a social and cultural ascendancy had come to inspire the thought of *Nuevomexicano* literates is seen in their invention and adoption of two terms meant to inspire their cause and uplift the social standing of *Nuevomexicanos* in general. It is clear that *los periodiqueros* consciously moved to create a space in the context of their publications for the use of the terms *Nuevomexicano, Neo-Mexicano,* and to a lesser degree, *Novo-Mexicano.* The widespread use of the Latinisms *Neo* and *Novo* among New Mexico's Spanish-language literates was a deliberate and conscious attempt to draw attention to a sense of progress and promise which *los periodiqueros* had come to believe was within the reach of all *Nuevomexicanos,* one they believed would break the bonds of social stultification. Sensing the magnitude of that promise and taking solace in recent efforts of Mexican youth to organize against the Díaz regime, Camilo Padilla exhorted his readers on *Cinco de Mayo,* 1892, "Let us celebrate the valor and intrepidity of the youth in the neighboring Republic of Mexico. And by this, filled with enthusiasm and patriotism we admonish, 'Why can not, *Neo-Mexicano* youth, do likewise?'" In provoking *Nuevomexicanos* to a sense of action, Padilla continues, "What is not possible for New (Neo) Mexican youth?—these young people who were not born to be dictated to by some or another corrupt politician—unite and organize yourselves, and by this make yourself known and respected." [23]

As is the case with Texas Mexicans, alternatively referred to as *méxico-tejanos* or simply *tejanos,* in the nineteenth century and who have variously been characterized by historians as "a people of paradox,"[24] *Nuevomexicanos* were also attempting to naturalize their social and cultural position within the United States through their use of the terms *Neo* and *Novo Mexicano.* While seeing themselves as *Mexicano* in *sentimiento,* thought, and culture, they necessarily felt the need to address the changing nature of the society they inhabited. In the face of the increased pressure to Americanize they brought into use the term *Neo-Mexicano.* Through the use of this neologism, *Nuevomexicanos* began to foster an image of themselves as a new and emerging group, heir on the one hand to the *Mexicano* culture of their forebears, and on the other, active in the technological and societal changes of the industrial age.

An item in *La Voz del Pueblo* in 1889 on the subject of territorial politics does not essentialize group membership exclusively along racial and ethnic lines in its use of the term. Clearly present in the minds of the editors of *La Voz* is the implicit idea that common ground could be had among Anglos and *nativos* if a clear respect for the region could be fostered between them.

The editors of *La Voz* began the item by declaring their solidarity with those groups identified with the region, "siempre abogaremos para que Nuevo México sea para los Neo Mexicanos" [we shall always advocate for New Mexico to be for New (Neo) Mexicans]." The article glosses out the meaning of *Neo-Mexicano,* ascribing the term primarily to *nativos,* but affording a space, at least in theory, for those individuals who over time could demonstrate commitment to the region, regardless of their racial or ethnic background, "these being of the American race or foreigners as we say, or these being native Mexican-Americans." And while *Neo-Mexicano* as a signifier surely meant many things to many people, the editors of *La Voz del Pueblo* noted that it had greatest significance as a term synonymous with the politics of home rule and self-governance. "No one can understand the affairs of a household like he who resides in it. The same is true of our Territory. Inasmuch we repeat and will always continue to repeat, "New Mexico for *Neo-Mexicanos*."[25] The identification with New Mexico as a homeland, is clearly at work here. It was an idea that would have a lasting and decisive impact on the formation of this and subsequent generations.

In ensuing decades the editors, proprietors, and correspondents of New Mexico's Spanish-language periodicals came to be known by the local populace and fellow journalists as *los periodiqueros.* The work of these *periodiqueros* over the next decades lead to the establishment of Spanish-language newspapers in every important township in New Mexico. By the turn of the century Spanish-language journalism flourished and prospered.

Los periodiqueros were responsible in fact for giving cohesion to a literary, cultural, and political movement among *Neo-Mexicanos* on a scale they had not experienced before. From the ranks of *los periodiqueros* came the first inklings of a native and indigenous intellectual tradition that coalesced in the work of a productive group of poets, writers, historians, and publishers. Within this group are to be found the earliest exponents of a Mexican-American narrative tradition and the first known native historian of the U.S. war with Mexico. It is abundantly clear that New Mexico's *periodiqueros* had every intention of producing works of history and a corpus of literary work with the aim of laying the foundation for a *nativo* school of history and a native literature in the Southwest.

Rarely, if ever, did these individuals have the luxury and means to dedicate themselves solely to literary pursuits and scholarship. Their time was one of dynamic social and political flux, and it was exceedingly rare for them to express their literary and humanistic ambitions apart from the social and political concerns that surrounded them. To their accomplishments can be added important achievements in politics throughout the period. For *Nuevomexicano* youth in the latter half of the nineteenth century, journalism often proved to be a springboard for launching careers in politics, business, and the law. *Neo-Mexicano* journalists would play important roles in politics, education, scholarship, letters, and business in New Mexico toward the end of the century. The long history of elected public officials and the legacy of *Hispano* participation in government and civil service that continues into the present may in fact be the most tangible and lasting legacy of the *periodiquero* movement of the late nineteenth century. One need only consider that New Mexico's second governor, Ezequiel C. de Baca, was a well-known and respected editor in Las Vegas, New Mexico. His associate editor, Antonio Lucero, served as the first secretary of state, and Nestor Montoya, the owner and editor of Albuquerque's *La Bandera Americana* was elected to the Congress of the United States in 1920. To the names of these individuals can be added those of an impressive roster of Spanish-language editors elected to local political office before and after New Mexico became a state.

As *Neo-Mexicano* print culture grew across the region it found form in the organizational networks established by this generation. La Prensa Asociada Hispano-Americana, a regional organization of newspapers, was the most important of these organizations. By 1900, member newspapers formed the vertebrae of a *Mexicano* culture of print along the spine of the railroad lines that criss-crossed the Southwest. The story of this organization, its development, and the culture of print it came to represent, is the subject of the next chapter.

3

Contesting Social and Historical Erasure

The Discursive Agency of La Prensa Asociada Hispano-Americana

> No one can doubt that the union of Hispano journalists will bring great benefits to the community they represent. It's about time that the apostles of journalism move to be respected and make their strength felt.
>
> —Camilo Padilla, Mora, New Mexico, 1892.

"Ya no es simplemente una posibilidad sino un hecho asegurado [No longer a mere possibility but a sure thing]," *La Voz del Pueblo* of Las Vegas announced in February 1892 in its report on the progress of Spanish-language journalists in their bid to organize a press association. As on prior occasions, New Mexico's Spanish-language journalists, or *periodiqueros,* were reiterating their shared belief that a well-organized regional press could, in their words, "bring us innumerable improvements." Pragmatic and prophetic, these editors saw their work in journalism as a way to inform but also to educate the masses of Spanish-speaking *nativos.* Here too was a means to contest the dehistoricizing tendencies of the 1848 Anglo-American conquest of their homeland.

As *La Voz del Pueblo* suggested, the moment was opportune: "The Hispano press *will* organize as it should and when this has been done, certainly, it will benefit, first, the Latin race in general, and second, it will facilitate great advantage for the journalists who represent that group."[1] Spanish-language weeklies in the 1890s enjoyed the advantage of being able to communicate with the majority of New Mexico's citizens who read almost exclusively in Spanish. Since early in the decade they had eclipsed the effectiveness of newspapers published in English. The enthusiasm of the decade led to the increase in quality and professionalism of member papers. José Escobar of *Las Dos Repúblicas* urged members to maintain a unified front and to desist from printing libelous attacks of a personal nature. Such things, he believed only weakened the overall aims of the Spanish-language press. He admonished his fellow journalists to commit their energies toward cultural integrity and professionalism. Escobar wrote:

> Colleagues of the press, *Las Dos Repúblicas* invites all of you to work with her: wherever there is a breech to defend; wherever a wall weakens and is in danger of caving in; wherever the enemy amasses his forces to attack our defenses with burning fire; there you will always find this newspaper defending its people, do not turn away from following it. But if among you there is someone that persists in useless whims, it would do you good to leave behind your editorial desk, to cast your pen to the fire, and to cease dishonoring the noble hosts of journalism.[2]

As the activity of the *Neo-Mexicano* press increased, journalists met in Las Vegas, New Mexico, in December 1891 to hold the first organizational meetings of La Prensa Asociada Hispano-Americana. When La Prensa Asociada met again, it would be to install its officers and draft a preamble and resolutions to guide the work of the organization. Victor L. Ochoa, editor of *El Hispano-Americano* of Las Vegas was elected president of La Prensa Asociada, and Camilo Padilla, editor of *El Mosquito* of Mora, became the organization's first vice president. La Prensa Asociada continued to draw other members to its ranks. *El Combate* of Albuquerque reported that several of the most prominent Spanish-language journalists in New Mexico, Colorado, and West Texas attended a meeting of La Prensa Asociada in Santa Fe in early July 1893. By this time membership included José Escobar of *El Combate* (Albuquerque), Teófilo Ocaña Caballero of *La Lucha* (El Paso, Texas), Marcial Valdez of *El Tiempo* (Las Cruces), Pedro G. de la Lama of *La Opinión Pública* (Albuquerque), M. Lerma of *La Flor del Valle* (Las Cruces), José Segura of *El Boletín Popular* (Santa Fe), and Manuel Salazar y Otero of *La Crónica de Valencia* (Socorro). At its July meeting the association approved memberships for Adelaido C. de Baca, associate editor of *La Crónica de Valencia,* M. Cisneros, editor of *El Cosmopolita* (Eagle Pass, Texas), Justo Cárdenas of *El Correo de Laredo* (Laredo, Texas), and G. E. Hosmer of the bilingual weekly *El Estandarte de Springer* (Springer, New Mexico). Region-wide meetings continued at Las Vegas, Santa Fe, Albuquerque, Las Cruces, and El Paso, and as the decade progressed the association met in earnest and with regularity. The Spanish-language press in these cities gave space to reporting on the activities of the organization and its membership. With its dynamic growth La Prensa Asociada rightfully began to describe itself as the first professional organization of its kind among the Spanish-speaking in the Southwest. By formalizing relationships among member editors, La Prensa Asociada was clearly bolstering the idea that Spanish-language journalists should move to establish a standing in both Anglo and Mexican societies as members of a respected profession—not an insignificant act in light of the dearth of such opportunities in the borderlands.

La Prensa Asociada was by no means ideologically or politically homogeneous. Even as the group espoused a defense of the interests of the community, the membership often held varying positions on how to solve societal problems. The strong personalities of certain editors often drove heated editorial exchanges that resulted in bitter quarrels that took years to reconcile. Member newspapers were drawn from the Democratic and Republican ranks and the political credo of individual editors was frequently a source of friction and political infighting. Still, the organization brought formal recognition to the idea that the Spanish-language press should act in concert to oppose injury to the community it represented, as expressed in its charter: "To reach consensus on the measure and means best suited and needed for the progress and betterment of the community it [the association] represents."[3] Tantamount to the call to unity issued by the organizers of La Prensa Asociada was the need for members to overcome factionalism so as to extend the benefits of print culture to outlying communities throughout the region.

It must be kept in mind that the emergence of a culture of print in Mexican-origin communities across the region came as an expression of post-1848 resistance and opposition to Anglo-American political, social, and cultural hegemony in the Southwest.

Fig. 5. Staff of *La Voz de Pueblo* at typesetting desk, circa 1898. Staff members from left to right: Eduardo?, Ignacio Gold, Lamberto Rivera, Francisco López, José García, Donato Rivera, Anastacio Coble. Donnelly Collection, New Mexico Highlands University. Courtesy of Las Vegas Committee for Historic Preservation.

The discourse activated by the conquest would remain contestatory and counterhegemonic and was by its nature subject to the subordination by the dominant group. Contained and never totally free, this culture of print, and those in whose name it spoke, were often coerced into angered posturing and defensive positioning, the result of antagonistic social and political policies. Writing in March 1892, Manuel C. de Baca of *El Sol de Mayo* (Las Vegas) saw in the existence of La Prensa Asociada an antidote to the threat of social and cultural erasure: "Our people will come to see," he wrote, "that the New Mexican [*Neo-Mexicano*] Press Association will take up the shield so as to do its duty . . . the time is right for the *Hispanos* to bring to an end the repeated injuries that all too frequently are directed against them."[4] Grounded in these concerns La Prensa Asociada Hispano-Americana assumed the role of guarantor of the community it served: "The Spanish-speaking press, by nature and by consequence, should be the trustee and defender of the race it represents."[5]

In the decade prior to the formation of La Prensa Asociada, Spanish-language editors often reprinted items from one another. They also spent much time citing the works of fellow journalists, which they praised or derided as occasion dictated, but La Prensa Asociada had the immediate effect of enhancing the exchange of information among its membership. A network of *canjes* created by the association improved exchange among member editors and provided *Nuevomexicano* editors with a steady and inexhaustible source of texts from member newspapers in northern Mexico, who in turn reprinted items from other Latin American sources. Their work would become an important factor in reinvigorating *Nuevomexicano* cultural identity at a moment of deepening crisis. The organization also pressed railroad, telegraph, and postal officials to provide association members and the communities they represented with improved service. The work of La Prensa Asociada was realized through the discursive practices of individual editors and is best seen in the impact wrought by the enterprises they established along the Río Grande.

Discourse and Ideological Alliance

> At the appointed time a large crowd had assembled, and it was not long in waiting, soon the noisy whistle of the locomotive announced the arrival of the train from the north. Upon stepping off the train, Sr. José Segura, the president of the Association, was received by a committee that introduced him to several ladies and gentlemen who were closest to him, and to the Women's Mutual Aid Society consisting of *Señoras* Armijo, García Lerma and *Señoritas* Ames, Yrlas, Rienhart. *Señoras* and *Señoritas* made a gift of some exquisite flowers to the members of the Press Association, pinning them to the left lapel of their jacket and, in addition, a magnificent bouquet was given to the President.

—"Prensa Asociada, Recepcion y baile con se le obsequio en Las Cruces [The Reception and Dance Given to the Spanish Press Association in Las Cruces]," *El Boletín Popular*, Santa Fe, 1894.

José Segura (1856–1908)

José Segura, the editor of *El Boletín Popular* in Santa Fe was among the founding members of La Prensa Asociada. During his lifetime Segura held no prominent political posts and seems to have exercised no other profession apart from that of a journalist. As a result, mention of Segura in newsprint nearly always appears in connection with his work as an editor, making it is safe to say that he emerges as the first full-time professional *Neo-Mexicano* journalist.

Throughout its twenty-five years in publication Segura's *El Boletín Popular* remained a powerful voice in *Neo-Mexicano* journalism. Located on East San Francisco Street, just up from St. Francis's Cathedral, the paper's impact and presence in Santa Fe was felt by all segments of the community. On the matter of *El Boletín's* readership, F. Stanley remarks, "*El Boletín Popular* commenced publication in 1885 and continued to 1910. This gave lie to the theory that New Mexicans did not want Spanish reading, or that they couldn't read Spanish. This latter may be true of the postwar generations of the two World Wars, but up to 1912 many Santa Feans read and wrote in Spanish" (1965, 171). Sensing *El Boletín's* influence among the Spanish-speaking, W. H. Manderfield, owner-editor of the *Santa Fe New Mexican*, responded by publishing a Spanish-language counterpart to his paper. To counter *El Boletín's* large circulation, Manderfield employed several *Nuevomexicanos* to edit *El Nuevo Mexicano*, which began publication in 1890.

El Boletín Popular's style proved to be its strength over time. The paper provided readers with local, regional, national, and international news. In addition, Segura devoted a segment of each issue to literature and the arts. In this regard, *El Boletín* served an intermediary function by publishing a wide array of literary works that intersected with the vibrant *Neo-Mexicano* oral culture. The texts published by Segura ranged from submissions by local *Neo-Mexicano* poets to regional works by *Mexicano* writers known in the Southwest to international works of literature, especially by renowned authors from Latin America and Spain. The careful editing and attention to detail José Segura brought to the paper reflects the increasing quality of Spanish-language publications in the 1890s.

El Boletín soon came to voice the concerns and aspirations of *Nuevomexicanos* of all classes and walks of life. Many of the most prominent voices in the *Nuevomexicano* community spoke through *El Boletín*. The paper featured submissions by J. M. H. Alarid, Eleuterio Baca, Benjamín M. Read, Camilo Padilla, and others, with Segura contributing editorial commentary that remains among the most important reflections of *Neo-Mexicano* concerns during the period. Segura embodied the aspirations of a generation intent on leaving a cultural legacy to its descendants. He was a member of La Sociedad Literaria y de Debates de la Ciudad de Santa Fe, a literary arts group made up of *Neo-Mexicanos* that met regularly to discuss literary topics, engage in debate, and promote the general cultural welfare of the capital city.

Segura's Jesuit education accounts in part for his knowledge of world literature, particularly that of Latin America. Added to this, his extensive travel in Mexico and the eastern United States assisted him in recognizing consequential and important literary and cultural trends, which he then imparted to his readership. As part of *El Boletín*'s efforts in this regard the paper often noted the arrival of significant and important publications from the eastern United States, Mexico, and other Latin American countries. In May 1894, Segura shared with his readership news of the arrival of the Mexican modernist journal, *La Revista Azul.* Summarizing the importance of the journal, Segura advised his readers, "The weekly needs no other recommendation than to say that it is edited by the Mexican writers Señores Gutiérrez Nájera, Carlos Díaz Dufoo, Luis G. Urbina, and others. The lovers of fine literature in our Territory, where the reading of good authors is so needed, should not miss the opportunity to subscribe to such an interesting publication."[6]

Segura's knowledge of world authors and literature had only a slight impact on the average *Nuevomexicano* villager. Nonetheless it is important to note that journalists played an extremely important role as print intermediaries and cultural go-betweens who kept alive the idea that New Mexico was tied to other parts of the Spanish-speaking world. Newspapers themselves represented a mediating text of the kind alluded to by print historian David Hall. Hall suggests that such texts were composed in a system of signs meaningful—that is to say, interpretable—to large segments of the unlearned. Hall's point that "like it or not" such populations came "in contact with the culture of the learned" (1983, 12) makes ready sense here. Thus in Segura's work we detect a new and distinct role for the *Neo-Mexicano* literates who now opted to use their special authority as *periodiqueros* to mediate the world of learning and books for a semiliterate society.

While cultural and literary events were exceedingly rare in New Mexico, *El Boletín* made every effort to call serious attention to them. For example, it printed a note on the visit of Mexican writer and diplomat Vicente Riva Palacio to Santa Fe in July 1886.[7] Riva Palacio, an adherent of romantic dicta in literature was well-known and well-published in Mexico. Segura worked to keep alive the memory of the Mexican writer's chance visit to Santa Fe in follow-up reports and in the frequent publication of Riva Palacio's poetry in the columns of *El Boletín.* José Segura not only drew from a Mexican literary foundation, but frequently used the presses of *El Boletín* to disseminate items of interest to his local readership. We know, for example, that the anthropologist Adolph Bandelier forwarded important historical narratives from the colonial period for republication in *El Boletín Popular*, and that Eusebio Chacón's novellas *El hijo de la tempestad* and *Tras la tormenta, la calma* were issued in a slim volume by La Imprenta Tipográfica de El Boletín in 1892.[8] Thus book publication and the reprinting of texts on New Mexico history by Segura illustrates yet again the role of the Spanish-language press as a print intermediary serving a population, a half to two-thirds of which did not read but, as can readily be imagined, *was read to* by literate members of the community.[9] In addition Segura made publication another venue through which he sought to display *nativo* achievement and promote the cultural potential of Spanish-speaking communities in the region.

Camilo Padilla (1864–1933)

> *Zum!* . . . *zu-u-um* . . . was the echo that was heard at a distance though I could not determine where the sound came from, that is, until, with my hand placed against my spacious forehead, (well it should be known that I certainly *do* have a brow upon which I can make the sign of the cross), I found a small bump and I realized that this was a mosquito, indeed it was so, at my side was the buzzing *Mosquito* of Mora.
>
> Its appearance gave me pleasure, indeed, and I conjecture that its continuance will assuredly be applauded, since in the sad and difficult times through which we pass, we need the appearance of a *Mosquito,* if only to remind us in our bewildering hours of hardships and solitude, that we are alive, because, although we may lament it, there are many among us who will not open their eyes until Death with its cold hand comes to close our eyes for us.
>
> —"A Friend Paints the Visit of *El Mosquito*," *El Mosquito*, Mora, New Mexico, December 10, 1891.

Active at the outset of the *periodiquero* movement Camilo Padilla would devote his life's energy to educating the populace by means of the press. As one of the last remaining Spanish-language publishers in New Mexico, Padilla continued the work begun by La Prensa Asociada as the organization's last president. Padilla, owner-editor of *El Mosquito* and Felix Martínez, owner of *La Voz del Pueblo,* were selected at La Prensa Asociada's first organizational meeting in 1891 to draft a set of resolutions to guide the work of the association. Martínez and Padilla's resolutions responded to what they saw as the failures of U.S. society to insure the rights guaranteed to *nativos* under the Constitution of the United States. Sensing the urgency of the work of the press, Padilla and Martínez introduced their resolutions with the following call to action:

> Inasmuch as the credo of society and of prevalent affairs in the United States of America have not proved satisfactory at this

> present time at keeping the standing which the rights of the American constitution guarantees us, it is incumbent upon us to form associations so that our capacities increase in equal measure to those of the rest of our fellow citizens with the goal that the dignity of our forebears and descendants be justly respected.[10]

Padilla was a well-read biliterate who took as many local and national newspapers in both English and Spanish as could be had. A seasoned traveler as well, Padilla had the opportunity to journey often to Washington, D.C., and other parts of the east coast. His travels were some of the earliest by *Nuevomexicanos* to the eastern states and to the nation's seat of government. In 1890 Padilla traveled to Washington, in the capacity of private secretary to Antonio Joseph, New Mexico's territorial delegate to the United States Congress. In the early years of the decade, Padilla had interspersed visits to Washington as Joseph's secretary with time working on newspapers in Mora County when Congress was not in session, but from 1898 to 1901 he resided continuously in the nation's capital where he was employed by the Government Printing Office.

In the early 1890s Padilla began to lay the foundation for his own work in journalism. From July to September 1890, he shared the editorship of *La Gaceta de Mora* with a cousin, Nepomuceno Segura, a resident of mountain village of Rociada above Las Vegas, New Mexico. In December 1891, he began publication of his own paper at town of Mora, the seat of county government. He gave his paper the feisty name *El Mosquito* and added its voice to the growing number of Prensa Asociada newspapers. Padilla moved to El Paso, Texas, in 1907, where he began the publication of *Revista Ilustrada,* the most important and best developed publication to be issued by any *Neo-Mexicano* editor and publisher up to that time. The complete record of Padilla's work as a publisher remains fragmented. Information regarding the issuance of his magazine is sketchy and incomplete, especially since few issues of his magazine made their way to libraries or archival repositories. The publishing history of *Revista Ilustrada* is also marred because it was alternately published at Santa Fe and El Paso and under the titles, *Sancho Panza* and *Revista Ilustrada.* During its first five years of publication (1907–12) Padilla published in El Paso. Beginning with and perhaps prompted by the granting of statehood for New Mexico, Padilla returned to Santa Fe in the fall of 1912 and issued *Revista Ilustrada* for a number of years thereafter from an office on San Francisco Street that housed both his magazine and the *Santa Fe Eagle.* Sometime after 1918, Padilla once again returned *Revista Ilustrada* to El Paso, first opening an office on Porfirio Diaz Street and later moving to 521 Prospect in that city. In the summer of 1925, Padilla moved the magazine one last time to Santa Fe, where it remained in publication until shortly before Padilla's death in 1933.

Padilla's collaborations with *Neo-Mexicano* periodicals began early in his life. Among his first submissions to Spanish-language newspapers is a letter to the editor of *La Voz del Pueblo* in Las Vegas in May of 1889. Printed with the title "Crónica nacional," the communiqué provides *La Voz* and its readership with news and information from Washington, D.C., where Padilla resided. During the early part of the decade, Padilla contributed many such items to Santa Fe's *El Boletín Popular*. Padilla's association with the Santa Fe paper was no doubt strengthened by family ties (José Segura was Camilo's first cousin). Through such communiqués—including editorial opinions, travel narratives, and cross-cultural observations—Padilla came to be regarded as the paper's official correspondent in Washington.

Nuevomexicanos had little information and few opportunities to understand the enormity of the socioeconomic disparity that existed between New Mexico and other parts of the United States. This lack of understanding was exacerbated by the air of haughtiness and superiority that conditioned Anglo-American interactions with the native populations of the territory. Padilla obviously sensed the importance of issuing his communiqués from Washington. His long absences from New Mexico gave Padilla a deeper reverence for his homeland. Recalling his time in Washington, Padilla's comments are filled with the longing and concern of the exile: "When finding ourselves far away from our beloved homeland, we thought often about this land which today, like an old plow is on the auction block; when, in company of the young patriot, Maximiliano Luna, we contemplated the future of our peaceful and righteous people, and thought about the discord of our fellow citizens,—which has arrived here like a plague."[11] But Padilla's concern often moved beyond nostalgia. Writing for *El Mosquito* in December 1892, Padilla lays out the true meaning of homeland to his readers: "The New Mexican earth, which is sprinkled and has been bought with the blood of our parents, should be as sacred to us as is the nation for the good patriot and citizen.... Therefore, when one sees a *Neo Mexicano* sell a piece of land to a foreigner, it seems a sacrilege, because the seller demonstrates how little he appreciates the inheritance bequeathed to him by his ancestors."[12]

Addressing the beleaguered condition of *nativos* Padilla submitted a short essay he titled "Nuestra única salvación [Our Only Hope]" to *El Boletín Popular* in April 1894. Padilla spoke of the disharmony and disunity he felt had become most pronounced among *Nuevomexicanos* in the twenty-year period between 1874 to 1894, which encompassed the coming of the railroad and the unprecedented immigration of *extranjeros*. It was clear to Padilla that racial and economic conflict was intensifying as *nativos* found themselves caught up in the machinations of political and economic rings. Padilla alludes to the political and cultural fissures that disfigured the contours of self-reliance that in his words characterized *Nuevomexicano* society of earlier times. Padilla suggests that if the tendency to factionalism is allowed to continue that the native population would find itself entirely at the mercy of Anglo-American interests. On another occasion he would write: "A *Nuevomexicano* should never feel alone in the land of his birth and among his people."[13] In a direct reference to the fraternalism inspired by *Nuevomexicano* lay religious organizations such as La Hermandad de Nuestro Padre Jesús (The Brotherhood of Our Father Jesus Christ), Padilla's exhorts his readers to work toward a return to cultural unity:

> The time that has transpired between these two dates—1874 and 1894—means much for us. Here we find the key to our situation. . . . During this interval of time a marked tendency to separatism has moved our conscience, a movement towards disunity that increases day to day with terrifying progression. Nowhere can be seen a communion of ideas; the great principles that brought unity to our actions and that established among men of the same race a kind of brotherhood have crumbled away or are threatened by ruin.
>
> The fateful result of this dissolution is envy, ambition, and the ill will we have for each other; [these things] have come to supplant and shrink the great principle of brotherhood that we inherited from our forefathers, even in matters of our very faith. Intrigue and falsehood—those monsters that keep company with the politics of the day—have come to overtake sincerity and truth. Individual concern has replaced the collective sentiment; the latter does not exist today, or if it exists, it is shamed by such treachery as lays hidden in the heart of one or another of us.[14]

Padilla turned to other forms of writing to distill reflections of a more personal nature, yet ones forged from cross-cultural interactions between *Americanos* and *Mexicanos.* He penned short stories with titles like "Camilo en Virgina" (Camilo in Virginia) (1889) and "Historia Original Neo-Mexicana: ¡Pobre Emilio!" (Original New Mexican Story: Wretched Emilio!) (1890). These items, published in the local press, offer the first writings that delineate a *Nuevomexicano* perspective concerned with the social and cultural boundaries that conditioned interpersonal relationships between *nativos* and Anglo Americans.

E. H. Salazar (1858–1915)

> Let nothing divert you from the path you have taken—neither politics, nor self-interest—and if by misfortune you should find the need to return to private life, you can do so with the sweet satisfaction that you have done your duty as a patriot—as does the man whose heart beats in consonance with the sentiments of a people.

—Camilo Padilla on the work of E. H. Salazar and *El Independiente*, Washington, 1894.

Journalists associated with La Prensa Asociada were unified by a cultural bond and such sentiment was often expressed in the professional fraternalism that greeted new publications into the fold of La Prensa membership. Language, culture, and identity provided a foundation for the unity of purpose that drove La Prensa Asociada's cultural agenda. The resulting dialogue and exchange fostered mutual support that encouraged the work and writing of association members. Professional fraternalism of this kind is reflected in the epigraph by Camilo Padilla above. The commentary is taken from a letter written in Washington D.C., in which Padilla valorizes the work of Enrique H. Salazar, editor of *El Independiente* of Las Vegas. Expressing pleasure at having a source to inform him in Washington of happenings in his native New Mexico, Padilla continues, "From here, from the banks of the Potomac, I applaud your patriotic efforts,"[15] and lauds the prophetic vision of Salazar's front page editorial essays, which offered a critical assessment of *Nuevomexicano* social decline resulting from Anglo-American economic and political domination. In his many editorials Salazar urged *nativos* to end "that fiction of racial inferiority which our enemies use to label us"[16] while insisting that derision along ethnic lines was a root cause of the political and economic marginalization of the Spanish-speaking. Salazar's editorial opinions are among the clearest articulations of La Prensa Asociada's sociocultural concern:

> Many are the discerning observers that note and comment on the anomalous position currently occupied by the Hispano population of this Territory, [and] with just reason are surprised by what is happening. This awe stems from the fact that the Hispanos are a majority and constitute four-fifths of the population of New Mexico, yet their social and political importance in most cases does not match [this] numerical superiority and it is necessary to confess that it [its importance] diminishes daily.[17]

Enrique H. Salazar's work at *El Independiente* also won him immediate praise from *El Boletín Popular*. Upon receiving the first issue of the paper, José Segura noted of the new publication: "We should say that our new colleague, beyond being elegantly printed, is written in good Castilian, a fact that has not always typified the politically oriented journalism of that county for many years."[18]

Enrique H. Salazar, a founding editor of *La Voz del Pueblo*, was drawn to the work of La Prensa Asociada from its inception in Las Vegas, New Mexico. As a young man in his early thirties, Salazar became associated with Nestor Montoya, a few years his junior, and together in 1889 they assumed ownership and management of *La Voz del Pueblo* in Santa Fe. *La Voz* had begun publication in the summer of 1888. At that time Hilario A. Ortiz, an influential citizen of Santa Fe, was listed along with Nestor Montoya as the editor of the paper. Enrique H. Salazar was listed as the paper's administrator. On February 2, 1889, Salazar and Montoya rededicated *La Voz* and continued to publish the paper in Santa Fe until June of the following year.

Throughout its many years of service to the *Nuevomexicano* community, *La Voz* would prove to have a Phoenixlike ability to rise up with renewed vigor and purpose at critical moments in its evolution. A year and a half after its founding Salazar announced to his readership that *La Voz* was relocating to Las Vegas. In August of the same year, Nestor Montoya, who had served as editor of *La Voz* since its inception, abruptly ended his association with Enrique H. Salazar. No explanation is given for the severing of the partnership. By all indications, however, the partnership dissolved amicably and Salazar expressed regret at Montoya's departure, vowing to guide the actions of the paper by the principles and ideals they had set forth as partners.[19]

With the removal of *La Voz* to Las Vegas in the summer of 1890, Enrique H. Salazar left Santa Fe, the city of his birth, to engage his life's ambition as a writer and journalist in Las Vegas, a city that at the beginning of the decade was teeming with new economic activity. By 1890 Las Vegas, the seat of San Miguel County, had become the largest city in New Mexico. Conversely, and despite the promise of economic growth and prosperity on the horizon, Las Vegas was also a city beset by tremendous political strife and cross-cultural conflict. Animosity between *Nuevomexicanos,* who comprised the majority population in the area, and succeeding waves of newly arriving Anglo Americans was intensifying. The roots of this deteriorating relationship between the groups can be traced to the rapid growth Las Vegas experienced in the years following the arrival of the railroad in New Mexico: "Las Vegas rose to the first rank of New Mexico cities and changed its cultural balance—'New Town' sprang up around the depot on the east side of the Gallinas river. The railroad heightened tensions between Hispano and Anglo and intensified competition for resources" (Rosenbaum 1984, 101).

Throughout his career as a journalist Salazar was keenly aware of the threat to the *Nuevomexicano* community represented by Anglo-American dominance of the region. As newcomers, Anglos knew little of the history of the area. Equipped with notions of cultural superiority, the newcomers seemed bent on political and economic appropriation. Ethnic tensions and conflict in every aspect of life were played out on a daily basis during this period on the streets, in the courthouse, and in hotel meeting rooms in Las Vegas. Ironically, Las Vegas, the city that was the point of entry and seat of Anglo-American commercial and banking interests in the 1890s, would also be associated with the most powerful challenges to Anglo-American political and cultural hegemony in the area. The year 1890 saw the rise of the Gorras Blancas movement in San Miguel and Mora counties. The same year, dissatisfaction with the existing political parties lead to the creation of the Partido del Pueblo Unido, which threatened to mobilize *Nuevomexicanos* into a strong third-party alternative to existing political parties. In subsequent years, outbreaks of racial violence such as the Billy Green disturbance in 1894[20] further eroded interethnic relationships in San Miguel County. Salazar, a staunch defender of *Nuevomexicano* economic, political, and cultural rights, strode headlong into the fray by relocating *La Voz del Pueblo* to Las Vegas, the vortex of cross-cultural debate and conflict.

Salazar was obviously aware of the strategic importance of relocating his paper. He described *La Voz*'s relocation to his readers as a tactical move, designed to position the paper where it would be most conducive to influencing public opinion and articulating a *Nuevomexicano* cultural and social agenda. In the last edition of *La Voz,* issued in Santa Fe, Salazar uses the language of the military strategist to make clear to his readership that *La Voz* was caught in a battle of transcendent proportion. Drawing on the imagery of battle, Salazar cast the paper's staff and management as "foot soldiers" who were preparing to defend the homeland from the aggressive designs of usurpers. Expounding on tropes of battle and engagement, Salazar writes,

> Our periodical, with the exception of its [present] location, will continue its watch to protect the interests, honor, and advancement of all the segments of our great Territory. The well-being of the people of New Mexico and principally of the native population will be at every instance the powerful motive that will impel with great vigor our efforts in the publication of our weekly. We are the foot soldiers of the community, guarding its rights; for this reason, believing that the battle nears, we wish to place our batteries where they are most effective and where they will cause the most damage to our enemies. This is, after all, the reason for our move to the city of Las Vegas.[21]

In the ensuing years after 1890 Enrique H. Salazar strove to maintain autonomy and independence and defend the interests of *el pueblo nativo.* After moving *La Voz* to Las Vegas he continued to administer and edit the paper, but gradually over the next three years he relinquished ownership of the paper to the rising business mogul, Felix Martínez. Martínez would then use *La Voz* to promote El Partido del Pueblo Unido (The United People's Party) in a bid to break the domination of the Republican political machine in San Miguel County.

Whatever Salazar's particular motives in selling *La Voz* to Martínez, they did not include a retreat from the arena of journalism. In 1894 Salazar launched a new paper in Las Vegas. His paper, *El Independiente,* would be published as a Spanish weekly for the next thirty-four years. In *El Independiente's* salutation, Salazar summarized the aim of his paper in the maxim "independiente en todo, neutro en nada [independent in all things, neutral in none]." Salazar further declared that the paper would not be affiliated with any political organization or party, saying that as a matter of editorial policy, the paper would not shy away from addressing matters of accountability, corruption, and favoritism among *nativo* and nonnative elected officials from both parties. As before, Salazar recommitted himself to work for the common good of the *Nuevomexicano* community. "This periodical," he announced, "shall dedicate itself to the advancement and enlightenment of the people and to the defense of the true and legitimate interests of San Miguel County and the Territory of New Mexico."[22] Salazar ended his salutation with a note that he and his staff would strive to issue a professional newspaper superior to those already established in Las Vegas. Salazar maintained that *El Independiente* would use its autonomy from political parties to better express the concerns of the entire Spanish-speaking populace.

Like the majority of his colleagues in the field of journalism, Salazar was a graduate of St. Michael's College. He later learned the printer's trade and became familiar with other aspects of the journalistic craft in the office of the *Santa Fe New Mexican*, which at the time was under the direction of W. H. Manderfield. After his apprenticeship at the *New Mexican*, Salazar worked for a time with Urbano Chacón, a well-known and respected journalist who had founded the Taos County paper, *El Espejo*. Salazar worked alongside Chacón from 1878 to 1879. Subsequently, he relocated for a time to Chihuahua, Mexico, where he was employed to manage a newspaper known as *Correos y Nuevas de Chihuahua*. Salazar returned to his native city of Santa Fe and married Agueda López, the daughter of the Lorenzo López, then sheriff of Las Vegas.

The nonaligned position Salazar espoused through *El Independiente* proved to be a great advantage to the paper. Throughout the 1890s, a period of intense infighting and political squabbles among *Neo-Mexicano* civic leadership, Salazar managed to stay above the fray and call the action with relative impunity. During Salazar's years with *La Voz* and as editor of *El Independiente*, nearly every issue of these newspapers carried on its front page masterful editorial essays penned by the hand of Enrique H. Salazar. Invariably, these essays took up as their subject the erosion of *Nuevomexicano* civic and social power.

When viewed cumulatively, the discourse established by Salazar in his editorial essays represents the clearest articulation of the La Prensa Asociada's sociocultural agenda. In his essays Salazar addressed every major issue of concern to the *Nuevomexicano* community. Salazar wrote on questions of history, education, literacy, the maintenance of language and culture among *Nuevomexicanos*, the land grant struggle, and many other subjects. Not only were these essays timely and descriptive of the sociocultural milieu of Salazar's time, but they were well-written, elaborated pieces that made use of figurative and metaphorical language built from a cultural episteme that spoke directly to his readership.

Both *La Voz del Pueblo* and *El Independiente* were members of La Prensa Asociada and both papers proved to be successful business ventures, each being published in Las Vegas for some thirty years. The staff at both papers claimed large readerships and good advertisement revenues, with subscribers lists for each in excess of three thousand names. An early photograph of the offices of *El Independiente* gives some idea of the paper's success as a business enterprise. The photograph shows the paper's office housed in an up-to-date building of the period. Above the office, in large, bold letters appears the name of the paper: EL INDEPENDIENTE. Pictured on the sidewalk are four members of the printing room staff and nine paper boys holding the latest issue of *El Independiente.* In the upper left hand corner, inscribed by an oval border, is the portrait of Enrique H. Salazar bearing the simple caption: "Fundador."

Salazar's work as a journalist was decisive in the founding and establishment of two of the most successful Spanish-language publications in the Southwest. He continued to edit *El Independiente* until September 1910 when he broke with Secundino Romero of Las Vegas, his business partner for a number of years.

Manuel C. de Baca (1853–1915)

Manuel C. de Baca viewed the effort to organize La Prensa Asociada as a bold and decisive move on the part of *Neo-Mexicano* editors and journalists. In March 1892, C. de Baca's paper, *El Sol de Mayo,* reprinted resolutions recently adopted by La Prensa Asociada. He added the following editorial comment to their publication: "[They] have as their motto the defense of our people and of our homeland; our lineage should by all means have use of good armament for its defense."[23]

Manuel C. de Baca began publication of *El Sol de Mayo* in Las Vegas, New Mexico on May 1, 1891. Aware of the lyricism of the paper's name, he orchestrated the appearance of its inaugural issue to coincide with the first of May. A staunch conservative, C. de Baca entered journalism ostensibly to deter corruption among public officials, sustain the merits of "honest men," and expose the misdeeds of those holding public office. He also took as his mission to end the corruption and widespread lawlessness that he believed had taken hold of San Miguel and Mora counties in the early 1890s.

El Sol's prospectus is a high-sounding introduction to a personalistic agenda of moral reform. The purifying rays of the spring sun emblazoned on the paper's masthead appealed to its readers. C. de Baca was quite aware that May was the month reserved for Marian devotions in New Mexico's Spanish-speaking communities, and he counted on this communal reverence to attract a predominately Catholic readership. Focusing on the name of his paper he explained, "El cual hemos adoptado esforzandonos armonizar tal nombre a las

Fig. 6. Manuel C. de Baca. Courtesy of Elba C. de Baca.

bellezas naturales del mes de Mayo. [We have adopted it (the name) in the effort to harmonize such a name with the natural beauty of the month of May.]"[24]

Manuel C. de Baca's career as a journalist was framed by his public charge as an attorney and prosecutor. In an age in which the social order of pre-American days began to give way to factionalism and divisive politics, he saw his role as moral guardian of an older, and to his mind, more peaceful time. In the arena of public morality and religious sentiment, much of his writing takes up where his public charge leaves off and reflects his desire to root out what he considered the moral lassitude and lawlessness he believed had come to plague society.

At the time Manuel C. de Baca came of age, the profound social, economic, and political changes underway in Las Vegas had dislodged the populace from its traditional, cyclical patterns of agrarian and pastoral life. In the late 1880s the Las Vegas-Mora area was plagued with the banditry and violence of Vicente Silva and a cohort of thugs. In his public charge C. de Baca prosecuted several members of the Silva gang, and in doing so he incurred the enmity and wrath of members of Vicente Silva's Sociedad de Bandidos (Society of Brigands). Later in his life, C. de Baca was fond of retelling the details of threats made against him and his family during those stormy years. His niece, Fabiola C. de Baca, a respected Southwestern author, would later write, "It was in this same patio that, during the Silva terror, that Uncle Manuel almost met his death. He and Uncle Ezequiel, who later became governor of New Mexico, were on Silva's blacklist. One night, as Uncle Manuel was leaving for an evening meeting, two masked men jumped from behind some lilac bushes. Don Manuel always carried a gun, but as he went to reach for it, the bandits fled" (Cabeza de Baca 1954, 95).

No sooner had the Silva matter subsided when in 1890 the Las Gorras Blancas movement took hold in San Miguel County. In contrast to the Silva gang, the aims and goals of the White Caps organization were political and social in nature. The railroad, which ended the isolation of the region, brought hundreds of Anglo-American émigrés to north central New Mexico. Gorras Blancas were for the most part land grant heirs who were being dispossessed by Anglo-American land companies and speculators who consorted with political rings to wrench control of Mexican and Spanish land grants. The Gorras Blancas movement grew in response to this outside encroachment on the Spanish and Mexican communal land grants held by *Nuevomexicanos* across northern New Mexico, but C. de Baca, who had premised his public life and actions on ideas of moral rectitude and personal character, had little sympathy for what he considered to be illegal methods espoused by the Gorras Blancas. In his paper he openly accused them of fence-cuttings, barn burnings, and similar acts directed at Anglo ranchers. Such was C. de Baca's aversion to the White Caps that he organized La Orden de Caballeros de Protección Mutua [The Order of Knights for Mutual Aid] to counter the aims of the White Caps.

As a journalist, and later as the author of two novelettes, Manuel C. de Baca showed himself to be at odds with the populist sentiment represented by the Gorras Blancas and its electoral counterpart, El Partido del Pueblo Unido. These movements, at times allied and at others not, championed causes with widespread support among the poorer classes of *Neo-Mexicano* society.

By the time Manuel C. de Baca began publication of *El Sol de Mayo*, Las Vegas had two other well-established Spanish-language newspapers. The longest running, *La Revista Católica,* was in its seventeenth year of publication. The other, the sectarian *La Voz de Pueblo,* had made its debut only the year prior to his own paper. C. de Baca brought forth *El Sol de Mayo* as a public challenge to the populist sentiments espoused by Felix Martínez and the staff of *La Voz del Pueblo.* In responding to these popular movements C. de Baca's actions are in accord with a kind of noblesse oblige tied to questions of prominence and family name in New Mexico.

Throughout 1890 and 1891 the editorial comments of *La Voz* reflected a tacit alliance and support of the Las Gorras Blancas. *La Voz,* too, had became a strong supporter of El Partido del Pueblo Unido. That Manuel C. de Baca did not fully share this concern may have resulted from his status as a member of the landed class, which in great measure sheltered him from the effects of land-grabbers.

News of Manuel C. de Baca's intention to publish another paper in Las Vegas was met with enthusiasm. The editorial staff at *La Voz del Pueblo* had greeted the news of the forthcoming publication of *El Sol de Mayo* with goodwill and professional fellowship. As was customary, *La Voz* published a note of welcome greeting the paper into the fold of *Nuevomexicano* newspapers. Manuel C. de Baca, however, left no doubt as to where he stood in regards to the Gorras Blancas movement and the politics ascribed to by *La Voz*'s owner, Felix Martínez. Manuel C. de Baca stated that as a matter of policy his paper would be equally intolerant of the Gorras Blancas, as of other political rings and cliques. His paper, he wrote, was about "pointing out the transgressions we are able to observe, be they of individuals or groups, our greatest enemies, which we do not lose from sight are our kin the Gorras Blancas, and the [other] Rings and political circles, the most pernicious and greatest enemies of the people."[25] With his May 1 prospectus, C. de Baca began what would be a long-running attack on populism in general, and on the most strident voice of that movement in San Miguel County—*La Voz del Pueblo.*

Between February and March of 1892 C. de Baca published a nine-part novelette in *El Sol de Mayo* openly critical of the Gorras Blancas movement. He entitled his text *Noches tenebrosas del Condado de San Miguel* [Dark Nights in San Miguel County]. The series was a narrative indictment of the movement. Perhaps due to Manuel C. de Baca's prior experience as a prosecutor, he equated the Gorras Blancas with the banditry, violence, and crimes that had been the work of the Silva band. His descriptions and assertions concerning Las Gorras Blancas invariably rested on the view that its members were brigands who operated outside the framework of the law. The novelette quickly came to the attention of many *Nuevomexicanos,* with other conservative papers singing the praises of *Noches tenebrosas.* Manderfield's *El Nuevo Mexicano* noted that with its publication *El Sol de Mayo* "is lending a great service to the cause of law and good order, and is worthy of the support and praise of the honest and decent men of the territory."[26]

Manuel C. de Baca published *El Sol de Mayo* for most of two years. Perhaps bowing to the pressure of other professional obligations, or perhaps fearing reprisal from his enemies, he turned over the editorship of the paper in March 1892 to Victor L. Ochoa who moved his own *Hispano-Americano* from southern New Mexico to merge it with *El Sol de Mayo*. During the years C. de Baca edited *El Sol de Mayo,* his hand is visible in frequent and bitter editorial attacks he made on the staff, management, and editors of *La Voz del Pueblo.* Often his accusations deteriorated into heated, racially charged attacks heaped onto the person of Felix Martínez. Manuel C. de Baca's intractable position is also visible in many of his poems of a didactic nature that appeared in *El Sol de Mayo*. Ironically, one of the first acts of Las Vegas editor Manuel Salazar y Otero, who took over the paper two years later in 1894, was to publish a short article praising C. de Baca's mortal enemy, Felix Martínez and repudiating his detractors. Such were the consequences of the volatile mix of journalism and politics in San Miguel County.

A Voice for the People: La Compañía Publicista de La Voz

> But there is none to do his work, none to speak his faiths and convictions, none to interpret his ideals, none to inherit his peculiarly felicitous eloquence, none to hold in hand at once all the vibrant fibers of intricate business organization, none to stand quite so typically as the representative and spokesman of two peoples, two races, two modes of thought, two schools of political philosophy—of each to the other.
>
> —Necrology for Felix Martínez, *Old Santa Fe Magazine,* Santa Fe, New Mexico, July 1916

Felix Martínez (1857–1916)

Although Felix Martínez, owner and proprietor of *La Voz del Pueblo* during most years of its publication, commanded great presence as a political orator in nineteenth-century New Mexico, he authored few literary or editorial texts. His contribution to *Nuevomexicano* journalism was nonetheless important because of his work as proprietor and entrepreneur. Present at the founding of La Prensa Asociada, Martínez helped draft the organization's resolutions and served the organization as vice president at one point in its early history.

With the purchase of *La Voz del Pueblo,* Martínez became proprietor and editor-in-chief of the first successful *Neo-Mexicano* printing company to emerge from the Spanish-language newspaper activity of the 1890s. Martínez ran the business end of the paper until his death in 1916. A shrewd businessman and investor, he employed Ezequiel C. de Baca and Antonio Lucero as associate editors, bringing to the staff of *La Voz* the finest and best-prepared

Fig. 7. Felix Martinez, circa 1895. Peterson, *Representative New Mexicans* (192).

journalists in the territory, and in turn provided them with a well-staffed printing room and the latest presses. Housed in one of the largest buildings on Douglas Street in Anglo East Las Vegas, *La Voz* would remain a profitable business throughout its thirty-seven years of publication. As a business venture it marked new possibilities for *Nuevomexicano* success in the field of printing and publishing. For example, the La Voz Publishing Company was responsible for the publication of several early works of Mexican-American literature, including *Vicente Silva y sus cuarenta bandidos: Sus crímenes y su retribución* (Vicente Silva and His Forty Thieves: Their Crimes and Their Retribution), authored by rival journalist Manuel C. de Baca and issued in serial form in 1896.

In many respects, Felix Martínez personified the potential and possibility of a new era in which the *Neo-Mexicano* culture and identity might emerge intact and be compatible with the institutional and technological advances of the age. Given his singular accomplishments amid the great inequities experienced by most *nativos,* his death in 1916 created a void that would not be filled again. [27] Martínez openly supported Las Gorras Blancas and El Partido del Pueblo Unido. As populist movements the base of support for these groups was in the poorest sectors of *Nuevomexicano* society and among those directly impacted by Anglo-American encroachment on the communal land grants, anti-*Mexicano* bias in the legal system, a dual wage system for Anglos and Mexicanos, and the unequal living standards between an Anglo East Las Vegas and *Mexicano* West Las Vegas. *La Voz del Pueblo,* a strong catalyst for change and reform, voiced the dissatisfaction of the Spanish-speaking with the social inequity around them. By placing these highly charged issues in the foreground, *La Voz del Pueblo* drew social disparity into sharp relief. *La Voz*'s criticism of class- and race-based inequity would not be without cost, and as such *La Voz* became the object of heated reactionary attacks from both within and without the *Mexicano* community. Martínez himself was forced to leave Las Vegas in 1898 and moved most of his business interests to El Paso, Texas.

In El Paso he held varied investments in real estate, banking, public works, newspapers, and water reclamation projects. He also remained owner and principal investor in *La Voz del Pueblo* and continued to invest heavily in English and Spanish newspapers. In Las Vegas, he held stock in the English-language *Optic,* and at Albuquerque he was among the founders of the Albuquerque Tribune-Citizen Company. He published the *El Paso Daily News* from 1899 to 1907 and was a founder of the *El Paso Times-Herald.* The support Martínez offered, removed writers and journalists from the day to day concerns of publishing and afforded them access to a well-established forum where they were able to wage a campaign of social and cultural advancement for *Nuevomexicanos.*

Martínez's associate editors, Ezequiel C. de Baca and Antonio Lucero, were lifelong friends and colleagues. As children they attended the same schools, and as young men they studied with the same instructors at the Jesuit College of Las Vegas. They shared similar ideals and sought similar channels to put their ideas into practice. As members of La Prensa Asociada they served their community as public spokesmen, leaders, and thinkers. Signing on to the staff of *La Voz del Pueblo* in 1891, Ezequiel and Antonio would find themselves at the center of contentious territorial politics for the next twenty-five years. Both would emerge from the political strife of these years as two of a handful of *Neo-Mexicanos* to hold elected offices in the newly organized state government of 1912.

Ezequiel C. de Baca (1864–1917)

In his initial years at *La Voz,* Ezequiel worked as a reporter and copy editor. Like others of his generation, however, he was particularly interested in fomenting education through the use literary and dramatic arts. Ezequiel belong to several civic and educational circles. *Neo-Mexicanos* in the city of Las Vegas had by this time organized La Sociedad Literaria y de Ayuda Mutua (The Literary and Mutual Aid Society), La Sociedad por la Protección de la Educación (The Society for the Protection of Education), and El Club Dramático de Las Vegas (The Las Vegas Drama Club). As a member of these groups, and through *La Voz,* he headed community efforts to extend learning to the populace-at-large.

The altruism, lofty sentiments, and ennobling notions of art and literature espoused by these organizations was offset by cross-cultural conflict, racial strife, and the intrigue of local and territorial politics. Fabiola C. de Baca would later write that Ezequiel, her uncle, "was a slave to the cause of the poor people. . . . In those days being a member of the political party to which my uncle belonged was indeed martyrdom" (1994 [1954], 163]. Ezequiel who vowed to defend the interest of "las masas de hombres pobres [the masses of the poor]" and Las Gorras Blancas, opposed the political views of his older brother, Manuel C. de Baca. The rift between the two was well-known. *El Defensor del Pueblo,* co-edited for a time in Albuquerque by former Gorras Blanca leader, Juan José Herrera, mocked Manuel C. de Baca in a satirical editorial. Speaking in the first-person "Manuel Caribe de Baca" is made to declare, "And those who are not with me are against me; this is my theme . . . , well, I declare my brother Ezequiel, a very intelligent, honest young man, with better judgment then I, a stranger to my family for the mere offense of being a collaborator of *La Voz de Pueblo,* a newspaper opposed to my interests."[28]

A brief period of reconciliation for the two brothers came on the heels of what would become known as the Billy Green matter, one of many episodes that strained race-relations in San Miguel County. The incident came to a head when Sheriff Lorenzo López and other local citizens attempted to apprehend Billy Green, an Anglo ruffian with a history of violence and criminal behavior, for the murder of Nestor Gallegos. The authority of Hispano lawmen involved in the arrest was undermined, when according to Robert Rosenbaum, "East Las Vegas Marshall T. F. Clay hurried across the Gallinas River to bring the three [Green and accomplices] into the more congenial custody of Anglo, 'new town' " (1981, 134). As public outrage grew in the aftermath of this event, a contingent of Army regulars was set against the Mexican residents of Las Vegas in what can only be described as a race war (Rosenbaum, 134).

For locals, the Billy Green matter made all the more apparent the need to set aside political and ideological factionalism in favor of cultural and ethnic unity. *Neo-Mexicano* leaders urged solidarity. Manuel Salazar y Otero of *El Sol de Mayo* ran an editorial praising the work of Felix Martínez. Ezequiel C.

Fig. 8. Portrait of Governor Ezequiel C. de Baca, 1916. Courtesy of Elba C. de Baca.

de Baca formalized the resolve of La Prensa Asociada to steer public sentiment toward unified political and cultural aims and ran front page editorials in *La Voz* with this aim in mind: "Unión y prosperidad: El pueblo de San Miguel se Une Bajo el Gremio de un Solo Partido [The People of San Miguel Unite Under the Guidance of a Single Party]."

In his work as journalist and community spokesman, Ezequiel C. de Baca had been at the center of political life in San Miguel County for twenty years before seeking public office. When finally he did so, it would be in the context of New Mexico's bid for statehood. C. de Baca wrested the gubernatorial race from the Republican candidate Holm O. Bursum in November of 1916.

Unfortunately for the citizens of the state Ezequiel C. de Baca was in office only a short time, succumbing forty-nine days after taking office as the second governor of the state to what was referred to at the time as "pernicious anemia." Fellow journalist Antonio Lucero delivered the eulogy at the state funeral. Invoking the spirit of duty embodied in C. de Baca's life, Lucero stressed the steadfast commitment the governor had shown to his origins: "I die poor, but I lived in honor."

The Lucero and C. de Baca editorial team enhanced the pages of a *La Voz del Pueblo* throughout many years. Its work represented the new level of sophistication and professionalism achieved by La Prensa Asociada after 1900. Through journalism both men came to be considered central figures in leadership circles within the *Neo-Mexicano* community. [29]

Antonio Lucero (1863–1921)

Neither Lucero nor Ezequiel C. de Baca were in the habit of including bylines to their work. It is therefore difficult to attribute authorship of specific writings to either editor. Some inferences can be made. Lucero often accepted invitations to speak at public and civic ceremonies and dedications, and the texts of these speeches, some given in Spanish, others in English, offer proof that Lucero was a gifted public speaker. Lucero's knowledge and awareness of authors and writers in the Latin American and Spanish tradition played a role in the selection of literary texts that peppered the columns of *La Voz.* Although he was employed as an editor, Lucero often channeled his commentaries on *Nuevomexicano* culture into other forums. In 1913 he was asked to address the Archeological Society of New Mexico in Santa Fe. He titled his talk "Homely Virtues of the Spanish Americans" and directed his comments to a largely English-speaking audience in an effort to improve cross-cultural relations. Lucero explained:

> We speak a language, the English, in which, I regret to say, it has been for so many years the fashion of many to write in ridicule of the Spanish-Americans of New Mexico, and to give so little credit, or no credit at all, to the work that their ancestors and the Catholic pioneers did for civilization in these parts, that I have often felt the want of a conscientious writer who would take up this subject and discuss it in the press with the idea in mind to displace fiction and put in its place a genuine and conservative narrative of the facts. (Lucero 1913, 443)

Lucero's article appeared in *Old Santa Fe Magazine* shortly after taking office as secretary of state in 1912. It is not surprising that the item would be picked up by the *Neo-Mexicano* press as well and a Spanish version, titled "El Hogar Hispano-Americano y sus virtudes," found its way to Albuquerque's *La Bandera Americana* in March 1913. But, importantly, Lucero was among the few *Neo-Mexicano* editors to "cross over" into the Anglo-dominated literary and cultural arts movement of the post-statehood era.

Antonio Lucero no doubt played a key role in determining the content, format, and style of *La Voz.* The paper touched on and brought into focus every major issue of concern to the *Nuevomexicano* community. By including the verbal arts of the community in each issue, *La Voz del Pueblo* was grounded in its commitment to *Nuevomexicanos.* Throughout its many years in publication its pages reflected the voice of *Neo-Mexicano* poets, writers, and the chroniclers of *nativo* traditions and history.

Linking the Borderlands: Binationalism and *La Prensa Asociada*

With some exceptions, the majority of Spanish-language journalists working in New Mexico at the end of the nineteenth century were, as might be expected, native born, but the strength and vigor of the *periodiquero* movement drew journalists from other Spanish-speaking regions of the Southwest, as well as other countries. Pedro García de la Lama, the editor of Albuquerque's *La Opinión Pública* from 1892 to 1895, was Mexican born. Oliveros V. Aoy, who worked for a time at *La Voz del Pueblo,* and José Jordí, who edited the columns of *La Bandera Americana* and other newspapers in the post-statehood era, were both natives of Spain. Another Spanish immigrant, José Montaner, settled in Taos and was editor of *La Revista de Taos,* a paper with a circulation of over five thousand subscribers. Montaner also issued *La Revista de Ilustrada Taos,* a literary arts magazine he began in June 1919. Montaner's assimilation through marriage into *Nuevomexicano* society, coupled with his years as editor of *La Revista de Taos,* laid the basis for his career as a state senator representing Taos County in the early years of statehood.

Victor L. Ochoa, Teófilo Ocaña Caballero, Rafael and Elfego N. Ronquillo, and José Antonio Escajeda were journalists who were strongly identified with northern Mexico and the U.S. Mexico border communities of West Texas and New Mexico. These journalists influenced Spanish-language journalism on both sides of the border.

Victor L. Ochoa

La Prensa Asociada's first president was Victor L. Ochoa. His election came within months of having moved his paper, *El Hispano-Americano,* from El Paso, Texas, to Las Vegas, New Mexico, in 1892. Under Ochoa's direction La Prensa Asociada immediately began to pursue a proactive agenda to secure the full participation of the Spanish-speaking in the affairs of government. At its May 9, 1892, meeting in Albuquerque, Prensa Asociada members passed numerous measures, among them one petitioning the territorial legislature to require that all legal and judicial documents be published in Spanish so that the *Nuevomexicano* community could "inform itself with knowledge that concerns its rights as citizens."[30] Ochoa's resolution had practical as well as cultural implications. Prensa Asociada members were very aware that public subsidies providing much-needed revenue went first to English papers. Stratton observes, "The general territorial public subsidy was monopolized by the Santa Fe *New Mexican* journalists" (1969, 35).

An activist as well as journalist, Ochoa soon found himself involved in the politics of the emerging class struggle in Mexico and did not remain president of La Prensa Asociada for long. Newspapers in New Mexico reported his departure from *El Hispano-Americano* in Las Vegas in 1894. Ochoa, it was reported, had joined the revolutionary struggle in Chihuahua then mobilizing to oppose the regime of the Mexican *caudillo,* Porfirio Díaz. Reports of "the knight errant of the Rio Grande," as he became known, continued to appear in New Mexico's newspapers for many years after his presumed death at the hands of *Carransistas.* Some reports had him aiding Villa's cause in the north, others had him serving time in a federal prison in New York for violating intervention laws, and inciting anti-Díaz revolutionary sentiments along the border. Other journalists used their papers to aid the revolutionary cause in Mexico, most notably Juan José Herrera and Pedro García de la Lama of *El Defensor del Pueblo* in Albuquerque.

Through the work of Ochoa and others the *periodiquero* movement in New Mexico was able to link efforts with other Spanish-language editors in California, Arizona, Texas, and Mexico. In particular, the El Paso and Las Cruces area became important conduits for the exchange of information into north central New Mexico from the border area and beyond.

Jesús Enrique Sosa (1856–1918)

Jesús Enrique Sosa was a young man when he chose to leave Mexico and emigrate to New Mexico. Throughout a long and active career in which Sosa edited and published several newspapers in New Mexico he became a respected *periodiquero.* Sosa's education and early formation in Mexico would set a pattern somewhat distinct from that of his *Neo-Mexicano* contemporaries.

Sosa was born in 1856 in Guadalajara, Mexico. He received a quality education in the public schools in Jalisco, but orphaned at age ten, he left his native state of Jalisco in 1871 and joined the Mexican Army by age fifteen. Sosa achieved the rank of captain and was known by that title later in his career as a publisher (Coan 1925, 258).

After his years in the military Sosa went on to study at Academia de San Carlos [St. Charles Academy] in Mexico City. San Carlos, housed in an elegant nineteenth-century building in the center of the Mexican capital, was the premier institution for the study of the Fine Arts. Students at San Carlos studied painting and sculpture after the fashion of European neoclassicism and realism. At San Carlos, Sosa trained to be a painter, an avocation he maintained throughout his life.

In 1888, Sosa moved to El Paso, Texas. Despite the fact that the U.S.-Mexican border at the time was quite open, Enrique Sosa sought and petitioned for legal immigration status. The formality was motivated by Sosa's desire to be a professional journalist in this country. One of his sponsors in El Paso was José Escobar, another Mexican exile who was a familiar figure among *Neo-Mexicano* journalists working at the time.[31]

Sosa remained in El Paso for five years and was employed by American railway companies in the area. In 1894 he moved to Las Cruces, but remained there for only a short time. About this time Sosa became active in journalism. In 1894, while living in Santa Fe, he founded the Spanish weekly, *El Gato,* a paper he qualified as "Semanario Independiente Joco-Serio, Amigo de la Verdad y del Progreso" (A jocular-serious and independent weekly, a friend of the truth and progress). Sosa added the following humorous

SANTA FÉ N. MÉX., VIÉRNES 20, DE JULIO DE 1894.

TOMO 1. NUMERO 12.

EL GATO.

Semanário Independiente, Joco-Serio, Amigo de la Verdad y el Progreso.

CONDICIONES: EL GATO maullará los Viérnes de cada semana en diversa variedad de tonos según las circunstancias. La suscrición por un mes 0.10 centavos, por 6 meses 50 centavos y los pagos deberán ser adelantados. Números sueltos 5 centavos. La persona que reciba dos números de ésto periódico sin devolverlo será considerada como suscritor

EL GATO Semanario Registrado en la Oficina de Correos como materia de Segunda Clase.

ENRIQUE SOSA, Editor
ANTONIO ORTIZ, Manejador

El Capitalista y el Obrero.

La presente y formidable lucha entre capitalistas y obreros, probará una vez más que el pueblo unido es invencible, y que cuando lucha por sus sagrados derechos, encuentra en si mismo una fuerza de que no sospechaba la existencia. Un solo esfuerzo hecho por los obreros unidos ha sido suficiente para paralizar en un momento el poderoso [illegible] pero en su necio orgullo aun cree que puede resistir el impulso de los obreros que unidos le reclaman el más sagrado de los derechos reconocidos por el hombre, esto es la justa retribución de su trabajo.

Por el orgullo de unos cuantos ricos ambiciosos y que ejercen influencia por su dinero sobre el ánimo del pequeño Cleveland y su administración, el país se encuentra en deplorable estado, los ferrocarriles paralizados casi en su totalidad, hacen imposible el tráfico; las factorías cerradas por falta de confianza y de elementos manufactureros, siembran la confusión y la miseria, los obreros reclamando equidad de los que les chupan la sangre no pueden atender á la manutención de sus familias y abunda la [illegible] en lo moral como en lo físico; cuanto pasara para que vuelva todo á su primitivo estado aun está también en duda pués las cosas se mantienen casi en igual estado que al principio ó mejor dicho se agravan cada dia los víveres escasean ya en algunas poblaciones, los pagos se detienen, los créditos se cierran y la confianza de empresas se pierde más y más.

Los obreros reciben cada dia nuevos y mayores elementos y el capital se ve á cada momento más aislado y más hostizado, en vista de lo cual podemos casi asegurar que la cuestión de un modo ú otro se resolverá á favor de los obreros.

La sociedad entera está interesada en ésta lucha, pués no sabe [illegible]

Fig. 9. Masthead of Enrique Sosa's *El Gato,* Santa Fe, New Mexico, July 29, 1894.

note to the conditions of the paper's publication, "*El Gato* maullará los Viernes de cada semana en diversa variedad de tonos según las circumstancias [*El Gato* will meow Fridays each week in a variety of tones as circumstances dictate]."

The year after his arrival in Santa Fe, Sosa married Luz Alderete, a native of Las Cruces. Soon after he established a second paper, *La Estrella de Nuevo México,* in Santa Fe, a publication he later relocated to Socorro in 1896. Later he produced *La Hormiga de Oro* at 740 West Railroad Avenue in Albuquerque, a paper he named after the famous Barcelona daily. Sosa edited the paper in Albuquerque for the next two years. Throughout this time he continued to work as an artist and ran ads in local papers offering his services as a painter. Sosa became a naturalized citizen sometime in the early 1890s, while still living in Santa Fe.

In 1898, Sosa moved his printing plant permanently to Mora, New Mexico, but continued his business association with *La Estrella de Nuevo México* and *La Hormiga de Oro* for several years. At Mora, thirty miles north of Las Vegas, New Mexico, Sosa founded *El Eco del Norte,* a paper he edited until his death in 1918.

During the years he spent in Mora, Sosa, his wife, and ten children came to be closely identified with that community. A fact confirmed by Sosa's obituary: "There is no doubt that the residents of Mora and neighboring areas have greatly felt the sudden departure of a man who worked for them, both financially and morally."[32]

Sosa, by those accounts available, was a businessman dedicated to the betterment of his community and his people. This, of course, meant that he was accustomed to privation and hardships imposed by trying to eke out a living in an economically marginal community. The Mora Valley, which had prospered for a time in the late 1890s, began to experience a marked decline in its agricultural economy at the turn of the century.

From the founding of *La Estrella de Nuevo México* in 1895, Enrique Sosa's newspapers were actively involved in La Prensa Asociada. Through business associations, Sosa fostered lasting newspaper enterprises in Albuquerque, Santa Fe, and Mora, New Mexico. Sosa's editorials were short and to the point and his style was one of a tempered and seasoned writer.

Sosa's paintings from when he was a student at San Carlos graced the Palacio Nacional in Mexico City, and once in New Mexico, he reportedly gave other paintings to the Museum Society in Santa Fe. Little is known of his work as a painter or as commercial photographer, although it can be assumed that throughout his years in the Mora area his camera would have been witness and visual chronicler of the community's countless baptisms, weddings, first communions, and political and social gatherings. At the time of his death, Nestor Montoya, president of La Prensa Asociada de Nuevo México (The New Mexico Press Association), paid a final tribute to Sosa.

Fig. 10. Portrait of Enrique Sosa. Courtesy of John Phillip Sosa.

Writing in *La Bandera Americana,* Montoya noted, "He was an honest man, positive in his ideas and given to uphold, with his pen, the character and esteem of the people of New Mexico, [as well as] to loyally support the principles of the American government.[33]

José "Joselín" Escobar

> It has become necessary for the Press—that splendid altar that modern civilization has erected to popular institutions—taking note of its high ministry and the importance it represents in those institutions, to abandon the frivolity which has come to weaken it, in favor of consciously attending to the intellectual development of the masses of Hispanos that still inhabit a part of the West and Southwest of this great republic of the North.
>
> —José Escobar, Denver, Colorado, 1896.

As near as can be determined, José Escobar immigrated from Mexico to New Mexico in the late 1880s. Otherwise, little is known about his place of birth, education, and formal training as a journalist. It was José Escobar who provided a letter of reference to immigration officials in El Paso on June 1, 1889, in support of the legal immigration of fellow journalist Jesús Enrique Sosa.[34] The letter speaks to the fact that Escobar had been living in the United States for a time and as such was in a position to vouch for others crossing into the United States. Escobar continued to assist Jesús Enrique Sosa and other Mexican journalist in founding newspapers in New Mexico.

Little is known about José Escobar's activities before 1889. Just as perplexing is the abrupt end of any mention of "Joselín" in New Mexico newspapers after 1898, when Escobar parted company with *El Combate,* a Socorro, New Mexico, newspaper he was editing (Meyer, 1978). The paucity of information on Escobar encourages conjecture as to why and to what end Escobar spent some ten or more years in New Mexico. Whether Escobar's move to New Mexico was initially motivated by political, economic, or personal motives remains unclear.

The quality and professionalism of his work suggests that he was trained in journalism and letters before coming to the United States. Escobar worked with various publications in towns and cities both in New Mexico and in Colorado and edited no less than fourteen different newspapers in ten separate communities.[35]

Several suppositions can be advanced to explain Escobar's frequent moves and abrupt departures from newspapers with which he associated. As a professional journalist, he was in a position to offer much needed expertise to fledgling newspapers that were springing up virtually in every Spanish-speaking township in the region. Surely he was induced by competing papers to change jobs often. Other evidence, however, suggests that Escobar was a controversial figure. His ideas brought him into contention with the owners and proprietors of several of the newspapers he was hired to edit (Meyer 1978). Still other news reports from the period paint Escobar as a charlatan and a fraud.

In May 1892, for example, *El Tiempo* of Las Cruces published a letter from one of its subscribers describing a business deal with Escobar. The letter was sent to the paper by a Román Bermúdez of Ciudad Juárez, Chihuahua. Mr. Bermúdez writes to warn other unsuspecting readers lest they find themselves bilked by a certain José Escobar. Escobar, according to Bermúdez, had been about the city selling subscriptions for *La Voz de Juárez,* a newspaper the former promised he was going to publish in the city in the near future. No paper ever appeared. Mr. Bermúdez's letter provides a succinct physical description of José Escobar, as well as an equally succinct, albeit, opinionated estimation of his moral character: "On January the first of this year, 1892, a certain José Escobar paid a personal visit to my home. [He is] fair skinned, skinny, a bungler, a cheat, and a swindler."[36] While the Bermúdez letter registers a minor squabble over the matter of a subscription, the designation of *lépero* (charlatan), apparently followed Escobar in his wanderings in New Mexico and Colorado.

Fig. 11. Masthead of *Las Dos Repúblicas,* Denver, Colorado, February 1, 1896.

Escobar attended the 1891 organizational meeting of La Prensa Asociada in Las Vegas as editor of the Trinidad, Colorado, newspaper, *El Progreso.* After working at several newspapers, he returned to Colorado in January 1896 to become editor of a Denver-based publication bankrolled by Casimiro Barela who had just been appointed Consul General of the Mexican Consulate at Denver. At the behest of the Barela, Escobar produced and edited *Las Dos Repúblicas*. The paper obviously benefited from the capital outlay provided by Casimiro Barela and the support of the Mexican Consulate. Superior in quality to many English and Spanish publications, *Las Dos Repúblicas* was published on a state-of-the-art press and was illustrated with "magnificent engravings," giving Escobar cause to boast: "I dare say, [these qualities] place this publication, if not in the lead, at least among the first line of publications in the West of this great North American Republic."[37]

Whatever his personal character and temperament, there is no doubt that José Escobar was an editor of talent who was well educated and well read. His time at *Las Dos Repúblicas* represents the pinnacle of his achievements as editor, essayist, and poet. While there he published a periodical that addressed an array of issues on the industrial, commercial, and scientific potential of trade and exchange between Mexico and the United States. He also published in-depth editorial opinions on the condition of the Mexican-origin communities in the Southwest.

In his program for *Las Dos Repúblicas*, Escobar outlined his aspirations and the utilitarian function of the paper: "This newspaper will dedicate itself principally to developing, to the degree possible, the commercial sectors of these two [Mexico and the United States] great republics, and, more particularly, those of this state, Colorado, with principal markets in Mexico." Acknowledging that his patronage came from Casimiro Barela and other Mexican and U.S. entrepreneurs, Escobar also declared his objective to publish important works of literature and art: "We are trying to make this weekly a useful and interesting sheet for all social classes, and that upon its columns the arts, science, literature, and novelties each have their appropriate place."[38]

Las Dos Repúblicas, subtitled *Periódico comercial, de artes, ciencia y literatura*, (A Business Periodical of Art, Science, and Literature) was a six-page, eight-column weekly. Escobar included the following literary-arts departments: "Plumadas," a section of news briefs of an historical, literary, and scientific bent; "Variedades," a series of poems, epigrams, and other literary selections; and "El Folletín, which regularly reprinted historical texts from Mexican and New Mexican papers. In its short life, the paper managed to disseminate an impressive number of historical and literary texts, including works by Eusebio Chacón and much of Escobar's own published poetry.[39] That Escobar was directly responsible for the high quality and professionalism of *Las Dos Repúblicas* is apparent in the marked drop in the overall quality of the paper following his departure from the newspaper in July 1896.

José Escobar is the first journalist in the region to offer substantial self-reflexive commentary on the work of the press and progress of *Neo-Mexicanos* in education and literacy. He summarized that literary progress in New Mexico in an essay he published in July 1896 titled "Progreso literario de Nuevo México" (New Mexico's Literary Progress). The purpose of the essay was to offer refutation to charges in the eastern press that the region's Spanish-speaking community was backward and indolent in matters concerning education and progress. More important, Escobar's essay documents the spread of print culture in *Mexicano* communities: "That very press has improved noticeably over the last few years, and in its editorials and bulletins one can observe something more than the embryonic style of a press in its infancy; [it can be seen] in its logical and well-conceived commentary that struggles, not as the party line, but rather, for something greater yet, for the betterment of the masses irrespective of political or religious belief."[40]

Escobar was not only a publisher but was also a writer and poet who played a decisive role in the cultural program sponsored by *Neo-Mexicano* journalism. Like his contemporaries he would extol the virtues of literacy as a means to liberate *Neo-Mexicano* potential, at one point, exhorting his colleagues, "Foment your noble desire for knowledge; persevere in your noble struggle."[41]

Isidoro Armijo (1871–1949)

Who's Who in New Mexico for 1937 lists Isidoro Armijo's profession as that of a newspaperman. The entry notes his accomplishments in education and public life and further describes him as the author of "Sixty Minutes in Hades," and other stories. The entry ends with the claim that Armijo had written over two thousand feature articles for English and Spanish newspapers,[42] a figure that at first view seems large despite Armijo's many years of participation in Spanish-language journalism in New Mexico and Colorado.

Isidoro Armijo first became associated with the *periodiquero* movement while working at Trinidad's *El Progreso* in 1898. From July to September 1898, Armijo is listed as editor of *El Progreso*. During this time he worked for the paper's proprietor Salomón C. García. Armijo's tenure as a journalist had by his own account begun only a short time earlier in 1896 when at age twenty-five he entered the field by working as an editor of an unnamed *Neo-Mexicano* newspaper (Read *Historia*, 448).

After graduating from the College of Agriculture and Mechanical Arts, Armijo worked as a school teacher in Doña Ana County for about two years. He then became associated with Las Cruces's oldest periodical, *El Tiempo* (1882), where he learned the business of publishing a newspaper. During the next six years Armijo traveled extensively in the United States and in Mexico. In 1899 he returned to Las Cruces and became active in local politics.

From 1900 to 1904 he was editor of *El Eco del Valle* and from 1904 to 1908 he edited another paper in the Mesilla Valley, *La Flor del Valle*. In 1908 he was elected to the territorial legislature and served that body as chief clerk. In 1910 Armijo was elected to serve as delegate from Doña Ana County to the New Mexico Constitutional Convention. The convention's delegates were charged with developing a constitution that, if adopted, would signal the end of New Mexico's territorial status and usher in statehood. Armijo's greatest accomplishment as a delegate to the convention was to have drafted the legislation requiring the incorporation of the Treaty of Guadalupe-Hidalgo into the state's constitution. Years later, New Mexico's *periodiqueros* would not let their readerships forget the importance of Armijo's action. And even as late as 1926, when rumors circulated across the state that moves were afoot to disenfranchise *Neo-Mexicanos* by taking away their right to vote, *La Estrella* of Las Cruces offered the following editorial reprinted from an Española, New Mexico, paper called *El Palito:*

> The enemies of our people will not succeed in trampling the natives, taking away their right to American citizenship, since at the Constitutional Convention, Isidoro Armijo wrote and presented before that convention the noble law and idea which was unanimously adopted, to include the Treaty of Guadalupe-Hidalgo as part of the Constitution.[43]

As a result of the prominence he gained as a delegate to the Constitutional Convention, Armijo became a well-known figure in political circles at the state level. After 1912 Armijo resided for extended periods in Santa Fe, Taos, and Albuquerque. During these years he interspersed public service with his work as an editor of several Spanish-language newspapers in the upper Río Grande corridor. He served a term in the New Mexico House of Representatives (1914) but returned to journalism in the 1920s. From 1920 to 1922 he was editor of both the *Taos Valley News* and *La Revista de Taos*. In 1926 he established and edited *El Eco del Río Grande*, a newspaper serving the counties of north-central New Mexico. In the 1920s he established the Armijo Bureau, a newspaper agency that acted as a clearinghouse and news service for Spanish-language newspapers throughout the state. The two thousand feature articles reported in *Who's Who in New Mexico* were most likely the result of the collective work of his agency.

Armijo's contribution to La Prensa Asociada came by way of his abilities as a writer and a businessman. By 1900 Armijo had become the leading *Nuevomexicano* journalist in southern New Mexico. His success in forging newspaper enterprises that spoke with the urgency of other well-established publications at Albuquerque, Santa Fe, and Las Vegas was built upon the work and efforts of many other *periodiqueros* who had been working in the area for at least a decade prior. Armijo's *El Eco del Valle*, for example, absorbed *El Tiempo*, the Mesilla Valley's oldest Spanish-language weekly in 1910. *La Estrella, El Eco del Valle*, and *La Flor del Valle* were also successful because Armijo was able to enlist a cadre of diverse and well-prepared journalists, writers, and collaborators to edit and produce them. He also often collaborated with several correspondents in Ciudad Juárez and Mexico City. In March 1911, for example, Armijo's *La Estrella* promoted itself by, among other things, touting the credentials of its staff. *La Estrella's* promotional read: "La Estrella. El mejor periódico Político que se publica en español en Nuevo México. Nuestro material es original. No plagiamos artículos. No llenamos nuestras columnas con puras copias como lo hacen otros periódicos [*La Estrella*, the best political paper published in Spanish in New Mexico. Our material is original. We do not plagiarize articles. We do not fill our columns with reprints as other papers do]."

Like Felix Martínez in Las Vegas, Isidoro Armijo built a publishing company around his newspaper activities. As president and proprietor, Armijo delegated work to others who were more aptly trained and inclined to specific editorial and writing tasks. Armijo also played a key role in bridging interests between the *Mexicano, Neo-Mexicano*, and the Anglo communities in southern New Mexico. For example, he published *La Estrella* in the print shop of the *Las Cruces Citizen*, a newspaper owned and operated by William LaPoint, a friend and associate of Armijo's and an influential citizen in Las Cruces. Collaborative efforts of this sort were more likely in the Mesilla Valley than in other areas of the territory, because both *Mexicanos* and Anglo-Americans began to populate the area in substantial numbers around the same time in the late 1870s. Disputes over prior land tenure and historical precedent were less volatile, although cultural conflict over politics, religion, and customs still consumed interests and divided concerns in southern New Mexico.

Nestor Montoya (1862–1923)

Nestor Montoya, a journalist in New Mexico for many years, was elected president of La Prensa Asociada Hispano-Americana in 1903. Like other *periodiqueros,* Montoya was known as a fine public speaker, an able editor, at home in both English and Spanish. Despite years of work in Spanish-language journalism, his political career would eventually overshadow his accomplishments as an editor and publisher.

After severing his partnership with Enrique H. Salazar and leaving *La Voz del Pueblo* in 1890, Montoya retired for a time from the newspaper business. In 1901, however, he found an opportunity to return to the field when he took over *El Nuevo Mundo,* a paper founded in Old Albuquerque in May 1897 and which had been edited by José Escobar, and later by Enrique Sosa. Montoya and Alejandro Sandoval of Albuquerque merged *El Nuevo Mundo* with *La Bandera Americana.* In the initial years after the merger Montoya assumed the position of editor and secretary. He maintained control of the paper for some twenty-two years, until his death in 1923. The merger also established La Compañía Publicista de la Bandera Americana (The Bandera Americana Publishing Company), whose board of directors shared many members from the leadership of the Republican party in Sandoval, Valencia, and Bernalillo counties.

La Bandera Americana added pragmatism in politics and economics to its cultural program of earlier years. Through successive changes in editors, the paper continued to lend space in its columns to items of a cultural nature. No doubt, Montoya's earlier collaborations with literary journalists such as Enrique H. Salazar, Enrique Sosa, and José Escobar influenced the content of his paper. Like so many other papers, *La Bandera* published the works of local poets and writers alongside works in the Latin American tradition. It was not uncommon for *La Bandera* to feature the works of local poets such as Felipe Maximiliano Chacón and Eleuterio Baca alongside those of luminaries in the Latin American tradition such as Sor Juana Inés de la Cruz, Ignacio Altamirano, Ruben Darío, and Salvador Díaz Mirón. *La Bandera* also printed notices on local literary and dramatic groups that regularly met and performed in Albuquerque neighborhoods such as Los Barelas, Los Duranes, and Old Albuquerque. Nestor Montoya's editorials were often brief and to the point, but they were timely and strident in speaking of problems affecting *Nuevomexicanos* in Albuquerque.

Fig. 12. Portrait of Nestor Montoya with signature. Read, *Historia Ilustrada de Nuevo Mexico* (497).

Countless other *Neo-Mexicano* journalists joined in the work of fomenting literacy and education through membership in La Prensa Asociada. While nineteenth-century *Neo-Mexicano* print culture remained loosely networked to La Prensa Asociada Hispano-Americana, inadequate systems of distribution, competition for commercial revenues and advertisement meant that the efforts of individual presses needed to be replicated over and over again at each new locale. While dramatically increasing in numbers, the impact of newspapers, whether published in Spanish or English, was restricted to the town in which they were published. The work of *Hispano* journalists was highly dependent on the work of a local editor-printer, who in the absence of consolidation remained the cornerstone of efforts to extend the influence of print culture to all. Throughout the period, depending on social and economic changes, *Neo-Mexicano* literates moved in and out of printing and publishing. Yet the movement, it seems clear, stuck to its aims. Not merely satisfied with utilizing the press for weekly information exchange, *Neo-Mexicanos* of this generation headed local efforts to publish books, specifically, books of history and literature. The work of *Neo-Mexicano* literates to shape the discourse of their social world by recovering a history of the region is the subject of the following chapter. For its part, La Prensa Asociada Hispano-Americana continued to channel the discursive interests of *periodiqueros* in the territorial period. When at last the organization suffered a decline it would be in the context of the hegemonic dissolution of a culture of print for *Mexicanos* and *Neo-Mexicanos* in the Southwest.

Part II

Neo-Mexicano Culture in Print

Notwithstanding *Neo-Mexicanos'* need to locate themselves as a people amidst the constriction of their social world, they in all likelihood could not fully comprehend the degree to which their acts of daily living represented a kind of cultural defiance in the face of Anglo American demands for conformity. Genaro Padilla notes that after the American conquest "most people retained the daily self-identificatory practices of language, social custom, and communal relations. The rupture produced a situation in which Mexican people were forced to adapt to an alien social economy while increasingly struggling to remember themselves with a culture and history of their own" (1993, 15). This dynamic, Padilla concludes, produced protracted and complex responses born of "social situations that made a necessity of multiregistered address" (ibid., 44).

Neo-Mexicano print journalism after 1848 would encode cultural articulations in the literary arts and texts of history that evince all manner of social contestation. Group disclosure, then, was to be found in those private and public forms of address still open to *Neo-Mexicanos.* Publication in Spanish provided a social space that habituated contestation, and which, importantly, made it the staple of daily reading for many *Neo-Mexicanos.* Through the press and in their native tongue *Neo-Mexicanos* breathed life into a culture pinned by the boot of conquest and dispossession.

Part II of this study looks at the ways in which *Neo-Mexicanos* represented their *cultura,* and how, having established print culture in their communities, *los periodiqueros* went about putting that culture in print.

4

News, Bio-Texts, and *Neo-Mexicano* Historiography

Writing Against Cultural Excision

> We hope now that education and learning is taking flight among the children of New Mexico, that the day will arrive when we will not have need to look beyond our midst to find authors sufficiently learned to write the history of our Territory with precision and clarity. . . . this, so all is not lost and relegated to darkness, and so, that individuals only recently identified with the Territory will not attempt to monopolize the historical field that concerns *Hispanos*, and ignore important events that preceded their arrival.
>
> —Enrique H. Salazar, Las Vegas, New Mexico, 1895

The kind of nineteenth-century liberal romanticism so apparent in the infatuation of *Neo-Mexicano* literates with the press as means of leveling social disparity naturalized this generation's inclination toward historical inquiry and heightened its awareness of the past and its relationship to the present. In substantial ways print discourse was changing what this generation of *Neo-Mexicanos* thought and understood about historical and cultural representation. Even in the most remote corners of New Mexico, the dialectic of ownership of the documentary record of past events figured squarely into matters of sociopolitical agency. As the epigraph above attests, the issue was of greatest concern to those for whom conquest signified historical banishment. As *los periodiqueros* sought to use the press to divulge knowledge of *Neo-Mexicano* culture and history, they were engaged in the process Hayden White sees as characteristic of nineteenth-century artists and historians who "went to history for their themes and appealed to 'historical consciousness' as a justification for their attempts at cultural palingenesis" (1978, 41). If print culture assisted in a cultural rebirth for *Neo-Mexicanos*, in doing so it also "changed the way men think" (Darnton 1989, 46). One obvious result was that *Neo-Mexicano* journalists became cognizant of being excised from sociohistorical and literary accounts. Another was that the thinking of many *periodiqueros* was shaped by axiological relationships that galvanized print culture to historiography.

Neo-Mexicanos easily transposed their expectations of the press onto the figure of the historian-chronicler. In the work of the historian they saw the promise of social ascendancy and the redemptive attributes of the social emancipator. Liberation through cultural representation, "so that all will not be relegated to oblivion and darkness," was vested in historians, because their work (then as now), as Hayden White reminds us, "seek[s] to refamiliarize us with events which have been forgotten either through accident, neglect or repression" (1978, 87). *Neo-Mexicanos* knew as much when calling on *nativo* historians to make use of the documentary record of the past to illuminate the social distress that plagued the present.

It is not surprising that history and its consequences occupied the thinking of a great many *Neo-Mexicanos* after 1848. Accident, neglect, and repression, they understood, had disfigured *Nuevomexicano* social, political, and cultural economy under the American regime. These conditions gave rise to prolonged and extensive discursive introspection, which lead *periodiqueros* to consider the root causes of *Neo-Mexicano* social malaise. Enrique H. Salazar of *El Independiente* was one *nativo* editor who consistently provided edito-

Fig. 13. Enrique H. Salazar (circa 1900) atop delivery wagon with unidentified members of his staff and several Las Vegas residents. Donnelly Collection, New Mexico Highlands University. Courtesy of Las Vegas Committee for Historic Preservation.

rial grist to his readership entreating the matter of *Nuevomexicano* social decline. Pointing to obvious changes, Salazar reminded his readers, "It is no surprise that each day the New Mexicans are found in a increasingly disadvantaged situation."[1] The will to counter political and social devaluation lead *los periodiqueros* to question the accuracy of the representations put forth of them by amateur and professional Anglo-American writers.

Nuevomexicano journalists seemed dogged by the question of where to lay blame for the continuing erosion of *nativos*' power, and at times their rhetoric appears contradictory. Time and again they had challenged the rhetoric of enfranchisement and progress by pointing out that poverty, lack of education and social progress, and class stratification continued to define their social circumstance. However, *Nuevomexicano* editors also recognized that poverty and repression perpetuated equally destructive tendencies among the *nativo* populace. These factors stilted initiative and induced passivity in some sectors of the *Nuevomexicano* community. Enrique H. Salazar attacked the lack of enterprise among *Neo-Mexicanos* with absolute candor:

> We have become so fond of the role of seconding plans that benefit outsiders that we have forgotten that our innate autonomy should be the guiding star of our proceedings. If those who use us as a tool, throw us aside when we are no longer useful and they despise us continually for our servility and subjugation. . . . Who should we blame if not ourselves?[2]

Editors appealed to the notion of individual responsibility and exhorted the populace to compete and strive toward entrepreneurship and educational attainment. If a "top down" ideology of political empowerment through statehood was continually thwarted by the politics of territoriality, it then behooved *Nuevomexicanos* to take the longer, and albeit more difficult, path and chart a vertical ascent to retain their civil rights and full participation in society. Salazar urged self-reliance:

> Moreover, since our collective attempt to rise to the level of other communities in the nation has failed through our own shortcomings and in order to preserve our rights—at least (as they exist) up to now—this [our failure] should not cause us to dispense with our individual efforts and let ourselves be defeated or driven out of the fields of material progress and intellectual endeavor, [which will lead to] the deterioration of our dignity as men and of our financial interests. We have at hand the mirror by which to see ourselves in the actions and procedures of the immigrants from other States who come here to plant themselves around us; they, whoever they may be in other regards, are

> worthy of praise for their flawless love of work and for their constant effort to better their situation. By imitating their virtues and ignoring their faults, the path to advancement and progress shall be open to us. [That path] is indispensable if we are to avoid relegation to the category of inferiors without autonomy and initiative, the sole means of arbitration being to obey dictates and await the crumbs that fall from the table of the master.[3]

Assessments such as these were widely held by the community at large and led *Nuevomexicano* editors to return time and again to the question of educational neglect among the "masses" of the Spanish-speaking. This precarious social position, they understood, had the potential to undermine a *Nuevomexicano* sense of self and of historical representation.

Neo-Mexicano journalists were convinced that plotting the history of their people was a means to resist becoming a "subordinate and inferior group." Resisting cultural devaluation, they reasoned, was another way to reaffirm *Nuevomexicano* civil rights: "As we go on advancing in the arts and industries of civilization, [we] will bring to an end the fiction of racial inferiority with which our enemies label us."[4]

Neo-Mexicano journalists asserted that their three-hundred- year-old history in the region merited scholarly attention. Knowledge of that history, they argued, should be divulged to the populace at large, "Siendo esta materia que naturalmente interesa á los hijos de Nuevo México, á aquellos cuyos antepasados exploraron y colonizaron esta tierra por más que 300 años, hicieron grandes sacrificios y pusieron muchísimos trabajos para conservarla, parécenos que no dejará llamar alguna atención [As it is the case that this material which naturally is of interest to the sons of New Mexico, whose forebears explored and colonized this land and who for more than three hundred years made great sacrifices and put forth many works to conserve it; it is our view that it will call up some interest]." These considerations took on special significance as *Nuevomexicanos* became aware that their history was subject to distortion and omission at the hands of historians entering the region for the first time.

Neo-Mexicano historical consciousness grew in response to the introduction of the popular press. The press fostered three principle modes of historiographic texts, which offered the first forms of Mexican-American self-representation in historical discourse in the United States. Newspapers generated editorial opinion and short narrative articles on history that circulated regularly in *Neo-Mexicano* communities. Second, encoded in newspapers were short biographical texts that eventually led to the development of more complete biographical narratives; and third, established writers would arch out of the newspaper publication and produce historical narratives in the form of books and compilations. José Escobar, Eusebio Chacón, Camilo

Padilla, Enrique H. Salazar, and Benjamín M. Read, familiar figures in the *Neo-Mexicano* cultural movement, produced early works representing their community through the various forms of historiography available to them.

News of History: The Axiology of the Past and Present

In routinely inserting historiographic materials into their cultural pages, Spanish-language newspapers fostered a deep and abiding sense of historical consciousness among the various social classes in New Mexico. *Neo-Mexicano* editors regularly ran historical items in their columns and articles, encoding history as news for a general readership. José Escobar of *Las Dos Repúblicas* referred to newspapers as "el verdadero libro de las classes populares," (the real book of the popular classes) and urged his colleagues, "let us seek to write sound newspapers for the good of popular learning."[5] Providing reading material on historical events spoke to this need to assist popular learning. Most *periodiqueros* were cognizant of the scarcity of books throughout the region and admonished their readership, "You should, we repeat, read, since it is not possible [to publish] thick volumes, at least the pages of periodicals that circulate locally."[6] Editors believed that as *nativos* were given items of local history readers would understand the true nature and merit of *Nuevomexicano* society as it existed beyond "satirical allusions and biting falsehoods of eastern journalists."[7]

Neo-Mexicano editors did not want for historical material to draw from. The materials they published spanned the course of several centuries of Spanish and Amerindian influence that had shaped the matrix of their culture. The historical discourse of Spanish-language newspapers included pre-Columbian mythos and history, the conquest of Mexico by Spain, the colonial exploration of the Southwest, the Mexican War of Independence, and the arrival of the Americans in the Southwest. And if this did not provide enough reading, editors often included biographical items drawn from the gallery of U.S. presidents or the Latin American emancipators Bolivar, Sucre, Hidalgo, and others. Some newspapers, such as *Las Dos Repúblicas* at Denver, gave form to this historical panoply in weekly columns. José Escobar featured such items in a column titled "El Folletín" (The Newspaper Serial). Other Spanish-language newspapers, however, simply juxtaposed items on history alongside the news of the day, drawing from a wide range of historical subjects as seen in the sampling of articles that follow:

"Aztecas y tezcucanos [Aztecs and Tezcucans]," *El Sol de Mayo,* Las Vegas, August 2, 1891.

"Discursos de Washington [Speeches by Washington]," *El Sol de Mayo,* Las Vegas, October 29, 1891.

"Mexicanos Ilustres: Cuatemoc [Illustrious Mexicans: Cuatemoc]," *El Boletín Popular,* Santa Fe, July 23, 1893.

"Los tres americanos [Three Americans—a comparison of Washington, Hidalgo, and Bolívar]," *El Independiente,* Las Vegas, August 24, 1895.

"El idioma más antiguo: evidencias que México es la cuna del hombre primitivo, [The Oldest Language: Proof that Mexico is the Birthplace of Primitive Man]," *El Independiente,* Las Vegas, September 7, 1895.

"¿Fué un bien o un mal el descubrimiento de América para la humanidad? [Was the Discovery of America Good or Bad for Humanity?]," *El Independiente,* Las Vegas, September 14, 1895.

"Proclamación de Donaciano Vigil, Febrero de 1847 [The Donociano Vigil Proclamation of February 1847]," *El Boletín Popular,* Santa Fe, February 6, 1896.

"Joaquín Murrieta," (episodes) *El Boletín Popular,* Santa Fe, May 14, 1896.

"México antiguo [Ancient Mexico]," *El Boletín Popular,* Santa Fe, September 3, 1896.

"Historia de la Malinche [History of Malinche]," *El Boletín Popular,* Santa Fe, July 9, 1896.

"Manifiesto [Miguel Hidalgo y Castillo's speech to the nation]," *El Tiempo,* Las Cruces, September 17, 1897.

"Los obispos de Nuevo México [The Bishops of New Mexico—a listing of the bishops of New Mexico from Settlement through Lamy]," *El Boletín Popular,* Santa Fe, December 2, 1897.

Materials chosen for newspaper publication reflect the enormity of the historical field that informed *Neo-Mexicano* antecedents in the region. Such items authenticated a past that Anglo-American observers preferred to ignore, and journalists inserted them onto the pages of their publications so that their readership might more readily measure *Mexicano* achievement in the past against its devaluation and excision from historical accounting in their own time. It was the American interruption in this historical flow of events the most concerned *Mexicano* editors. This very real threat of historical erasure moved *Neo-Mexicano* literates to produce historiographic representation of the Southwest because they were aware that as more of the history of the region came under the purview and monopolization of *los extranjeros,* the very means of representation itself that was at stake.

Consequently the notion of a homeland lent force to the energies of *Neo-Mexicano* literates to historicize the particulars of their corner of the world. Concern in the face of dehistorization naturalized the underlying desire of much of this writing to reinscribe the epic proportions of the history of that homeland as chronicled in the myth, legend, and ethnopoetics of the colonial period. *Los periodiqueros* turned to the "glorious" deeds of the Spanish colonial enterprise. Filled with pure *fabula,* the sixteenth-century exploits of *conquistadores* provided the *periodiquero* generation with a powerful master narrative to counter Anglo-American pretensions to primacy in the region. Essentialist in this regard, the emphasis on the colonial narratives overshadowed the complexities of social and class formation in New Mexico tied to its *mestizo, genízaro,* and Indian past. As it was, nineteenth-century historicism attributed great history to the actions of great men, and following this line of reasoning, the monumental stature of the colonial epic was proof that Anglo-American achievement paled in comparison to that of "los bizarros conquistadores," (the gallant conquistadors) of a bygone age. For these, Enrique H. Salazar admonished, had been, "the true explorers of this continent and there is no comparison with the Pikes, the Clarks, the Fremonts, and other American explorers whose travels and explorations in this century have been so pondered and given over to fame, but which truly are child's play in comparison to the actions undertaken by the Spaniards more than two hundred years earlier."[8]

Neo-Mexicanos indeed had cause to worry. In the face of cultural exclusion, a new history of the region was being fashioned by Anglo-American observers and historians. This reshaping of the historical field followed the precept of Manifest Destiny and provided a justification for the territorial expansion of the United States into the western territories. As it worked to enshrine the Anglo-American pioneer epic as historical truth, this historical revision in turned devalued the history of native peoples. Enrique H. Salazar, feigning incredulity, ironized such maneuvering by attributing it to the inexperience of Anglo historians about whom he observed, "unintentionally, but simply in their ignorance of all these matters, and not having the aptitude to study them further, [they] have limited themselves to relate a few well-known facts about some prominent individuals who entered the territory since and after the American Annexation."[9] But as cultural misrepresentation in the eastern press became more pronounced, *nativo* editors were quick to point out the serious implications of such trends.

One instance that raised Salazar's ire was the legend surrounding local scout and Indian fighter, Kit Carson. The inflation of American adventurers to the rank of folk heros crystalized important elements of a dialectic that had become the cornerstone of *Neo-Mexicano* social discourse.

Enrique H. Salazar saw clear historical falsification at work in the postulation of Carson as a heroic figure for New Mexico and New Mexicans. Salazar suggested to his readers in July 1897 that the makeover had been orchestrated by the eastern press: "Carson's life [story] began to grow principally owing to books written as tributes, in these, very ardent accounts were given of his life and deeds; and while these books did not make much of a splash [here] and were nearly totally unknown in the Territory, they did find a following in the states of the east and west, whereby Carson's fame was established."[10]

Enshrining Kit Carson had become "the pretense of many to impose him on our community as the titular hero of New Mexico," actions which, Salazar stressed, represented, "a kind of usurpation that falsifies the facts and history and uses a false pretext to perpetuate a falsehood that belies *Neo-Mexicano* annuals." At one point in his essay Salazar asks, "Who are the legitimate heroes of a people?" and argues vehemently that moves to honor Kit Carson with a statue in Santa Fe are the work of a self-interested group of "friends and admirers," who by design show contempt for *Neo-Mexicano* participation in the history of the region. Salazar concludes, "If our fellow citizens embrace a desire to immortalize the deeds and acts of illustrious men of note in their history, they have within their view an ample field from whence to select without having to pay to strangers the tributes that belong to their own fellow citizens."[11]

The dialectic over which history should be told figured prominently in the Mexicano struggle for social recognition at the end of the nineteenth century. In an effort to counter dehistorization, *Neo-Mexicanos* appealed to historical precedent as means to assert their own participation in history. They reasoned that prior achievement authenticated the legitimacy of their claims to land, language, and cultural rights. Affirming this, *Neo-Mexicano* writers and journalists embraced history with particular fervor, not as Chautauqua, nor as a way to "make the past a living presence to their contemporaries" (White 1978, 41). Rather, they embraced historical discourse because they believed that it provided irrefutable evidence that would vindicate their society, protecting them from the ravages of conquest. The historical record, they believed, would convince their Anglo-American counterparts of their merit and worth as fellow citizens. *Nuevomexicanos* reasoned that the concreteness of their experience in the region provided evidence that their contributions and achievements were beyond censure. *Neo-Mexicano* literates had taken nineteenth-century liberal ideas to heart, believing history to be an objective, impartial, and irrefutable witness—a final arbiter, which like some deus ex machina would deliver them from the ravages of conquest and dispossession, and provide them a cornerstone upon which to reconstruct their sense of self and a means by which to reaffirm their cultural existence. History, *Nuevomexicanos* believed, was authority itself. Of this *Neo-Mexicano* biographer José E. Fernández was convinced when he wrote, "History is the narration of true facts" (1911, xii).

The incessant devaluation of *Nuevomexicano* culture and history made writers and journalists aware of the necessity for a comprehensive and definitive history of New Mexico and the Southwest from a *nativo* perspective. Here again print culture was suggesting the means for social empowerment. Producing a history of New Mexico that would self-consciously focus on the agency of *Nuevomexicanos* and whose a primary object was to liberate *Nuevomexicanos* from the burden of conquest and dispossession would require years of work. Nonetheless, the urgency to provide historical validation to counter misinterpretation by Anglo-American writers became the rallying cry of this generation. Nowhere is this concern more succinctly registered than in the front page editorial of *El Independiente* for March 6, 1895.

The editorial, written by Enrique H. Salazar, begins by speaking of the great many amateur historians who since 1850 had taken up New Mexico history as their subject. The primary failing of these authors, in Salazar's view, had been a disregard for *Nuevomexicanos* and their culture. Salazar suggests that the best known of these histories, *El Gringo* (1857) by W. W. H. Davies, was flawed by its omissions of fact and by its bias against the native population. Salazar wrote, "It contains so many errors and inventions and in many places displays such partiality against the native settlers of the land and their forebears, that its value as history is nil."[12] Salazar is unequivocal in declaring that the task of correcting this kind of misrepresentation fell to a native of the territory:

> This work properly belongs to a son of the homeland [who should] be filled with the required zeal and patriotism of similar endeavors. At the same time it should be well equipped with the work, instruction and criteria needed, so as to give birth to a history that is not built on errors and lies, one which will bear out the deeds of our forebears, [speak] of the obstacles they overcame and the dangers which with great perseverance and integrity they have borne for over three centuries.[13]

Editors whose intent had been to promote a positive sense of the community through literary and intellectual endeavor made historical discourse a part of their work in journalism. While texts produced by *Nuevomexicanos* were localized and concerned themselves with the Southwest, the idea that a sense of historical consciousness might be fostered through art as well as history did not run contrary to the theoretical dicta of the nineteenth century, which held that the work of the artist and historian was inextricably bound. White notes, "Historians of the second half of the nineteenth century continued to see their work as a combination of art and science, they saw it as a combination of romantic art on the one hand and scientific positivism on the other" (1978, 42). These macrotrends in nineteenth-century historical discourse were in a sense naturalized by the long- standing tradition among *Nuevomexicanos*, who employed ethnopoetic texts to encode historical narration. On the one hand, narrative forms such as the *décima* and the *corrido*, which often portrayed events in real time, were embedded in *Nuevomexicano* ethnopoetics. These forms were traditionally employed to authenticate, but also to enhance, the telling of lived experience. On the other hand, *Nuevomexicanos* had only to see that most important event of their history, the settlement of New Mexico by Spanish-Mexican colonists in 1598, had been chronicled in Gaspar Pérez de Villagrá's epic poem *Historia de la Conquista de la Nuevo México* (History of the Conquest of New Mexico) of 1612.

Evidence that historical consciousness was well ingrained in the thinking of this generation is found in the numerous historiographic projects that were launched by its members. In 1889 José Segura opened the pages of *El Boletín Popular* to Adolph F. Bandelier. The noted anthropologist reproduced the Fray Marcos de Niza chronicle on the exploration of New Mexico for the benefit of Spanish readers.[14] In 1896, Francisco De Thoma, a Spanish immigrant to New Mexico, and the editor of *El Nuevo Mundo* in Albuquerque, published a work titled *Historia Popular de Nuevo México.* De Thoma based his history on works by Hubert H. Bancroft and those of several Mexican authorities compiled in the tome *México através de los siglos* (Mexico Across the Centuries). Similar works would follow.

Bio-Narrative Credentialing: Projections Onto History

"Biografiar es historiar [to write biography is to write history]," declared José E. Fernández as preface to his 1911 biography of the southern Colorado legislator, Casimiro Barela. Contemporary theorists of historical narrative might readily agree with Fernández when considering the discursive strategies that constitute bio-narrative disclosure. New historicists, on the other hand, would be much less concerned about whether the subject of the narrative deals with real or imagined events, with truth or invented truth. The stance of such theoreticians gives Hayden White cause to state, "In point of fact, history—the real world as it evolves in time—is made sense of in the way the poet or the novelist tries to make sense of it" (White 98). José E. Fernández, on the other hand, a nineteenth-century *Neo-Mexicano* biographer, was not thinking of the philosophy surrounding historical narrative, rather his intent was to convince his readers that the authority of his narrative rested squarely upon the factual record. From what is known of Fernández, and considering the circumstances in which he wrote, it is safe to assume that his writing purports to cut from real life. The biographer's desire to equate biography as history locates *Cuarenta años de legislador, o la biografía del Senador Casimiro Barela* (Forty Years as a Legislator, or The Biography of Casimiro Barela) squarely within the cultural program of the *periodiquero* movement. The work, like numerous other historiographies of the day, was conceived as documentation, a means to leave to posterity some record of *Neo-Mexicano* collective (historical) and individual (biographical) experience.

Biography provided a particularly attractive means to document *Nuevomexicano* achievement over time. The bio-text familiarized history for a community of readers in a way other writing could not. Editors found that through the eyelet of an individual life and agency could be threaded sociohistorical events affecting *Nuevomexicanos* in general. Bakhtin has noted that the capacity of biography is to form axiological relationships that graft

José E. Fernandez

Fig. 14. Biographer, José Fernández. Read, *Illustrated History of New Mexico* (750).

the actions of the biographical subject to the world he or she shares with a group or nation (1990, 154).

Neo-Mexicano biographical profiles emerge in the print discourse of *Neo-Mexicano* newspapers as an extremely important field of representation that register *nativo* civic participation in the affairs of their society. These texts, which at their core are self-reflexive, celebrate in unabashed and laudatory terms the lives of those whom the community selects as worthy of emulation; thus, one result is the authentication of positive self-representation in the face of hegemonic effacement.

Biographical *bocetos* (short narrative profiles) prescribe models of behavior and validate the historicity of actions undertaken by members of the community. The practice of profiling the lives of prominent individuals in short bio-texts was a common occurrence in both the English and Spanish language press in the late nineteenth century. Ostensibly the practice owed as much to politics as it did to historical consciousness of the newspaper editors. *Bocetos* were used to inform readers about the qualifications and character of political office seekers and were published routinely as political campaigns for territorial offices intensified. The *boceto* demonstrates in tangible ways how print had come to shape communitarian expression, for unlike the *corrido* and other oral narratives, such texts produce expositional narration and move away from the lyrical embellishment that is characteristic of oral narratives. The value of these political sketches resides in the schemata they provide of model citizenship and exemplary accomplishment. For *Neo-Mexicanos* these questions were further complicated by a politics of conquest, which explains the heightened emphasis given in *Neo-Mexicano* biographical material to genealogy and the affinity of the biographical subject to local community. Many of these *bocetos* became the basis for longer biographical compilations such as those appended in Read's *Historia Ilustrada de Nuevo México* (1910) and in Peterson's *Representative New Mexicans* (1912).

The following *boceto* of my great-uncle, Tito Meléndez, typical of others from the period, was occasioned by his bid for the office as treasurer and tax collector of Mora County in 1908:

> Señor Meléndez was born in Mora, his honorable, though poor parents educated him at the Christian Brothers College, called the College of St. Mary's.
>
> He began to work at Mr. Roa's sawmill and in a short time he gained the confidence and esteem of his boss in such measure that he [Roa] sold him the entire business on payments.
>
> With his efforts and business, Señor Meléndez paid up in a short time, and with his intelligence and perseverance he has managed to have one of the best mills in the County. He is generous with his help, he pays on time, and keeps his promises as stipulated.
>
> He took interest in politics and was among those that won the administration, freeing it from the Democrats who used [it] to their own ends. He was then elected as a County Commissioner and managed through his efforts and good management to wipe away the opinions and bad reputation that circulated about the County's finances: since then in convention after convention he has been sought out for different nominations, but he ceded his rights for the good of the party, and with his help, influence and money he has supported others in the positions he was offered.
>
> In 1903, at the insistence of his friends, he accepted the nomination for County Sheriff and was elected by a large majority over his competitor, and he has discharged that position, much to his credit and to that of his constituents.

> Now he has agreed to accept the candidacy as Treasurer and Tax Collector; a man of talent, knowledge, honor and confidence is needed in this position. Señor Meléndez possesses all these virtues and the people in giving him their vote can be confident that in Señor Meléndez they have a faithful servant and an honorable person deserving of their confidence. Do not forget that Don Tito is one of the bright sons of the County, he is not prideful, despite his merits, he is generous in his business dealings and he is attentive and courteous with everyone. On voting for Señor Meléndez the voters of [the] county are voting for their benefit and for the honor and good name of the County.[15]

Enrique Sosa, the editor of *El Eco del Norte,* wherein the *boceto* appears, no doubt thought his first responsibility was to inform readers about the candidate, but the bio-text he printed forms a kind of group portraiture. For the text's close identification with the subject is tied to the aims, beliefs, and values that derive their meaning from the overall social good of the community. As such, the profile is encoded with expectations held in common by *Neo-Mexicano* rural society. While, on one plane, the residents of Mora County are provided information to judge the merits of a particular candidate, on another the information is meaningful only to the extent that it confirms the values they themselves hold to be important.

The *boceto* operates as a microtext since what it discloses is as much about personal ambition as it is a primer on the ethical norms of the community. As is typical of the *boceto,* the Meléndez bio-text privileges affiliation and identification with the welfare of the community as criteria sine qua non public trust and confidence is all but impossible to secure. Beyond individual merit it prescribes that office seekers have a shared genealogy, honorable parentage, a Christian-Catholic foundation, initiative and industry, a sense of fair play and justice, selflessness, honesty, reliability, and humility.

The tendency of *Neo-Mexicano* editors to preface local *bocetos* with laudatory introductions more fitting of a royal edict likewise belies a desire to project individual and collective ascendancy on the transcendent plane of social history. For these textual "snapshots" are taken from a *Neo-Mexicano* vantage point, and their subtext suggests a communitarian will to historical and cultural presence. Thus the elements outlined above become essential to sociobiographical credentialing along the lines of communitarian values of individual agency within *Neo-Mexicano* communities after 1848.

Historical Biography

Among the first historiographic projects to be touted in the *Neo-Mexicano* press was José Escobar's "Nuevo México y sus hombres Ilustres. 1530–1894" ([Illustrious Men of New Mexico, 1530–1894). In October 1893 *El Boletín*

Popular of Santa Fe ran the item, "De interés para los Neo-mexicanos" (Of Interest to New Mexicans). Escobar forwarded the note to *El Boletín*, which announced the forthcoming publication of the work. This work, reported *El Boletín*, was to be a collaboration between Trinidad editor José Escobar and Trinidad attorney Eusebio Chacón and was set to be published by *El Progreso* in the same city. Mindful of questions of self-representation, Escobar promoted the book as one that would register the historical precedent of *Nuevomexicanos* upon their native soil in a dignified way, apropos to the merit of the subject. Escobar writes:

> Confident in those actions that tend to accompany the betterment and prosperity of a race of people, we hope that those who are fond of literature will read the book, which we have talked about in *El Progreso*. [We hope this is the case] so that when it has been elegantly bound and adorned with fine and beautiful illustrations that represent the ancient and modern monuments upon our New Mexican soil, as well as with the portraits of the illustrious sons of the territory; [its readers] will be sure to obtain a personal copy.[16]

History, but also the practical matter of who among them should author (read authorize) that history, was on the minds of *Neo-Mexicano* literates. Print culture and the attendant personal and professional struggles over intellectual property and the turfs it produced was the cause of heated debate. Rivalries ensued.

Not long after announcing the book project, Escobar left *El Progreso* and formed a partnership with Pedro García de la Lama, the editor of *La Opinión Pública* in Albuquerque. Escobar's association with García de la Lama seems to have led to the dissatisfaction Eusebio Chacón expressed soon after toward the continuation of the history project. In January 1894, Eusebio Chacón wrote Pedro G. de la Lama to inform him that he was disavowing any participation in the writing of the history. Chacón also sent a letter on the matter to *El Boletín Popular*. Ostensibly, he objected to the fact that he was not consulted about the direction and the ultimate form of the book. Chacón wrote:

> This work was begun without consulting with me, without my knowing about it, and without my consent. Inasmuch, I do not consent that my name be given as a partner and I pray you will remove it immediately, wherever it appears. By the same token, since the work you are engaged in is not in accordance with the one we originally had thought of writing, I choose to part company with Señor Escobar; in the future, I alone shall take up the writing of the History of New Mexico.[17]

Undeterred José Escobar continued to promote the work of history he planned to publish. Originally planned as a book, "Nuevo México y sus Hombres Ilustres" was now projected to appear in serial form in a magazine to be called *Revista Histórica Quicenal* (Biweekly Historical Review).[18]

Escobar and García de Lama responded to Eusebio Chacón's public charges of professional impropriety by reiterating that their intent was simply to write a short historical sketch "whose main objective is to in some way assist our national literature and at the same time will provide New Mexican youth with a brief synopsis of the pinnacles of its history, so that they can find in them a means to learn about the civic merits of their forebears."[19] Escobar, who had been in New Mexico for a relatively short time, had become aware of the need and desire on the part of many *Nuevomexicanos* to see such work in print.

It seems clear that the inscription of *Neo-Mexicano* historiography remained part of José Escobar's publishing agenda over the next several years.[20] As late as January 1895 Escobar continued to promote his biographical history project. Although by this date Escobar had gone through two other newspapers, having left *La Opinión Pública* in Albuquerque to found *La Voz de Nuevo México* in the same township. This paper was short-lived. *El Boletín Popular* reported in January 1895 that Escobar had suspended publication of *La Voz de Nuevo México* and was relocating its presses to Los Lunas, a community just south of Albuquerque. According to the report, Escobar planned to continue the "Nuevo México y sus Hombres Ilustres" project there. Fortuitous events returned Escobar to Colorado in January 1896, where he assumed the editorship of *Las Dos Repúblicas*, a newspaper founded and supported by Casimiro Barela in Denver. As editor of *Las Dos Repúblicas*, Escobar remained interested in promoting *Neo-Mexicano* historiography and he again approached Eusebio Chacón to collaborate on the history project begun years before.

Eusebio Chacón's socioliterary avocation had lead him to compile important historical documentation over a number of years. He collected such materials on travels to Mexico, and presumably, other important documents and records were entrusted to him by friends and associates. Chacón put aside his earlier disagreement with Escobar on the matter of authoring a history of New Mexico and offered himself to a new collaboration. The renewed effort was fortified by business and family ties, since it was Chacón's father-in-law, Casimiro Barela, who had brought José Escobar into his employ as editor of *Las Dos Repúblicas*.

Chacón's own attempts at producing a history of New Mexico were well-known by this time. Santa Fe's *El Boletín Popular* reported in October 1894 that Eusebio Chacón was at work on a history of New Mexico and had made a trip to Guadalajara for the purpose of researching historical materials there. Escobar and García de la Lama had earlier acknowledged Chacón's work in print, saying, "We wish you true success and triumph with what you plan to publish."[21] By this date Chacón had become known for his work in literature as the author of two novelettes and scores of poems published in *La Voz de Pueblo* at Las Vegas as well as other papers in New Mexico. Responding to the call raised among his contemporaries for a history of the Southwest to be written by a native writer, Chacón's passion and interest in writing historical narrative grew.

Chacón was but one among many other *nativo* and non-*nativo* writers who had taken up the challenge. José Escobar viewed this development as a sign that education and learning were having a desirable effect among the Spanish-speaking population of Colorado and New Mexico. In July 1896 *Las Dos Repúblicas* reported, "In the last few years distinguished writers such as his excellency Archbishop J. B. Salpointe, the knowledgeable archeologist Adolph Bandelier, and the reverend J. Defouri have taken charge of writing the history of the New Mexican Church; and talents as brilliant as that of young lawyer E. Chacón have decidedly begun to write the first historical dissertations in Spanish."[22]

Like other voices in the cultural movement of the late nineteenth century, Eusebio Chacón had first begun to articulate his historical observations in relation to *Neo-Mexicano* destitution and material poverty. Chacón shared the belief that the codifying of *Neo-Mexicano* history was key to building renewed confidence in the future, for it was also a means to map the social ascendancy of his people.

From January to July 1896, Escobar published a six-part history authored by Chacón entitled, "Descubrimiento y conquista de Nuevo México en 1540 por los españoles. Disertaciones de Historia Patria" (Discovery and Conquest of New Mexico in 1540 by the Spanish—Dissertations on the History of the Homeland). This indeed, may be the closest Escobar came to collaborating on a history project of the magnitude he had envisioned for his "Nuevo México y sus Hombres Ilustres."

Chacón's six-part history begins with the accounts of exploration and incursions by the Spanish into North America and the Southwest. The first installment of Chacón's work in *Las Dos Repúblicas* is missing from available collections: part two continues as an evidentiary account of Alvar Núñez Cabeza de Vaca's adventures into the interior of North America. Later installments of Chacón's history recount the Fray Marcos de Niza expedition of 1539 and Francisco de Coronado's journeys to the Colorado, through Cíbola (New Mexico) and to Quivira (Kansas). The series ends with Coronado's withdrawal from New Mexico and his decommissioning in Mexico.

Although it is not known if Chacón documented history beyond the Spanish colonial period, it is a matter of record that he possessed an important cache of original manuscripts pertaining to New Mexico history that he drew upon for other writing projects. One use was for the republication of historical documents in Spanish-language newspapers in New Mexico and southern Colorado.[23] Trinidad's *El Progreso,* for example, initiated publication of Gaspar Pérez de Villagrá's account-in-verse of the Juan de Oñate expedition,

"Historia de la Nuevo México" (History of New Mexico) at Chacón's request in July 1898. Isidoro Armijo, editor of *El Progreso,* aware of the value of this material, prefaced its publication by saying, " 'The History of New Mexico' by Don Gaspar de Villagrá is a work of 34 cantos in free verse which was published in Alcalá de Henares by the bookseller Luis Martínez Grande in 1610. The only copy that exists in New Mexico is the property of Attorney Eusebio Chacón and he has a magnificent collection of documents on the history of New Mexico. [The History] will be published in editions that follow."[24]

As late as 1915, however, the Spanish-language press continued to solicit Chacón's works and observations on the New Mexican past. Chacón, for example, sent a text titled "Cosas raras de nuestra Historia de Nuevo Mexico: Los tres votos" (Rare Aspects of Our History of New Mexico: The Three Vows) to Camilo Padilla at *Revista Ilustrada.* The article, light in tenor and tone, uses self-mocking humor to explain how *Nuevomexicanos* came to be typified by the virtues of poverty, chastity, and obedience. In the piece, Chacón delves into obscure manuscripts for antecedents that explained the poor hand New Mexico had been dealt throughout its history. It leads Chacón to conclude in tongue-in-cheek fashion that poverty, humility, and servitude seemed to characterize the disposition of the greater part of its citizenry.

From *Boceto* to Biographical *Communitas*

> History, like a holy reliquary, holds in its bosom the good and evil acts of men: the first that we might imitate them and the latter so we might avoid their repetition.
>
> —José E. Fernández, 1911

Biography remained a fertile field for *Neo-Mexicano* self-representation and self-objectification. It permitted a kind of factual conflation of past and present through which the deeds of *Neo-Mexicanos* long dead might be compared to the lives of contemporary men and women. More precisely biography also filled the desire to historicize the circumstances of the present moment, an idea wholly consistent with creating a code of ethics, a morality of community around the aestheticized, the biographed life (as the epigraph above suggests). At the center of *Neo-Mexicano* bio-historical discursivity remains the intent to strengthen a reciprocal system of meaning connecting the biographical subject to community. At various levels of signification, the potential in biography for self-reflexivity and self-objectification "proceeds in indissoluble unity with the collective of others, it is interpreted, constructed and organized (with respect to all the constituents it shares with the world of others) on the plane of another's possible consciousness [this] life; a life is perceived and constructed as a possible story that might be told about it by the other to still others (to descendants)" (Bakhtin 1990, 153).

The best early example Bakhtin's dictum in the Neo-Mexicano community was *Cuarenta años de legislador, o la biografía del Senador Casimiro Barela* [Forty Years as a Legislator, Or the Biography of Senator Casimiro Barela].[25] The work, compiled and written by José E. Fernández of Trinidad, Colorado,[26] was published in 1911 by Barela's own El Progreso Publishing Company of Trinidad. Benjamín Read, who had profiled Barela in *Historia Ilustrada,* consented to write the introduction for the book.

Barela's 504-page biography revolves around the same kind of bio-discursive credentialing that informs the *bocetos* of local *Neo-Mexicano* political figures. Even Barela's vanity in having commissioned the biography is masked by the work's emphasis on community building. Barela's biography is, after all, about a life aestheticized in the name of *communitas.* Biographer Fernández declares, "Esta obra no está escrita por el sentimiento de la adulación, está escrita para que el pueblo conozca actos dignos de imitarse [This work is not written out of a sentiment of adulation, it is written so that the people might come to know actions worthy of imitation]" (Fernández 1915, xii). As with political *bocetos* the elements selected for retelling reflect the prevailing sense of *communitas* for *Mexicanos* in the Southwest at the end of the nineteenth century. Here as in other instances, genealogy, honorable parentage, a Christian-Catholic foundation, and the other aspects of moral character constituted the dominant themes in the emplotment of life narratives.

Barela's origins in the Embudo-Mora area gave his biographer cause to remark, "Aquí hallarán como un joven de humilde cuna, de limitada educación y pobre de recursos ha llegado a distinguirse no solamente entre sus paisanos sino ante el mundo entero [Here (readers) will find how a young man of humble birth, with limited education and financially impoverished (background), has come to distinguish himself not only among his (*Nuevomexicano*) countrymen, but before all the world]" (Fernández 1915, xii).

According to Fernández, Barela's genealogy included forebears who were among the colonists who settled San Francisco, San José, and Los Angeles, California. It was their descendants who later traveled east, opting to settle south of Albuquerque at the ranching community of Tomé. The family relocated to Taos, New Mexico, in 1839, where Barela was born amid the chaos of the American invasion and the Taos revolt, Fernández writes:

> As there were terrible persecutions, like those that are recalled with horror at Fernández de Taos, so it was that the family of Don José María Barela, which made its home in Mora, had to leave and take refuge at El Embudo in Río Arriba County, New Mexico, where it was destined by the Supreme Architect that Señora María de Jesús Abeyta de Barela would present her husband on March 4, 1847, the child who we today call Senator Casimiro Barela.[27]

Fernández takes up in turn other elements of biographical credentialing, recounting the details of Barela's formation as a student of Christian Brothers in Mora, New Mexico; his apprenticeship under the Reverend Juan B. Salpointe; his rags-to-riches ascent from a humble freighter of goods to a wealthy landowner in southern Colorado; and his election to the territorial legislature of Colorado at age twenty-five in 1871. Laced throughout the narrative are numerous references to Barela's moral character and, as if this were not enough to convince any reader that here are "actos dignos de imitarse" (acts worthy of emulation), Fernández adds a twenty-one page conclusion, a gushing tribute really, in which the author enumerates the virtues of his biographical subject as family man, entrepreneur, politician, civil libertarian, community and church leader, and so forth. Throughout, Fernández does not pretend to offer impartial and objective account of the public and private life of his biographical subject, but rather reflects a perspective quite in keeping with biographical narrative, one that, as Bakhtin's observes, remains grounded in the idea that "what the hero believes in, the author as hero believes in as well; what the hero regards as good, the author regards as good" (1990, 163).

Several elements regarding the sociohistorical value of *Cuarenta años de legislador* and its axiological signification to *communitas* return us to a discussion of print culture, the history of books, and the effect such development was having on *Neo-Mexicano* social formation. Among these, Fernández's adulation and panegyrical discourse in the retelling of his subject's life is cause to look for the meaning of the work within and outside the text. Bakhtin theorizes, "Biographical values are values that are shared in common by life and by art, that is, they are capable of determining practical acts in the capacity of the ends these acts strive to attain" (1989, 152). While Fernández's high praise of Casimiro Barela may ring hollow to the contemporary readers, it is axiomatic to *Neo-Mexicano* sociohistorical disposition in its intense desire for a reintegration of *communitas*, even as that sense of communitarianism is precariously positioned within the body politic of U.S. society after 1848.

In becoming the vehicle for that reintegration, biography as narrative inscription must to some degree indulge in the high praise for the biographical subject, but it must not forget its debt to the factual field of representation, for its authority ultimately derives from the tacit understanding that all that is presented in the narrative is subject to its value as social good. In this sense Bakhtin believes that "biographical form is the most 'realistic' of forms, for it contains the least amount of constituents that isolate and consummate" (1990, 152).

Biography, however exuberant, must be buoyed by factual information, which makes the sociopolitical and historical discourse of the struggle for civil and cultural rights among the Spanish-speaking of southern Colorado an unwa-

Fig. 15. Portrait engraving of Casimiro Barela, 1888.

vering point of reference in Barela's life story. To this end his account reproduces momentous events in that struggle, all the while pointing—in the way the *boceto* points to shared aspirations—to Barela as the foremost spokesman and political leader of the *Neo-Mexicano* community of southern Colorado.

Barela's life as told by Fernández is styled apropos an age wherein the progress of society and civilization was attributed to extraordinary individual achievement. Barela's record as lawmaker and his participation in the development of Colorado suffice to make his story worth telling. *Cuarenta años,* too, is the record of a legislative and political career filled with firsts for *Neo-Mexicanos.* Among Barela's accomplishments is his election as president pro tempore of the Colorado Senate in 1893, his appointment in the same year by the Mexican Government as Mexican Consul in Denver, and to a similar post by the Costa Rican government in 1897. Above all, Barela as steadfast advocate for the Spanish-speaking community of southern Colorado through various terms of office ties the biography to the sociohistorical events of his day. This is particularly important given the fact that racial hostility and discrimination toward *Nuevomexicanos* was considerably more evident in Colorado, a state where anti-Mexican sentiments ran high and often resulted in intimidation and open violence against the Spanish-speaking. This was a condition that often lead Barela to assert, "Al tratarse de mi raza, especialmente si se trata de discriminar, abdico mis ideas en política y me dedico á su defensa en todo tiempo y lugar [If it concerns my race, especially if it is a matter of discrimination, I abdicated my political ideologies and dedicate myself to its defense at all times and in all places]" (Fernández 1915, xvi).

In introducing the biography, Benjamín Read was confident that its reading would improve *Neo-Mexicano* self-esteem and identity, because it held up to public scrutiny an example of success and attainment. "As a result," Read wrote, "I who for many years have had the honor to include myself among his [Barela's] close friends, find it a sincere joy to grant the wish of the author, and write these notes in the form of an introduction to a work that is destined to be perpetuated in the hearts of the *Hispanos* of Colorado and New Mexico, the great service and innumerable benefits that has come to them from one of the most loyal and selfless of its countrymen, [he is] blood of our blood—We *New* Mexicans recognize and appreciate him as a son of this earth, which in effect he is, and of that we are proud."[28]

Even Eusebio Chacón's review of the book points to the idea of shared valuation when he remarks, "Mr. Fernández paints all with good result, placing here and there a light commentary of his own, adding at another point a deep felt apostrophe, and ending with some sentence of admiration."[29]

Benjamín M. Read (1853–1927), *Neo-Mexicano* Chronicler-Historian

> In the treatment of the subject you appear as a philosopher as well as a historian.
>
> —L. Bradford Prince in Congratulating Benjamín Read, July 1910, Santa Fe, New Mexico

Benjamín M. Read, a native of Santa Fe was the first *Neo-Mexicano* to produce a historical narrative that took the *Nuevomexicano* experience in the Southwest as the subject of its discourse. In Read *Neo-Mexicano* literates found the embodiment of the historian-chronicler who would "establish the value of the past, not as an end in itself, but as a way of providing perspectives on the present that contribute to the solution of problems particular to the present" (White 1989, 41). Regarded as the most authoritative and articulate spokesman in the *Neo-Mexicano* community, Read established himself as a leading figure in the civic life of New Mexico through many years of work

LIC. BENJAMIN M. READ,
Autor.

Fig. 16. Benjamín M. Read. Read, *Historia Ilustrada de Nuevo Mexico.*

and service in law and politics, gaining public prominence late in his life as an author interested in presenting a *Nuevomexicano* perspective in history. Throughout his long legal career he maintained close association with many *periodiqueros* and writers of the period. Involved from the outset of the *periodiquero* movement, he galvanized the sentiments of his generation in its pursuit of a *Nuevomexicano* presence in public life during the territorial period.

Benjamín M. Read, was of mixed Anglo-Mexican parentage, a *coyote,* in the vernacular of New Mexico Spanish. His father, Benjamin Franklin Read, a native of Baltimore, had immigrated to New Mexico in 1846. The elder Read was employed as an agent for the U.S. Government and later was appointed superintendent in charge of the construction of the Federal Building in Santa Fe. After moving to New Mexico, Benjamín's father married

Ignacia Cano. The Canos had moved to Santa Fe from Mexico and became well-known in the area. Much of their fame derived from the discovery by Ignacia's father of the celebrated gold and silver producing El Real de Dolores mine in the vicinity of Cerrillos, New Mexico. Benjamín (inflected with the Spanish pronunciation) was the second child born to the marriage. His brothers, Alexander and Larkin, also became well-known as jurists and lawyers in New Mexico. When Benjamín's father died in 1857 Ignacia was left with three sons to raise and support. Benjamín later credited his mother for his achievements and success in life. His identification and regard for his mother is evident in the dedication of *Historia Ilustrada de Nuevo México.* The prefatory poem, written after Ignacia's death, which opens the book, reads:

> A LA MEMORIA DE MI MADRE,
> DONA IGNACIA CANO.
> A la mejor de las madres,
> La más fiel y más virtuosa,
> Más amante y cariñosa,
> Con lágrimas y emoción;
> Esta obra le dedico
> De mi pobre ingenio fruto,
> Como amoroso tributo
> Que ofrece mi corazón.
> El Autor.
>
> [TO THE MEMORY OF MY MOTHER
> DONA IGNACIA CANO.
> To the best,
> the most faithful and virtuous of mothers,
> the most loving and endearing,
> With tears and emotion;
> I dedicate this work to her
> which is the fruit of my poor intellect,
> In loving tribute
> Offered from my heart
> The Author] (Read 1911)

With her remarriage to Mateo Ortiz, Ignacia drew her family even closer into the embrace of *Nuevomexicano* society and culture. Ignacia's children from both her marriages knew no other cultural affiliation than that imparted to them from their mother's ancestry. Benjamín's service to the *Neo-Mexicano* community touched even the lives of his *hermanos maternos,* his half-brothers Modesto, Luis, and Juan who received their education at St. Michael's College during the time Read was preceptor there (Read 1911, 514).

Read's antecedents on his father's side—his father claimed to have descended from George Read, a participant in the Revolutionary War—did not bring him special privilege or assuage the need to make his own way in life. It is more the case that Read was estranged from Anglo society because he was of mixed parentage. Read's formative experience came from the predominantly Catholic, Spanish-speaking community with which he identified. As a young man Read's first job was as a section hand for the Atchison, Topeka, and Santa Fe Railroad. Later, through the intercession of friends, his mother enrolled Benjamín in St. Michael's College. After finishing his schooling, Read worked as a translator for the legislative assembly of the territory. In the years that followed he served as private secretary to territorial governors Marsh Giddings and Lionel A. Sheldon. About the same time he was appointed teacher and later preceptor of St. Michael's College. In 1885 Read was admitted to the New Mexico bar and while he held other minor political posts, his main occupation was his private law practice.

Read gravitated to the study of history in order to tell the complete story of New Mexico's development. Beginning around 1893 he developed an intense passion for researching and collecting documents on New Mexico history. He procured historical documents from Spain and Mexico, as well as some from private collections in New Mexico. Read was aware of the value of written materials that were carefully guarded and kept in many *Nuevomexicano* households. At the time of his death Read's biographer noted that he had "acquired from old families their possession in the way of letters and documents."[30] His research fueled an active correspondence with several *Neo-Mexicano* editors and others interested in historical documentation,[31] while his efforts to recover and document events related to the Spanish colonial and the Mexican period in New Mexico proved invaluable to later historians.

Read lamented the slanted and biased view expressed by most Anglo-American historians toward *Neo-Mexicano* society and its Spanish-Mexican antecedents, and he often challenged misrepresentations in matters of culture and history. This overriding concern, shared with other *Neo-Mexicano* literates, was the subject of much of his correspondence and contributions to Spanish-language periodicals. A close friend and associate of Enrique H. Salazar at *El Independiente*, Read was no doubt among those whom Salazar alluded to in his writings as capable of taking up the task of writing a *Neo-Mexicano* history.

Read was obviously aware of the Anglo-American fascination with the history of the Southwest. Historian Hubert Howe Bancroft had sent his field workers to New Mexico in search of historical documentation on the region. Likewise, the archeologist Adolph F. Bandelier had been at work describing the Pueblo Indian cultures of the middle Río Grande area, and Charles F. Lummis's popular accounts of the region were already in mass circulation.

Read himself was elected a fellow of the New Mexico Historical Society and was a personal friend of Governor L. Bradford Prince, the society's president for a number of years. Read also had been involved at the outset of the founding of the Archeological Society of New Mexico and was a contributor to its journal, *El Palacio*. But it was not until later in his life that Read gave up his law practice entirely and devoted himself to historical research and writing.[32]

Read published *Guerra México-Americana* (The Mexican American War) in 1910, only two years before New Mexico became a state. *Guerra México-Americana* documents the U.S. War with Mexico from the perspective of the *Mexicano* population living in the dispossessed lands taken in the war of 1846. In his prologue to *Guerra México-Americana,* Read declares his goal is to bring into discussion the work of Mexican historians that had not figured in Anglo-American accounts of the origins and causes of the U.S. invasion of the Mexican republic. Read proposed to examine the roots of the Mexican American War, beginning with the Adams-Onis treaty of 1821, which ceded Florida to the United States. For Read this event set in motion animosities between the U.S. and Mexico. "Ahí originó el odio racial, etc., [There began the racial hatred, etc.]," writes Read. Taking the 1821 event as a point of departure, Read's book offers "a virtual chain of incontrovertible acts as proof of the unjust [nature] of that war [una verdera cadena de hechos incontravertibles en prueba de lo injusto de esa guerra]" (1910, 6). The prologue to *Guerra México-Americana* mentions Read's forthcoming work, *Historia Ilustrada de Nuevo México* (Illustrated History of New Mexico) and adds the note that it is the first history written "por un hijo nativo de Nuevo México [by a native son of New Mexico]."

A circular printed in June of 1911 by the Compañía Impresora del Nuevo Mexicano (New Mexican Printing Company) lauded Read's *History of New Mexico*, calling it, "The Latest Up-to-Date History of New Mexico." The circular includes comments and letters from notables such as the Archbishop of Santa Fe Juan B. Pitavel, prominent Hispano political leader Octaviano A. Larrazolo, and L. Bradford Prince, all of whom praise the book's merits. Prince, then ex-governor and presiding president of the New Mexico Historical Society, had himself authored a history of New Mexico in 1895, a work touted in the New Mexican circular as "the standard history of this commonwealth." Prince spoke of Read's courage and forthrightness in expressing the *Nuevomexicano* viewpoint, acknowledging that the work made some uneasy as it overturned certain assumptions about New Mexico history: "All the value of a history comes from its perfect honesty; and no one can read your *Historia* without being struck by the extreme care you have given to accuracy, and your fearlessness in stating facts even when they overthrow cherished ideas and traditions."[33]

Read's *Historia Ilustrada* appeared in two limited editions in 1911, Its publisher, La Compañía Impresora del Nuevo Mexicano, promised a second edition of the work to be followed by an English translation by Eleuterio Baca of Las Vegas. Read's work spanned history from the pre-Conquest of Mexico by the Spaniards in 1521 through the end of the territorial period in New Mexico. Read organized the work around four historical time periods (pre-Columbian, Spanish, Mexican, American.)

Read's historiography offers a distinctly *Neo-Mexicano* perspective on historical antecedents, the "truth" of which, for Read, lay astride or between, "the very evident lack of agreement between those [Anglo] historians and Mexican historians" (1911, 7). The approach repositions historical subjectivity to account for a Mexican-American perspective. Even as Read reiterates his disdain for inaccuracy in English-language histories ("the English-speaking authors have copied and plagiarized each other to the degree that there are no two of them that concur in their translations, from this comes great confusion in the exposition of historical incidents and events" [1911, 7]), he also suggests that Mexican historians "allende el Bravo [on the other side of the Rio Grande]" have been slow to censure "the American government of those days for the unjust shedding of innocent blood" (1910, 3). In suggesting oversight and neglect from both quarters, Read announces what would become a familiar theme in Mexican-American culture studies—the often neglected Chicano point of view as the orphaned citizens of the U.S. war with Mexico. The predicament of not belonging to either the American or Mexican historical field is registered in the prologue to *Guerra México-Americana*, but fearing readers might misinterpret his motives, Read takes great pains to rationalize his localizing of certain events:

> The last two chapters are of a different sort from those that precede them; from a certain point of view [this] makes them seem as though they lack unity and form, since they deal with events and incidents, which having occurred in New Mexico (then a province of Mexico) will look at first sight, [as if] they have no connection with the work, but when they have been read with the necessary attention it will be seen that those events and incidents are nothing more than a part of the affects resulting from the same cause, they were some of the many ramifications of the original cancer.[34]

Read's concern in explicating his choice of historical perspective and geographical locus is also a way to suggest to his contemporaries that when these sections are "read with [the] necessary attention," they will disclose a third vantage point that is neither Anglo nor Mexican, but one uniquely Mexican American.

Part four of Benjamín Read's *Historia Ilustrada de Nuevo Mexico* (1910) is interesting because it illustrates the idea that biography illuminated historical *communitas*, or a sense of shared experience. Composed of 146 biographical sketches of contemporary men and women along with those of notable personages from *Neo-Mexicano* history, Read's biographical section provided readers with the rare opportunity to read and learn about the accomplishments of their contemporaries, and thus added popular appeal to the book.[35] The inclusion of this material in a book of history was a strategy meant to reverse the intense negativism of the eastern press toward New Mexico and *Neo-Mexicanos*.

The weight of proving the merit, worth, loyalty, and accomplishments of *Nuevomexicanos* within Anglo society had been cast upon *nativos* since the American conquest. The sting of discrimination determined to a large degree the social station *Nuevomexicanos* occupied during the period. *Nuevomexicano* aptitudes and qualifications as citizens were continually judged by a small, but powerful Anglo elite. Read and other members of his generation could not escape the urgency to "put one's best foot forward"; hence this public biographical tally of the accomplishments of *Neo-Mexicanos* in diverse walks of life. As Read intimates in his prologue to *Historia Ilustrada*, here again is the way to make history: "This last book carries some appendices and the biographical sketches of many of the sons and prominent citizens of the Territory along with the photos of many and other illustrations *of extreme historical importance*" (emphasis added) (Read 1911, 8).

Despite the work undertaken by Read and others, the trend to discount and undervalue the merits and accomplishments of New Mexico's *nativos* would prove to be tenacious and would outlive Benjamín M. Read. In a real sense he himself would be victim of this insidious form of cultural hegemony. Upon Read's death, the author of his obituary in the *New Mexico Historical Review* took a dim view of his work, finding two reasons to deride Read. First, notes the biographer, Read was an amateur historian whose "lack of scientific training barred him from the recognition which his zeal and persistent endeavor should have brought him." Second, the writer declares, Read's writings "hardly struck a popular chord."[36] In rather terse and unceremonious terms, the author of this obituary reduced Read's work of well over thirty years to relative insignificance. And yet, it was not out of the ordinary at the time for historical writers to come to history having been trained in other professions. Both Charles Coan and Ralph Emerson Twitchell, whose histories of New Mexico are contemporary with Read's, had been trained as lawyers, not researchers. On the matter of Read's lack of popularity, the biographer's charge is more specious. His comments were not directed at narrative logic or style, rather at Read's having "thought and wrote in Spanish." In the mind of the reviewer "popular" equated to the availability of the work to an English-speaking readership, but the New Mexican Publishing Company circular of 1911 suggests otherwise. It notes that the first edition of Read's history, written in Spanish, had sold out upon being published.

And if we judge the merit of the censure in light of the testimonials that accompany the circular, it is also clear that the work received high praise across a wide spectrum of the community. Given the short shrift paid to Read's writings here, one can only conclude that the influential readership of *New Mexico Historical Review,* wherein the necrology appeared, was left with little or no compulsion to seriously entertain Read's work further.

Read's speeches, historical writings, and pronouncements on the condition of *el pueblo nativo* frequently appeared in major Spanish-language publications and often his writing moved beyond *Hispano* themes. For example, *La Bandera Americana* printed a short historical tract titled, "Antigua descripción de la tribu navajo por Benjamín Read [An Ancient Description of the Navajo Tribe by Benjamín Read]" in May 1920. He authored articles that continued to circulate in print after his death. One such item, a biographical text entitled "Taos en la época del Padre Martínez: Bosquejo del Presbítero A. José Martínez" (Taos during the Padre Martínez Era: A Profile of the Presbyter A. José Martínez), was reprinted in *El Nuevo Mexicano* as late as August 1945. His leadership in the *Nuevomexicano* community also made him the frequent object of articles and news items in the English weeklies as well.[37] Tributes came from both *Nuevomexicanos* and Anglo Americans, from the prominent and the humble alike.[38]

Read followed the publication of *Historia Ilustrada* with the publication of *Popular Elementary History of New Mexico* (1914), a brief history in English that became a standard text in the public schools of the state. Read continued to work on other projects in the years just after statehood. One project centered on the life of Hernán Cortez. According to reports in *La Bandera Americana,* around this same time, Read's biography, *La Vida de Hernán Cortez* (The Life of Hernán Cortez), had been accepted for publication by an editorial house in Boston early in 1923. A second work was titled "Sidelights of New Mexico History," excerpts of which were published in the Spanish-language press. Read also compiled "Documentos inéditos del archivo de las Indias" (Unpublished Documents from the Archives of the Indies), a bibliography of the documents Read had uncovered through years of research. *La Revista de Taos* suggested in February 1921 that Read be named the state historian. *La Bandera Americana* also noted that Read was about to publish a work titled *Nuevo México en las guerras de la unión* (New Mexico and the Wars of the Union), a work which Read announced would take as its subject the military record and participation of *Neo-Mexicano* soldiers in the military conflicts of the United States. *La Bandera Americana* glossed the contents of the book: "[The book] narrates the role that New Mexico has taken in the wars with the Indians, the Civil War, the war with Spain and the World War."[39] Reportedly, these titles were published, although copies of them have yet to be recovered.

Much of the information that is available today regarding the ascendancy of *Neo-Mexicano* literates and their work in journalism comes directly from

Read's writings and compilation of materials. In addition to the wealth of information in the biographical profiles in part four of *Historia Ilustrada,* Read appends detailed lists of all newspapers, Spanish and English, being published in New Mexico. Read's compilation includes the names of 134 newspapers published in 1911, noting the names of their editors and the political affiliation of each paper. Read summarized the work of the press in a section of his work titled "Sociedad Histórica y Prensa Periodica" (The Historical Society and the Press), saying "The press in New Mexico, in both languages, has progressed in marvelous fashion" (1911, 379). Read's documentation of the work of *los periodiqueros* and descriptions of the growing stature of the Spanish-language press in New Mexico remained the only mention of this press in the historical formation of the region until recent years.

Benjamín Read became a member of the American Historical Association in January 1917. This recognition, however, was long supplanted by Read's personal mission to write "in favor of the unjustly treated Latin race." The altruism he expressed in such declarations held great appeal for his generation. Read took his reward from whatever transcendence his writing might have in society: "Si con mis insignificantes escritos se realiza mi ideal, redundando en ellos en honor de la verdad y la honra de los hijos de Nuevo México, quedarán mis deseos ampliamente recompensados. [If with my insignificant writings my ideal is realized, to the advantage of the honor of the truth and the tribute of the sons of New Mexico, my desires will be amply paid]" (1910, 6).

High on the list of rewards, as *Neo-Mexicano* literates saw them, was New Mexico's entrance as a state into the Union, a matter that was being considered in the Congress at the moment Read's *Historia Ilustrada* went to press in 1911. Read viewed statehood as a complement to his years of struggle in that cause. Writing in *La Revista de Taos* in January 1911, only days after the ratification of New Mexico's state constitution by popular referendum, Read notes:

> And since 1846 hence, how many efforts have been made to obtain the ideal of our liberty? Great in truth is our good fortune. The patriotism which pushed our loyal fellow citizens to battle courageously against those who placed so much effort to prevent our autonomy is deserving of admiration. It was a magnificent spectacle to see throughout the hard struggle the good sons of New Mexico become true patriots and from patriots become orators, all speaking with an eloquence that is possible only at times when the life or liberty of an entire people is threatened.[40]

Staking out a place for *Neo-Mexicanos* to see themselves represented in the body politic of the nation had by Read's time come to mean forging a state out of an ancestral homeland. This ideological positioning was never meant to supplant the idea of homeland, but rather turned on the idea of allegiance to homeland, and *Neo-Mexicano* literates were charged in advocating for the best interests of the people of that homeland, which was seen as the incorporation of the territory into a state of the Union.

Hayden White points out that historical narratives are produced much in the same way that other narratives, even literary narratives, are produced. At least in purely formal ways, the matter of making sense of real or imagined events involves similar narrative strategies, the most apparent of which is a shared use of figurative language (White 1979, 82). To the extent that this is true, it can be argued that all writings produced by *Nuevomexicanos* and other *Mexicano*-origin groups in the Southwest in the nineteenth and early twentieth century are at their core historiographic, that is, they are as concerned with the problem of the historical representation as with offering up evidentiary texts whose aim, ultimately, is to vindicate their culture and society from the effects of accident, neglect, and repression.

Tejano scholar Américo Paredes, and more recently Ramón Saldívar, indicate that this is indeed the case with forms such as the *corrido.*[41] Seen in this way, Jesús María Hilario Alarid's call for "language rights," Severino Trujillo's call for the establishment of a vigorous press to counter "the lack of instruction of the masses of the people," and Enrique H. Salazar's call for a *nativo* history are all texts issued from the specificity of a common and shared experience. These examples show *Neo-Mexicanos* engaged in a common effort to make sense of their society and the social moment they occupy. To accomplish this they appealed as much to the literary arts as to historiography. What this suggests is that the polysemic articulations of the popular press—whether literal or figurative, whether in the form of poem, essay, or narrative—are all efforts at self-representation, and that writings on *Neo-Mexicano* culture were inscribed with the intent to show the nature and merit of *Neo-Mexicano* society. As with historical emplotment, *Neo-Mexicanos* also positioned themselves in the post-1848 era to create a space for representing themselves in the literary arts. By fashioning an expressive identity in letters, *Nuevomexicanos* bequeathed a verbal image of the reality they lived to the generations to follow. They called the literary movement they created and sustained "una literatura nacional [a national literature]," the formation of which is the subject of the next chapter.

5

The Poetics of Self-Representation in *Neo-Mexicano* Literary Discourse

Una literatura nacional

> Poets are lutes that sound across the winds; lakes that change hues with the passing of each cloud; there is something enigmatic about them, like prophecies, like premonitions, like dreams.
>
> —*El Eco del Norte,* Mora, New Mexico, December 1908.

In contrast to the figure of the historian-chronicler whose task, in the view of nineteenth-century *Mexicano* literates, was to tell a story from factual evidence, the role of the creative writer is not nearly so plain. Complicating the host of clouded notions held of the writer is the thick overlay of Latin American romanticism that was inflected onto poetry and the literary arts in New Mexico in the nineteenth century. The wish to showcase *Neo-Mexicano* poets and writers in the columns of newspapers and magazines grew out of the same necessity that prompted *periodiqueros* to call for a *nativo* historian. In each case the inscription of texts by native editors was driven by the desire to ward off the disparagement of *Neo-Mexicano* culture and society that swirled around it. But, where the historian could be relied upon to produce a straightforward and literal narrative, the same could not be said of the poet or novelist, who was held up to be "un ser misterioso, indefinible, que escapa análisis [a mysterious, indefinable being, who escapes analysis]." To ask a "creature" who "se va por las alturas etéreas en busca de la luz [goes across ethereal heights in search of light]"[1] to stay a predetermined course was not in keeping with the poetics of an age in which characterizations of the poet and novelist rested on figurative and symbolic associations. Most often turgid displays of emotion, passion, and *sentimiento* reigned over terse restraint in the literary endeavors. The *Neo-Mexicano* worldview revealed itself as a kind of literary portraiture that required a lyrical *desgarramiento* (a wrenching of the heart): an externalization of deeply held belief through the voice of the writer.

This suggests that the tropics—to borrow a term from Hayden White—of *Neo-Mexicano* literary production (excluding traditional oral forms) borrowed widely from Latin American (late) romanticism and modernism (that is, print culture reintroduced the literary fashions of Latin American into the Southwest). This literary mimesis was filled by the desire of *Neo-Mexicano* writers to see themselves as fully formed *literatos* or authors. So too this literary fashioning fleshes out the biographical notes of many of the writers profiled in this chapter.

These thoughts on the literary tastes of the era serve as a preface to a discussion of the wider implications of this literary movement among *Neo-Mexicano* literates. The point is not to argue the merits of style nor the appliqué of literary formalism in a remote, sparsely populated, underdeveloped corner of the Borderlands, but rather to show that regardless of the high aspirations of *Neo-Mexicano* literates, of whatever flights "across ethereal heights" they may have entertained, it is the sociohistorical reality of newspaper publication—the only available "communications circuit"—that ultimately determined the limits of their movement.

As has been noted, *Neo-Mexicano* literary expression, like the print culture that had inspired it, remained throughout the years of its existence a movement held in check and contained by Anglo-American hegemony. In this context, this chapter seeks to examine the extent to which the movement figures as resistance to sociohistorical imposition, and the degree to which it extended self-representation and stabilized a *Mexicano* cultural episteme in the Southwest that would last well into the twentieth century.

Foundational Texts in *Neo-Mexicano*/Chicano Literature

The large *nativo* population residing in New Mexico in the years following the Mexican American War decisively restrained the massive and wholesale vigilante terrorism of the type that had been unleashed against *Tejanos* after 1836 or against *Californios* after 1848.[2] In those regions armies of henchmen and quasi-military units in the employ of Anglo-American business and economic interests waged a war of terror and violence against the original residents (Paredes 1958; Acuña 1971).

Notwithstanding the obvious differences, the eastern press and its agents in New Mexico waged a heated campaign of derision against the cultural practices of *Nuevomexicanos.* After the armed resistance at Embudo, Mora, and Taos had been put down in February 1847, the struggle for the hearts and minds of *Neo-Mexicanos* increasingly became a war of words, an ideological battle that pitted the idea of Anglo-American primacy in the West against the tenacity of *Neo-Mexicano* self-image and self-representation. As has been seen in the previous chapter, the task of proving the moral and social inferiority of *Mexicano* society in the Southwest went to Anglo-American writers and journalists entering the region for the first time. Beginning with W. W. H. Davis, *Nuevomexicanos* were described as "lacking the stability of character and soundness of intellect that give such vast superiority to the Anglo-Saxon race over every other people" (Davis [1857] 1982, 217).

Amid such negative typecasting many *periodiqueros* aimed to create a literary tradition to reflect the sociohistorical experience of *Nuevomexicanos* and other *Mexicano*-origin communities of the Southwest. Most editors did not need to be convinced of the benefits to be derived from such development. Well-known journalist José Escobar countered Davis and others like him by insisting that the press and its literary production was fostering "the positive progress of the Hispanic-American race in the United States." Echoing a belief widely held by his colleagues in the press, Escobar declared that all things were possible to *Neo-Mexicanos* owing to "las claras inteligencias de los neo-mexicanos, poseedores en su mayoría de un magnífico talento natural (the clear faculties of the *New* Mexicans, the possessors in the main of a magnificent natural talent)." In describing the region as backward and its inhabitants as ignorant, newcomers provoked *Neo-Mexicanos* to mobilize their social, economic, and literary resources against such attacks. As with history, literature was presented as evidence of the intellectual potential of their generation. For, as *Neo-Mexicano* literates assured themselves, "with deeds [literary works] of this kind we can vanquish the unjust charges and warped slander of the *tourists*."[3]

At the center of that literary agency resided a creative imagination that produced nonviolent acts of resistance to domination and cultural derision. It became a matter of utmost importance for *Nuevomexicanos* to prove themselves a people capable of producing a literature. Newspapers referred to the coming literary production as *una literatura nacional* (a national literature). The designation registered a bold affirmation of cultural will that had immediate effects. The most important was to allow *Nuevomexicanos* to hold on to a positive view of themselves in spite of the campaign of derision and denigration being waged against them by the eastern press.

The movement was multilayered and drew from a wide spectrum of letters in the Latin American tradition as well as from the oral poetics of the region. Anglo Americans railed against the supposed inferiority of *Mexicano* culture, but the cultivation of the literary arts and the unbroken ethnopoetics of *Mexicano* communities provided woof to the weave of *Mexicano* sociohistorical experience. In the verbal arts lay the cultural touchstones, the "showings" that distilled a people's experience and became the undergirth that insured the survivability of *Nuevomexicano* cultural life. As such, textual reliquia from the vernacular and lettered traditions were invoked to stave off a derisive discourse filled by the "satirical allusions and scathing slander of eastern newspapers."[4]

The concept of *una literatura nacional* created new expectations among the *periodiquero* generation. The phrase suggests that even by this early date the Spanish-speaking of the Southwest had begun to see themselves as a national minority. This sense of group identification on a regional scale (New Mexico, Colorado, Texas, and Arizona) was closely bound up in the work of La Prensa Asociada Hispano-Americana, which had long described itself as "the organization of Hispanic-American journalists, writers and poets in the United States."[5]

And yet, *una literatura nacional* was less an appeal to nationalism and nation-building than a means to mobilize community resources and engage them in literary codification by which questions of ethnicity, identity, and group participation might reflect the status of Mexican Americans in the national life of the country. Among the master narratives of their Spanish/Mexican literary inheritance *los periodiqueros* began to insert texts that were authored locally.

By the 1890s several *periodiqueros* had begun to assess the progress of print culture in the region. Pragmatic and sober in their estimations, they gauged such work in light of the history of arresting social forces that limited its pace of development. In speaking of the education in the region, Eusebio Chacón unmasked the hypocrisy of territorial politics. "The government which today calls so much attention to educating the Cubans, Puerto Ricans and Filipinos," he declared, "has done nothing to disseminate education among us. The few educational institutions that are among us are the work of our labor, built with our savings and maintained at our cost. There is not one cent of federal money there."[6] With such issues framing the sociopolitical backdrop of territorial New Mexico, *Neo-Mexicanos* took pride in their accomplishments in print and offered tempered views that gauged its development against that of other parts of the country. In pointing to New Mexico's "frontier" formation, José Escobar suggested that it would be unfair to compare the progress of press and literature in New Mexico to that of more developed regions without considering the circumstances impinging on its development: "It is a mistake . . . to want that a people, who for totally anomalous circumstances dedicated itself more to the exercise of arms than to instruction in literature, to show the interest that completely civilized and cultured societies show."[7]

Irrespective of the mean-spirited view propagated by *los extranjeros*, intellectual promise was apparent among many *nativos*. In 1896 José Escobar noted that even the most isolated mountain villages of New Mexico had been effected by a vigorous press, an impact that often led to the founding of literary and debate societies. These developments stirred dramatic changes, "As [is the case] with the press, in the literary circles of that alluring land [New Mexico] have for a time made for a radical change, today, in the cities and small hamlets there are literary and debate societies where the youth frequently go to practice."[8] Five years later poet and novelist Eusebio Chacón would remark, "Although, as of yet the name of not a single New Mexican has filled the orb with his fame, we are not so abandoned here by God as we are painted by some writers who go among us like the horsemen of the apocalypse with a cup of mire in one hand and the sickle of hate in the other."[9] Chacón, the author of *Tras la tormenta, la calma* (The Calm After the Storm) and *El hijo de la tempestad* (The Son of the Storm, 1892), and a principal figure in this emerging literary movement, was the first writer to offer originality and creativity as the cornerstones of a literary movement. He declared his own work to be "the sincere creation of my own imagination and have not been stolen nor borrowed" (Chacón 1892, 2). By insisting on autonomy, and by positing imagination and creativity as the key elements of its endogamy, Chacón encoded self-referentialty and self-consciousness into the movement. Through such declarations *Neo-Mexicanos* were marking the road to social ascendancy that they believed would be opened through the writing of high literature.

Credo and Desire Among *Neo-Mexicano* Literates: The Progress of *Belles Lettres* Upon High Deserts of Representation

> The most important of all the sciences truly slept in lethargy, while in other localities of our own country, the very justified ambition of development in letters was active in all languages, in the production of writers, poetry, novels, histories, realistic novels, etc., while in this poor and forgotten New Mexico of ours it seemed that this most important of the sciences slept the sleep of death; but as all places and localities have periods of regression and progress, so too fate seems to have set for us a day of light and advancement.
>
> —"Progreso de las letras en Nuevo México," *La Voz del Pueblo*, Las Vegas, 1896

Sensing the importance of maintaining the momentum of recent years in "this poor and forgotten New Mexico of ours," journalists also began to chronicle the work of the press. At *Las Dos Repúblicas*, José Escobar summarized the literary progress of *Neo-Mexicanos* in an editorial published in July 1896, which is among the first essays to offer a literary critique and credo of the *periodiquero* movement. Escobar introduced his subject, saying "we are going to involve ourselves in something that for all of us is truly a pleasure: the progress of literature in the neighboring territory of New Mexico."[10] Turning to the early history of the press in New Mexico, Escobar concludes that Padre José Antonio Martínez at Taos had only a minimal effect in achieving his stated goal to "give impetus to literature and the education of the masses." Escobar points to the poverty and geographic isolation of New Mexico as the principle factors that have retarded the education of the populace.

Escobar attributes the progress of recent times to: 1) the liberal laws of the American government, 2) the establishment of parochial and secular schools in the territory, and 3) the natural inclination of the populace to seek enlightenment. These developments were producing visible change. "Our young people," Escobar reports, "would leave their remote villages to go to those institutions where they earnestly drank of the blessed and sweet waters of those precious fountains, which in short time would bear fruit in [the form of] the bright intellect of the New Mexicans; who possessed magnificent natural talent."[11] Observing the cross-cultural tensions in the territory, Escobar suggests that the great efforts being made by *Neo-Mexicanos* in literacy and education were denigrated by the rash and hasty observations of foreigners. Moreover, Escobar notes, these *extranjeros* failed to see that a multitude of socioeconomic difficulties had conditioned the development of the area since its earliest settlement:

> Those travelers who at present traverse the high mountains, the fertile valleys and the expansive plains of this territory in comfortable sleeper cars, cannot appreciate the favorable change that the genius of progress has made in this land; but he who is familiar with the history of this heroic and hospitable country cannot do less then admire the energy of the native and the foreign settler.[12]

Escobar points to the work of *La Revista Católica, La Voz del Pueblo, El Nuevo Mexicano,* and *El Boletín Popular.* The improvements in the quality of these publications offer much hope:

> That very press has improved noticeably over the last few years, and in its editorials and bulletins one can observe something more than the embryonic style of a press in its infancy; in its logical and well conceived commentary that struggles, not for political ideologies, but rather, for something greater yet: for the betterment of the masses irrespective of political or religious belief.[13]

Escobar saw the organization of literary and debate societies in communities with good newspapers as catalysts that gave rise to work on a number of cultural fronts. Escobar's observations suggests that *los periodiqueros* were aware that their work represented the genesis of a literary and intellectual tradition meant to bring forth the writings of poets, historians, critics, and novelists:

> And, at present, in the cities as in the small villages, there are literary and debating societies which the young people attend to practice the melancholy inspiration of the poet or the reasoned thought of the historian; or perhaps [to learn] the cutting meta-

> phor of criticism or the intricate design of the slice-of-life novel; or the novel, filled with emotion, of *our national literature* [emphasis added].[14]

For Escobar two authors in particular, Manuel C. de Baca and Eusebio Chacón, were laying the groundwork for the development of a *Neo-Mexicano* tradition in the novel. Their writings, he insists, are tied to the Latin American *costumbrista* (novel of social custom and tradition) genre. Calling Chacón the first *Neo-Mexicano* to issue a work in prose, Escobar compares *Tras la tormenta, la calma* and *El hijo de la tempestad* to the work of the Spanish *costumbrista* Juan Valera and to the Mexican writer Padre Coloma, saying "one notes immediately the ease of style and the writer's amazing force of imagination; so much so that in this the second [novel] *Tras la tormenta, la calma,* one can observe after reading a few pages the early development of a superior talent that has reasoned and observed much from a young age."[15]

Escobar noted promise in Manuel C. de Baca's *Vicente Silva y sus cuarenta bandidos: Sus crímenes y su retribución,* a narrative recounting Vicente Silva's reign of banditry in San Miguel County in the early 1890s, which was only days from being published.[16] Having perused a copy of the work provided by the author, Escobar ventures the following summary and preview for his readers:

> The book that Attorney Baca has just written, is in our mind, the first to meet the rules and standards of the novel of tradition and custom and yet has the peculiar element of having been written in the typical style of *our national literature.* The truth of the story has been placed with all accuracy in the pages of this book; and its plot is so interesting and so deftly woven by its skillful author that after one has read the first few pages, one has the desire to read and read and read until one consumes those pages, which [contain], in addition to their good taste and uncomplicated style, a great moral teaching for young people. [emphasis added][17]

Like *Neo-Mexicano* writers and thinkers, Escobar argues that the fruits of New Mexico's literary progress will bring about the social and cultural betterment of all classes of *nativos.* It is Escobar's view that the movement's autonomy and energy would provide the social authority to dispel accusations and typecast views of *Mexicano* culture:

> In the meantime, Attorney Baca shall receive our warm and sincere best wishes for this literary achievement of real social worth, and we hope that his example stimulates native youth, so that with similar acts of this type, we might be able to rid ourselves of the unjust allegations and the crude slandering made [of

> us] by the passing tourist, who without bothering to know us—save what he might have seen as his train flies by—accuses us of lacking culture and of lacking talent.[18]

In Escobar's commentary on literary production can be heard the figuration of the literary critic voicing the promise of *Neo-Mexicano* cultural unity and identificatory self-coherence. Escobar's initial postulations moved other *periodiqueros* in turn to try their hand at offering critical assessment and commentary. This dialogical discourse appears in various newspapers (as in the epigraph from *La Voz del Pueblo* that begins this section) and signals vitality in the movement. From Escobar's work critical discourse widens so as to include criticism from fellow *periodiqueros*. A communiqué to *El Boletín Popular* the subsequent year, sent by a writer identified only as Adelfa, alludes to "el cantor de Popé," a name given to Escobar for his work in poetry. Adelfa's communiqué is a tongue-in-cheek chastisement of Escobar's review of *Nuevomexicano* literary works. In a thinly veiled dig, Adelfa offers Escobar the following advise in very unflattering terms:

> We have asked the farmers for a bail of alfalfa for a certain newspaperman who promises to amuse us a great deal with some critiques of certain "tempestuous novels." Since our in-house horn blowers know just how to blast out a note, we suggest "el cantor de Popé" use caution as it could turn out that this will backfire on him. And so, *au revoir monsieur*.[19]

Joselín, "El Cantor de Popé"

In addition to his work as a journalist and editorial writer, Escobar produced several works of poetry. His writings suggest that the Spanish-speaking communities of the Southwest were directly impacted by post-romantic and modernist poetics in the Latin American tradition. Doris Meyer, for example, considers Escobar a pivotal figure, one whose work must be reconsidered against the staid views offered in most cultural histories of *Mexicano* cultural practices in the late nineteenth century. Meyer contends that Escobar was "clearly aware of the innovative poetic trends in neighboring Mexico and was an admirer of the modern poets there who, like himself, were involved in journalism and contributed to newspapers and literary reviews" (1978, 33). Meyer's view debunks the notion that *Mexicanos* in the Southwest had no literary tradition to draw upon.

The poems Meyer identifies were all published in *El Defensor del Pueblo*, a paper founded in Albuquerque and which Escobar edited from 1891 to 1892. She suggests that spring 1892 represented an especially productive time for Escobar in terms of the publication of his poetry. Beyond his work at *El Defensor del Pueblo* lies a much fuller portrait of Escobar as poet. *El Independiente* of Las Vegas and other New Mexico papers regularly featured Escobar's poetry after 1894, and his poetic contributions to *Las Dos Repúblicas* in 1896 represent a much higher watermark of his work.

While editor of *Las Dos Repúblicas,* Escobar punctuated the departments of the paper with *epigramas,* or couplets, that enlivened the format. In more formal incursions into literary matters Escobar explored themes of love, rejection, and exile, subjects that reveal his temperament as a poet. In general, a romantic attachment to pathos and exaggerated displays of emotion characterize his lyrical musings. His poems "Calla (A Luz)" (Hush), "Negro y blanco" (Black and White), "Perdón" (Forgive Me), "Remember," and "Entre sombras" (Among the Shadows) are tinged by brooding introspection, melancholy, and lamentation, and indulge in the verbose opulence of the Latin American modernist aesthetic.

In addition to poems disclosing *sentimiento* bound by personal experience, he delves into his own condition as an exile from the land of his birth, a circumstance that figured in poems where the reoccurrence of memory triggers nostalgia for Mexico. In "Desde el destierro" (From Exile), published in *El Defensor del Pueblo* in 1892, Escobar casts his eyes toward the motherland to visit the transformations that have changed his homeland in the years of his absence:

I
Hasta el lejano y extranjero suelo
donde calma no encuentra mi dolor,
llegan en raudo y caprichoso vuelo
como aves blancas en nublado cielo
las sombras de mi patria y mi amor.

II
Lleno de dulce y triste arrobamiento
recorro el diapasón de mi memoria;
despierta mi dormido pensamiento
y sin querer, recuerdo en un momento
todas las horas de mi amarga historia.

I
[The rapid and impulsive flight of
the shadows of my country and my love
arrive like white birds in a cloudy sky
at this far and distant land
where my pain has known no relief.

II
Filled with sweet and sad rapture
I go over the fingerboard of my memories;
my thoughts awaken
and against my will, I remember
each hour of my bitter story.][20]

While Escobar never severed his attachment and identification with Mexico,[21] his poetry and editorial essays in his later years in New Mexico begin to speak to the concerns of the *Mexicano* community residing in the United States. We have already seen his interest in documenting the history of Mexico's lost lands to the north. Escobar shared an appreciation for the epic proportions of the history of the Southwest with his *Neo-Mexicano* counterparts, which was first manifest in his "Nuevo México y sus hombres ilustres: 1530–1894" history project. Escobar carried this interest over to at least one major historical poem on New Mexico, which he conceived as ten-part epic poem called "Leyendas Neo-Mexicanas" [*New* Mexican Legends].[22] The poem takes as its subject, Popé, the Pueblo Indian leader of the 1680 Pueblo Revolt in New Mexico. Of the ten cantos that comprised the poem, cantos III, IV, V, VI, VII, and VIII survive. These five sections are extremely important as examples of a mestizo consciousness at work in the writing. Each of the surviving cantos chronicles the condition and causes of the Pueblo Indian insurrection against Spanish colonial rule. As a chronicle it is one of the few works to document the Pueblo Revolt as the first successful large-scale revolt against a colonial power in the Americas.

In the poem, Popé emerges as a commanding and heroic figure who embodies the spirit of indigenous resistance to colonial subjugation. The Spaniards in turn are depicted as despotic and tyrannical overlords who unjustly enslaved the Pueblo people. Canto IV frames the conflict of the two races and casts the opposing figures of the Spanish governor Antonio Otermín and Popé in historic proportions:

Hasta la soberana cámara
de don Antonio Otermín
Entrególe aquellas cartas
En las que el Padre Velasco
Relación sucinta daba
Del complot que Tupatú
Catití, Francisco y Jaca,
Teniendo a Popé por jefe
En silencio preparaban
Para expulsar de esa rica
y subyugada comarca
A los pocos españoles
Que por fuerza escaparan
De la cólera y el odio
De aquella nación esclava
Que abruma de dolores
Y sediente de venganza,
Iban de nuevo a luchar
Frente á frente y cara á cara
Con el despótico ibero
Que en época no lejana
Con la humillante cadena
De la esclavitud amarga
Había mantenido cruel
A toda esa noble raza
Que por único delito
Y por vergonzosa mancha
Tenía la de haber nacido
En la cuna libre y santa
De los bosques tropicales
De la tierra americana.

[Arriving at an august chamber
of don Antonio Otermín
he turned over the letters
in which Padre Velasco
gave a precise account
of the plot prepared in silence
by Tupatú, Catití,
Francisco and Jaca,
and with Popé to lead them,
would push the few Spaniards
that might be spared its rage and anger
out of that rich and subjugated province
belonging to an enslaved nation
which is filled with suffering
and thrists for vengence;
They would fight face to face
against the despotic Iberian
who in the recent past
had humbled that noble race
with the chain of bitter slavery
whose only crime
whose only shameful sin
had been to have been born
at a free and sacred site
in the tropical forests
of the Americas.][23]

The quality of Escobar's work is comparable to the work of poets published in Mexico and Latin America during his lifetime. No doubt but what Escobar's years of exile in New Mexico, a region whose frontier formation was not conducive to literary aspirations, effectively distanced him from a literary career and the recognition he might otherwise have received. His years in New Mexico and Colorado, however, contributed enormously to the work of *los periodiqueros* and their emerging literary renaissance. Much is owed to Escobar, for his work as a journalist raised the quality and level of journalism, provided a direct link to the literary circles in Mexico, and added important texts to the *Neo-Mexicano* literary movement.

José Escobar's association with *Las Dos Repúblicas* ended shortly after the paper relocated to Trinidad, Colorado, in August 1896. The new editor of *Las Dos Repúblicas* suddenly and in no uncertain terms inserted the following in the October 3 issue of the paper: "We bring to the attention of the public, that from this date forward, Don José Escobar has no connection whatsoever with our periodical: J. A. Hermedia, prop."[24]

Almost immediately upon leaving *Las Dos Repúblicas,* Escobar published *El Independiente* at Walsenburg, Colorado, some fifty miles to the north of Trinidad. Within the month, however Escobar was on the move again, and in December 1896 was issuing *El Amigo del Pueblo* in Raton, New Mexico, with a partner identified only as Señor Arellano. Escobar's erratic movements and abrupt departures from other newspaper ventures continued in the months that followed. Within months he collaborated on three newspapers in two different Río Abajo communities: *El Nuevo Mundo* at Albuquerque, *El Defensor de Socorro,* and *El Combate* (the last two both at Socorro, New Mexico) each list Escobar as their editor for a brief time.

As we have seen José Escobar had difficulties in New Mexico and these were beginning to come to a head. In January 1898, José Segura the well-respected editor of *El Boletín Popular* publicly announced that he would no longer be associated with La Prensa Asociada Hispano-Americana, ostensibly because José Escobar was then a member of the organization.[25] Segura's public declaration seems to confirm the growing reluctance among other *periodiqueros* to work with Escobar. Whatever the root of José Escobar's troubles, these continued to grow into the spring 1898. Doris Meyer suggests that these troubles resulted from accusations that Escobar had accepted money from political bosses in New Mexico and that the public disclosure forced him to resign his post as editor of *El Nuevo Mundo* (Meyer 1978). Although the particulars of the incident are unclear, it does seem apparent that Escobar had incurred the disfavor of influential and powerful political figures, making his work untenable in New Mexico. There is mention of José Escobar leaving New Mexico in Socorro's *El Combate* in January 1898. Returning to El Paso, Escobar started up *Las Dos Américas,* a paper he began to edit in the March 1898.

A number of possibilities explain Escobar's abrupt departure from New Mexico. Exile, business failures, broken partnerships with fellow *periodiqueros* all seem to have played a hand in "Joselín's" sudden removal from public life in New Mexico. After nearly a decade of involvement with Spanish-language journalism in New Mexico, José Escobar's voice was absent, his pen stilled, and his presses silent, but its seems "Joselín" was not totally ostracized from *Neo-Mexicano* circles, nor was he at odds with all his colleagues in the upper Río Grande. In July 1898, Escobar made a trip by train up the Río Grande and stopped at San Marcial, Socorro, and other towns he knew well. Arriving at Las Vegas he reported to his readers in El Paso, "Fue grande mi satisfacción al estrechar la mano de muchas personas á quienes tengo verdadero estima y de las que, sin ser acreedor á ellas, me han distinguido siempre con sus consideraciones [Great was my satisfaction in extending my hand to so many people for whom I have real appreciation, and of whom—without being in their debt—I can say have always given me their consideration].[26] It seems the song and spirit of "El Cantor de Popé" had not been entirely extinguished by the political squabbles of early days.

Eusebio Chacón, Neo-Mexicano *Novelist:* *"True Jewel in our National Literature"*

Eusebio Chacón's accomplishments as an orator, interpreter, poet, historian, and novelist had long been noted and celebrated in the Spanish-language press in New Mexico, his parents' birthplace, and in Colorado, where Eusebio and his family resided for the greater part of his life.

Eusebio was born into a family with a decided inclination to public life and literary endeavor. Eusebio's father, Rafaél Chacón, was a noted military figure who rose to the rank of major in the U.S. cavalry. Rafaél's brother, Urbano Chacón, was the founder and editor of important newspapers in New Mexico. Urbano's son, Felipe Maximiliano Chacón, was also a gifted poet and writer.

Rafaél Chacón gives an account in his memoirs of a series of commercial endeavors undertaken to support a wife and two children after his discharge from the U.S. Army following the Civil War Battle of Valverde in 1865. He writes that in February 1871, with Eusebio still less then a year old, he set up a homestead in the Ojo Verde area, about twenty-five miles outside Trinidad, Colorado. Although the elder Chacón was a man reaching middle age and was hampered by persistent health problems, this move proved to be the beginning of a period of struggle that eventually brought a measure of prosperity. Jacqueline Meketa notes that these were decisive years for the Chacón family:

> The battle was not without pain, hard work, fear, and disappointments, but buoyed up by an undeviating faith in God and an indomitable perseverance, Rafaél Chacón established a home in

> Colorado, provided many advantages to his children, contributed much to his community and his fellow men, and eventually became a much-loved and respected patriarch of Trinidad. (Meketa 1986, 307)

Among the advantages Rafaél worked diligently to give his children, and in particular to Eusebio, was the benefit of an education few *Nuevomexicanos* of the period could imagine. Eusebio attended primary schools in Trinidad, a prosperous and bustling community in the 1870s. Rafaél then sent Eusebio to the Jesuit College in Las Vegas, New Mexico. Later Eusebio and younger brother Ladislao, were then sent to South Bend, Indiana, to pursue studies at Notre Dame University, where the brothers enrolled in the fall of 1887. Eusebio went on to graduate with a law degree from Norte Dame University in 1889. Ladislao left his university studies after two years and returned to Trinidad (Read 1911, 460).

At Notre Dame, Eusebio excelled as a student and was recognized for his intelligence and eloquence in addressing public forums. Just before his graduation, he was selected to deliver a welcoming speech to the Pan American Congress, which met in St. Paul, Minnesota, in 1889, and in the role of ombudsman greeted various delegations from Central and South America.

After graduation Eusebio took a position as a teacher of English at Colegio Guadalupano in Durango, Mexico. He eventually was appointed vice director of the college, but was obliged by poor health to return to the U.S. He returned to Trinidad in November 1891. The year changed Eusebio's personal and public life. Shortly after returning to Trinidad he was made a member of the Colorado state bar and set up a law practice in his hometown, and in the same year he married Sofía Barela, the daughter of Colorado state senator Casimiro Barela. He was appointed interpreter for the U.S. Court of Private Land Claims, which had begun to hold hearings in Santa Fe on the matter of adjudicating contentious land titles in New Mexico. For the next several years Eusebio, Sofía, and a growing family alternated their place of residence between Santa Fe and Trinidad. In 1894 Eusebio was admitted to the bar of the New Mexico Territory. Throughout a lifetime of public service, Eusebio practiced law in both New Mexico and Colorado. For a time after 1899 Chacón resided in Las Vegas, New Mexico, returning to Trinidad after 1900 where the family remained until Eusebio's death in 1948.

Eusebio's *don de la palabra,* his gift of the word, manifested itself early in his life.[27] In 1884, while still only a child, Eusebio addressed the local *mutualista* chapter in Las Animas County. Notice of Eusebio's talk was published in Santa Fe's *La Aurora*. The short item read, in part, "It is with great pleasure that *La Aurora* congratulates young Eusebio Chacón of Trinidad for the beautiful and well-crafted talk he gave to La Asociación de mutuo adelantamiento del condado de las Animas [The Association of Mutual Advancement of Las

Fig. 17. Eusebio Chacón. Read, *Historia Ilustrada de Nuevo Mexico* (460).

Animas County] on the 6th of this month. The youngster is only thirteen years old and shows surprising talent which will open a vast field where he will gather praise in a future that promises to be happy and prosperous."[28] Eusebio's talent and eloquence became much talked about in towns and hamlets throughout New Mexico and Colorado.

A *letrilla*, a rather flexible verse form, bearing the initials "E. C." appeared in *La Voz del Pueblo* in February 1891 and is among the earliest of Chacón's published works. The poem, distinctive in style, marks the beginning of fifteen years of sustained writing for Chacón. The following year he published his novelettes, *Tras la tormenta la calma* and *El hijo de la tempestad* in a slender volume that carries the imprimatur of José Segura's Tipografía de El Boletín Popular. The book remains among the first published narratives by a Mexican-American author in the Southwest, and the first edited and published by a *Neo-Mexicano* newspaper concern.

Chacón's interest in literature went beyond his own personal ambition. Like others of his generation, he was convinced of the need among *Neo-Mexicanos* to create, edify, and sustain a literary movement that would instruct, but also delight. Chacón, himself the beneficiary of a good education, believed that the education of the populace of New Mexico and southern Colorado could only be achieved through the liberating possibilities of what he began to call, "una literatura nacional," a term coined to describe the *Neo-Mexicano* movement in letters. Chacón's words in the introduction to his novelettes, declarative in nature, sound a call to other *Nuevomexicanos* of his generation to follow suit in establishing upon New Mexican soil a corpus of original and creative literary works that would unveil the intellectual capacities of his people to the larger society. Chacón is adamant in his introduction, making clear that his own work is the product of his own creativity and originality:

> [My writings] are the sincere creation of my own imagination and have not been stolen nor borrowed from *gabachos* [Anglos] or foreigners. Upon New Mexican soil, I dare lay the seed of a literature meant for [the] pleasure [of the reader] so that, if other authors with greater intellect than mine follow this path, they will be able to look back and point to me as the first to undertake this difficult road.[29]

Chacón's work in the novel was also the first conscious effort to set forth a literary credo other *Neo-Mexicanos* might follow. Four years after their appearance, José Escobar noted of Chacón's style, "One is surprised by the talent of the young man of letters: at times he is sarcastic and mocking, and at others he is elevated, philosophical and highly moralistic. In conclusion: Chacón's small book, although unknown among many *nativos*, is *a true jewel in our national literature*" [emphasis added].[30]

Fantasy and Social Transgression: "The earth parted and swallowed her"

Chacón's "dos novelitas originales," (two original novelettes), *El hijo de la tempestad* and *Tras la tormenta, la calma,* say a great deal to the contemporary reader about how *Neo-Mexicanos* viewed their art, their society, and themselves as literate members of their community. Chacón saw the two works as "literature to be read for pleasure" and, at least on the surface, eschews ideological or political motives in his writing. This authorial stance, much in keeping with nineteenth-century poetics and formalism, explains Chacón's ideations and choice of setting, plot, and characterization in his works.

El hijo de la tempestad reflects elements of literature of the fantastic and the story functions as an allegory that explores the dynamic interplay of good and evil, order and chaos, and civility and barbarism. Chacón makes no attempt to historicize or add local color to his narrative, and the novel offers only a weak allusion to the reign of terror instigated by Vicente Silva and his cohorts in New Mexico at the beginning of the decade.[31]

The story begins with the fantastical birth of a child known only as "Hijo de la Tempestad." His birth occurs as his parents take refuge from a violent thunderstorm in a mountain cave. The opening sequences of the novel are replete with foreboding. "El Hijo's" mother dies in childbirth and his father abandons him to a gypsy woman who has already prophesied a life of crime and immorality for the child. While "El Hijo" is still in the care of the gypsy, the pair is visited by "Sombra de la Luz" (Shadow of the Light), a sinister hag who battles Lucifer for dominion over "El Hijo," only to be cast into the fiery depths as "the earth parted and swallowed her" (Chacón, 1892, 12).

The second half of the novelette narrates the protagonist's reign of terror and banditry. For "El Hijo" as prophesied has become a completely despicable figure, "convertido en capitán de bandoleros, asolaba los campos y destruía los pueblos [having becoming a captain of bandits, he razed the countryside and destroyed the villages]." In a raid on an excursion of townspeople on a summer outing, "El Hijo" captures a young woman and her father. He retreats to his labyrinth of cave dungeons where he enslaves daughter and father. After months of torture and deprivation the young woman assents to "El Hijo's" constant demands to marry. As the orgiastic wedding banquet unfolds, a group of soldiers, who had skirmished with the bandits the day before, happen upon the cave as they look for refuge from another violent mountain storm. A battle between the bandits and the soldiers ensues, and an impenitent "El Hijo," with "blasphemy on his lips," is killed by the captain of the government troops. Predictably, the young woman is saved from dishonor and in the last lines of the novel we learn the fate of "El Hijo's" gypsy step-mother. The captain reports that she has been taken by the Devil to the depths of hell where: "Tiénela allí barriendo el aposento que deben ocupar ciertos politicastros que traen a la patria muy revuelta [He has her there, sweeping the chamber that should be occupied by certain petty politicians who keep the country in a state of upheaval]" (Chacón 1892, 29).

Chacón's *Tras la tormenta, la calma* shares certain axiological values with the first work, in the sense that issues of honor, decorum, and transgressions of moral character underpin the motives of protagonists of both stories. But in *Tras la tormenta, la calma* Chacón locates the meaning and details of the plot squarely within the realm of local experience. *El hijo de la tempestad* is set in a fantastic unnamed region, vaguely resembling the mountain villages of New Mexico; it is a locale populated by gypsies, fortune-tellers, monkeys, bandits, vengeful deities, and demons. *Tras la tormenta, la calma*, on the other hand, unfolds in the New Mexican capital, Santa Fe, and the action is set in Chacón's own lifetime. Whereas the characters in *El hijo de la tempestad* transgress both cosmic harmony (they tempt fate) and moral law, the characters in the second story are more earthly subjects. Chacón sees their sexual transgressions as part of a pattern of human frailty and weakness in matters of the heart. He reminds his readers that "there are indiscretions that result in serious and tangled consequences, and still they continue to be committed, to the contrary they are the source of more and greater ones [indiscretions]" (Chacón 1892, 31). Whereas "El Hijo" and his associates are punished with violent death and eternal damnation, communitarian restitution and the reestablishment of societal order await the protagonists of the second tale.

Tras la tormenta, la calma begins with a description of the budding relationship between Lola and Pablo. The young lovers are "of humble origins" and have grown up together, their relationship is naturalized by bonds of shared experience: "The imagination of these two children had developed simultaneously and, with the suitability of their disposition, they loved, desired, wanted, admired the same thing; they were in agreement in all things, even in the sweetness and charm of their temperaments" (Chacón 1892, 34).

The idyllic relationship between Lola and Pablo is broken when Luciano, a student at St. Michael's College, hears of Lola's remarkable beauty and decides to pursue her. Like Don Quijote in Cervantes's novel, Luciano is incited by certain works of literature as he undertakes this conquest. Luciano is particularly fond of the romantic writers, most particular Lord Byron and the Spanish poet Gustavo Adolfo Bécquer. The narrator informs us that such readings have caused Luciano to act "in such a way that they awoke his fantasy by which he singularly desired the occasion to prove himself a daring Don Juan or a Felix of Montemar." Luciano is eventually successful in seducing Lola with insistent promises of love. But, in a final scene, the lovers are found out by Pablo, who aided by Lola's aunt, forces public humiliation on Luciano by making him run half-naked through the streets of Santa Fe. A disgraced Luciano is brought back to marry Lola in an impromptu ceremony witnessed by the barrio residents.

Tras la tormenta, la calma provides an interesting example of self-reflexivity among *Neo-Mexicano* literates not only because the work is imbued with local color, but because it explores notions of literacy and social power in the context of class and gender. Lola, who lives in one of the poorer barrios in Santa Fe, is described as "una de esas morenas que endiablan a uno con sus miradas [one of those dark-skinned women who bedevil one with their looks]." Pablo is said to be "poor, but his poverty pushes him to work to struggle to improve his lot in life" (33). Chacón is present in the story in the voice of the omniscient narrator who interjects subjectivity by his admission of having personal knowledge of the events, and by assigning blame and responsibility to his characters for their part in moral and social transgression.

His metacommentary and authorial digressions suggest that the ultimate significance of the story has to do with the role of learning, literacy, and education among New Mexico's *nativos.* Chacón seems cognizant of the degree to which education and print culture have impacted his society. His intertextual references to classic works of literature suggests the change from scarcity to abundance in the reading matter available to nineteenth-century *Neo-Mexicanos.* Didactic in his views, Chacón moralizes against the "Lucianos" of his generation ("No era un estudiante aplicado, ciertamente no era un modelo [He was not a dedicated student, he certainly was not a model]") who misapply and abuse their learning and education. At issue for Chacón is the

SRA. SOFÍA B. CHACÓN.
y sus niñas Josefina Enriqueta y Ernestina.

Fig. 18. "Sofía B. Chacón y sus niñas Josefina Enriqueta and Ernestina"—the women of the Chacón household circa 1898. Fernández, *Cuarenta Años de Legislador* (107).

edifying use of learning and literature in a social milieu where Lola and Pablo, "los hijos del pueblo" (children of the people) have only their good name and honesty to stay them through life. *Tras la tormenta, la calma* offers social commentary on a world constrained by limited access to education. It is a social world where the old transgressions of the rich upon the poor, of the *patrón* against *peón* are now masked as self-evidential displays of learning. Read in this way Chacón's novelette provides self-referencing fictional disclosure about the nature of books and their potential to alter society, with Chacón reserving his greatest remonstrance for those who misuse the privilege of their education.

From 1892 to 1899, the years he worked as interpreter for the Court of Private Land Claims in New Mexico, Chacón continued to submit poems and other literary texts for publication in Spanish-language newspapers in New Mexico and Colorado. One of the most emotive lyrical renderings by any *Neo-Mexicano* poet of the period is found in his poem, "A Enriqueta," which appeared in *El Boletín Popular* in 1893. The poem is a tribute to Eusebio's first born daughter, Josefina Enriqueta. In the poem, Chacón creates finely wrought images of a dreamlike scene in which the conception of the beautiful child Enriqueta is drawn forth from her parents' passion and love:

De mi tiempo en la jornada
Cuando el mundo estaba oscuro,
Tuve un sueño puro
Del que sueña en la ilusión
Hija del ardiente estío,
Por los genios arullada,
Sobre una flor perfumada
Vi que una gota nació.
Y era gota del rocío
Tan hermosa como pura,
Y sentí feliz ternura,
Y sentí un inmenso amor,
Y hoy pensando sobre el sueño
Digo que la gota era ella,
Mi Enriqueta, dulce y bella,
Yo el estío y tú la flor.

[Child of the burning summer
child, cradled by humors
I have had a perfect dream,
from my time along this journey,
the dream of one who dreams idylic;
Upon a sweet flower
I saw a droplet's birth.
It was a drop of dew,
pure and beautiful,
and I felt gentle joy
and I felt great love;
And as I think about the dream
I say that the dew drop was she;
Enriqueta, sweet and lovely;
I was the summer heat and
you were the flower.][32]

Chacón's writings are not limited in style and aesthetic; but move between social concern on the one hand, and personal introspection on the other. His poetry can be as lyrical as "A Enriqueta," or as provocative as "A la patria," a sociohistorical poem that appeared in print in 1897, and in which he explores his own estrangement as a *Neo-Mexicano* from a tie to the Mexican nation. Clearly, this vein in Chacón's work stems from his understanding of history and from his own travels and experiences.

Chacón's admiration for "Mexico and the Mexicans" is seen in two works published after his trip to Guadalajara in 1894. Chacón published "Ocotlán" in January of the following year. The text is a short travel narrative, a tribute to the flora and fauna of the Mexican countryside.

Chacón's most distilled view of Mexico as cultural homeland, however, is found in "A la patria." The poem is evidence that forty years after the signing of the Treaty of Guadalupe-Hidalgo, the effects of that historical disjuncture produced by the American occupation of the Southwest still continued to disturb the consciousness of some *Neo-Mexicano* poets and writers. Ties of language, culture, religion, and sociopolitical ancestry were recognizable cultural traits that bonded *Nueśomexicanos'* geographical and political attachments to a pre-American frame of reference.

As with his incursion into the novel, Chacón's work as a poet, breaks ground by bringing into sharp relief elements closely identified with the Mexican-American or Chicano experience, an identity at the interstices of borders and historical junctures. Like Chacón's verses to his daughter, "A la patria," is a poem of homage and tribute. In this latter example, the object of the poem is the spirit and ethos of Mexico, both as it was defined by national boundaries in Chacón's day and as it once encompassed the northern frontiers of New Mexico, Texas, Arizona, and California. "A la patria" evokes a post-1848 repositioning of *Neo-Mexicano* cultural subjectivity by inscribing a powerful assertion of identity and cultural continuity in the face of Anglo-American hegemony in the Southwest. In the poem, the poet speaks to this question and exhorts,

O, mi patria, ¿por qué yo no he sabido
Lo que es vivir bajo tu suelo hermoso?

[Oh, my homeland, why have I not known what it's like
to live on your lovely soil?]

The second strophe alludes to war, conquest, and dispossession, the historical determinants that have sealed the fate of *Nuevomexicanos.* Chacón inscribes his subjective and personal account of discontinuity, documenting in this way collective *Neo-Mexicano* discontent with the sociopolitical reality of conquest and subordination:

Yo no nací en el nido que formaron
Las áquilas valientes que te hicieron
Y aunque mis padres por tu honor pelearon
Y en tus lides intrépidos murieron,
Bajo aquellos nací que te humillaron
Cuando tu frente con su planta hirieren
Bajo aquellos nací que te han quitado
La Méjico novel, mi suelo amado.

[I was not born in the nest made
by the courageous eagles that formed you
Even though my fathers fought for your honor
and died in your fierce struggles,
I was born under those who defeated you
when they trampled upon your head,
I was born under those who took from you,
novel Mexico, my beloved homeland.][33]

Chacón's "A la patria" inscribes into the poetic text personal circumstance viewed against the backdrop of sociopolitical change. The poem's allusions, tied as they are to history as the subject of its discourse, sets in motion a lyrical retracing of deep psychological scars that had come to disfigure *Neo-Mexicano* cultural subjectivity after 1848. The subject matter remains, however, a unique referencing of Mexico as a cultural matrix among the writings of other *Neo-Mexicanos*. The poem's sense of historical linkage between New Mexico and Mexico is derived from Chacón's knowledge of his own family's participation in events in Mexican history. But what is truly remarkable is that Chacón is moved to introspection by the ramifications of the historical break occasioned by the U.S. war with Mexico and its continuing legacy of dispossession as played out on daily basis in relations between Anglo and *Mexicanos* in the reconfigured lands of the Southwest.

Chacón and members of his generation were well-aware of this incessant undermining of the cultural integrity of their society. In November 1901, while residing in Las Vegas, New Mexico, Eusebio Chacón found himself at the vertiginous confluence of one such attack on the character and cultural practices of his community. The incident stemmed from a campaign of inflammatory rhetoric launched by Nellie Snider, a Protestant missionary working in the Las Vegas area. Ms. Snider's affronts were directed at the largely Catholic *Nuevomexicano* population of the city. Snider's observations, built on typecast views of *Nuevomexicanos*, incurred the community's ire when she concluded that Las Vegas's Mexican citizens were an "ignorant, dirty, degraded people of mixed Indian and Iberian blood." *Neo-Mexicanos* responded by calling for "una junta de indignación," a mass meeting to draft a set of resolutions to rebuff the falsehoods in Snider's article and to demand an apology from the editor of the English language *Daily Review* who published the libelous attacks (Arellano, 1985).

In attendance at the meeting were members of Las Vegas's distinguished core of *Neo-Mexicano* journalists: Antonio Lucero and Ezequiel C. de Baca of *La Voz del Pueblo*, Enrique H. Salazar of *El Independiente*, and Manuel Salazar y Otero of *El Sol de Mayo*. Asked to speak on the issue, Chacón challenged Snider's assumptions, refuting her stereotypical portrayals of the New Mexican community. His observations were delivered with the wit, grace, and style that had become the trademark of his writing. The complete text of Chacón's speech appeared in *La Voz del Pueblo* on November 2, 1902, with the title "Elocuente discurso: Caballeroso sí, pero picante" (Eloquent Lecture: Cavalier, Yes, But Spicy). Chicano literary critic Francisco Lomelí sees in the text of the speech "a breadth of knowledge, an assertive determination, and a keen appreciation of the historical significance of the situation" (Lomelí 1989, 150).

Chacón argues vehemently that the author of the slanderous attacks on the community simply had not taken the time to come to know the community. At issue in Chacón's estimation was not only xenophobia, but a flawed method of observation: "She purports to arrive at generalizations from individual premises. This person does not know us; if she did, she would not speak in this manner."[34]

Chacón established his cultural authority by countering Snider's remarks with the knowledge of the insider. Only through close intimacy and understanding, Chacón argued, could a distinction be drawn between the depravation painted by Snider and the generosity of spirit that he asserts is the true measure of *Nuevomexicano* communities: "In the country home where the necessities of life are simpler, there are no alabaster lamps, nor white velvet sofas that make our homes look like miniature palaces. But the table is set in abundance, and [they are places] where hospitality sweetens the fate of the traveler, where Christian charity never denies a bed where the weary foreigner may rest his head."[35] To Snider's harangues on "squalor, immorality, the indigestible *tortillas*," and "the shock of fiery chili," Chacón responds, "But if this Lady, had truly seen the inside of one of our residences, she would have noted that we always have a good table and a good bed; that our children grow surrounded by all the amenities that love can bestow."[36]

Chacón channeled the indignation of his fellow *Nuevomexicanos* into a coherent and incisive rebuff of the missionary's ignorance and biased perception of the *Mexicano* populace of Las Vegas. He puts the territory on notice that *Neo-Mexicanos* would not tolerate the racial attacks from xenophobic zealots and uninitiated observers. The speech unified the sentiments of the offended townspeople and galvanized their resolve to repulse the slanderous accusations made by outsiders.

From Chacón's oratorical displays as a boy, to his contributions in Camilo Padilla's *Revista Ilustrada* in the 1930s, he remained a central figure in this precursive movement in the arts and literature among *Mexicano*-origin communities in the Southwest. Unbound by the constraints of proprietorship, editorship, and the entrepreneurial side of newspaper publication, Chacón can then rightfully be considered the first *Neo-Mexicano* professional writer. His work embodied the aspirations of many other *periodiqueros* and editors whose mission had resulted in a first planting on New Mexican soil of the seeds of literary endeavor.

Camilo Padilla, Original Neo-Mexicano *Storist*

Camilo Padilla, born in Santa Fe in 1864, was the only member of his generation to publish and promote *Neo-Mexicano* literary works through the publication of *Revista Ilustrada*, a literary magazine published in Santa Fe and El

Paso. In issuing the magazine, Padilla took a qualitative step forward in the *Neo-Mexicano* cultural movement. The importance of *Revista Ilustrada* as a medium of cultural diffusion is a subject more fully explored in the next chapter. For the moment it is important to note Camilo Padilla's years of involvement with print journalism.

As a journalist, poet, and essayist, Padilla was a constant force in *Neo-Mexicano* print culture. He is among the first *Neo-Mexicanos* to explore the way in which fiction might serve to express social and cultural concerns. This work begins with "Historia Original Neo-Mexicana, -Pobre Emilio!" (An Original New Mexican Story—Wretched Emilio!) a short story published in 1890.

"Historia Original" interjects Padilla's autobiographical experience and explores the profound attachment of *Neo-Mexicanos* to their homeland. As editor of the Mora paper, *El Mosquito*, Padilla often made reference to his residence in Washington, D.C., and to the longing to be back in New Mexico that he and other *Neo-Mexicanos* experienced. Recounting one instance for his readership, Padilla calls forth the time he and Maximiliano Luna, the scion of a prominent Río Abajo family, were both living in Washington. Padilla writes, "When in company of the young patriot, Maximiliano Luna, we contemplated the [fate] that awaited our peaceful and benign homeland."[37] Though he and Luna came from different class backgrounds, this fact is overshadowed by a mutual concern for New Mexico that draws them together. Over a number of months their longing and concern for the region grows: "And on those occasions more than one tear came to blur our eyes—a humble offering by a couple of young men who may have many faults, but in whose chests also burns the torch of patriotism."[38]

Padilla draws on the question of identity and ethno-communitarian values to encode social history and literary representation in "Historia original." For one thing, Padilla's "Historia Original" predates other efforts by *Neo-Mexicano* writers to create foundational texts in literature. The story appears two years in advance of Eusebio Chacón's novelettes. Of greater significance here is that Padilla's text points to a *Neo-Mexicano* reality circumscribed socially, politically, and historically by Anglo-American society. The simple and straightforward story of Emilio may be the earliest narrative to mediate the truth of the world as viewed by *Nuevomexicanos* through the figurative ideations of literary discourse.

"Historia Original" is the story of a young man who, we are told, is a close friend of the narrator. The friend is about to embark on a journey that will take him *al oriente* (to the East) to work in the nation's capital. Camilo Padilla's own travel and work in Washington obviously inform the details of Emilio's story.

Upon taking his leave of Emilio at the train station in Santa Fe, the author reflects on the possibility that this separation will forever change their lives. The narrator's intuition will prove to be prophetic. Two years later, the narrator makes a trip to Washington where he has the opportunity to visit his friend once again. The two rekindle their friendship and indulge in long conversations about New Mexico:

> I obtained a room close to Emilio's and each night we would get together to talk or to take a walk.
>
> Oh what memorable times those were!
>
> Now, we would talk about New Mexico and the New Mexican race, now about the beautiful city and its attractions.
>
> Blessed talks, which like uncaring birds have taken flight and will never return again! While those conversations lasted my friend's beautiful dark eyes were bathed in tears. I remember a chapter regarding his stay in that place, of which I shall give some idea in the following narration:[39]

But indeed, things had changed. Emilio relates how he has fallen madly in love with a young woman in the capital. He is willing to give up everything in order to have her love: "Sacrificaré religión, familia, honor, futuro—todo por ti" [I will sacrifice everything, religion, family, honor, the future, all for you]," he declares upon asking her one evening to marry him. But she has already told him, "Tu eres católico; yo presbiteriana. Es imposible para mi cambiar de credo religioso, asi como tambièn lo es para ti [You are Catholic, I am Presbyterian. It is impossible for me to change my religious beliefs, just as it is impossible for you to do so]."

Emilio, dejected and torn, is given to bouts of depression. He confesses to his friend his folly at believing he could cross the cultural divide into the Anglo world by seeking the hand of this Anglo woman. Despondency invades his spirit and his conversations are filled with nostalgia for New Mexico, in particular, for New Mexican women. The narrator relates those moments of intimate disclosure when Emilio confesses all to him:

> Many times he would say to me: "Oh, in this world there aren't women as tender, passionate, sincere as our women—the Mexican women. Indeed our cousins here are quite the opposite—cold, hard, speculative. Mexican women, noble women. God bless you all a thousand times!" And when he would come to this, he would affirm that he truly felt what he had said by shedding a tear for them.[40]

Emilio, though no longer infatuated with the young woman, cannot rid himself of the humiliation at being spurned by the woman he loves. One day, having made the decision to kill himself, Emilio takes up a revolver and at the moment when he is about to end his life, a vision suddenly appears before him. The vision is of two shadows or shapes, which represent his most cherished ideals. In one he sees a vision of the homeland, of New Mexico, in the other he sees the image of his own mother. Emilio's dream occasions a profound transformation and change in the young man. Emilio confesses to his friend the following:

> At that moment he placed the revolver on the table and kneeling and crying he said, "If it were not for the both of you, my homeland and my beloved mother, I would blow off the top of my head! But it being the case that you may have need of my humble services, I am obliged to hide my pain beneath a false smile and defend you with my voice, my pen, and my sword. I am with you beloved homeland, to you I am betrothed and it is only because of you that I live.[41]

Although Emilio's story is cast in the mold of a nineteenth- century romantic narrative filled with melancholic undertones and overstated pathos, it nonetheless accords emotional valence to the profound identification of *Nuevomexicanos* to a homeland and a cultural inheritance distinct and at times at variance with Anglo-American sensibilities. While Padilla's protagonists appear as emotional caricatures suspended in the contrived situation of unrequited love, the subtext of "Historia Original" has everything to do with the clash of cultural values between *Nuevomexicanos* and the Anglo-American social order. The story's overt symbolism centers on themes revered in *Mexicano* culture. It is no coincidence that questions of religion, honor, motherhood, homeland, the idealization of the feminine, and a culturally prescribed abhorrence of suicide should figure so prominently in the psychological dilemma young Emilio confronts. From the vantage point of cross-cultural dissonance, the story, then, is less about personal sentimentality than it is about the exploration of contrasting worldviews and ideologies.

In other writings Padilla contrasts Anglo-American social custom with *Neo-Mexicano* cultural practice. Writing on seemingly innocuous matters Padilla was quick to point out that the dissolution of *Nuevomexicano* tradition, custom, and celebrations undermined the cultural group they represent and presage the death of a *Nuevomexicano* way of life. In his essay, "Nuestra única salvación" (Our Only Hope) Padilla writes that *Nuevomexicanos* had been made to feel shame for practicing their way of life: "We still remember those days when we were not ashamed to say our brothers had gone to hunt buffalo or that we had eaten empanaditas [mincemeat turnovers]; those days when we delighted freely dancing the *Indita*."[42] Padilla selects three distinguishing features of traditional rural New Mexican life to illustrate his point. At another writing Padilla speaks of the values of such practices aggregated and matrixed in the celebration of *La Navidad* among *Nuevomexicanos*. Reflecting the strong religious connotations of such observances within the typical *Nuevomexicano* household, Padilla remarks, "As long as there is respect for the customs of the home among us, there is hope that we can save ourselves from the elements that wish to dismember us. As long as a man respects his wife, a son respects his parents, and we see in each countryman a brother, The Christ Child be praised! [for] we will not have to fear our future."[43] Camilo Padilla continued to foster this kind of socioliterary agency in other submissions to newspapers across New Mexico and would do so more forcefully as editor of *Revista Ilustrada* in Santa Fe.

J. R. Ribera, "I too wish to leave my offering . . ."

Over the course of some five years, José Segura published the work of a poet he identified to the readership of *El Boletín Popular* as "J. R. Ribera of Wallace, New Mexico." Ribera's poetry stands apart from that of local *trovadores* because of its formal nature. In form and diction his poems represent the work of someone possessing a strong foundation in a lettered tradition. Because the accomplishments of the learned were so often subjects favored by the popular press in an era when "learning was not only professed by the true gentlemen by was expected of him by the populace" (Issac 1989, 245), the scant mention of Ribera in *El Boletín Popular*—with the exception of brief mentions of his visits to Santa Fe and other cities—is a puzzling omission.[44] No other reference is ever made in this or any other Spanish-language newspaper of the time about the personal or occupational habits of their author, an omission made all the more apparent by the literary acclaim ascribed to J. R. Ribera at the end of his life when it was reported, "He dedicated himself to poetry becoming New Mexico's privileged barb and troubadour."[45] Stray bits of biographical information in newspapers offer little information, but an unexpected source, the journals of the ethnographer Adolph F. Bandelier, record important junctures in Rivera's life.

Adolph Bandelier began his work at Cochití and the Pueblos of the middle Río Grande in 1882 with the assistance of José Rómulo Ribera, the parish priest, at the nearby town of Peña Blanca. Bandelier notes, "The Vicar-General has favored me with the books of the church, and when I shall be through here,— then Padre Rómulo Ribera at Peña Blanca expects me at his parish.—There I shall be among the pueblos of the "Queres" language,—Santo Domingo, San Ana, San Miguel" (Bandelier [1889–92] 1984, 37).

Bandelier, taken by the priest's extensive knowledge of Pueblo life and custom, used Ribera to arrange certain introductions and entrées among the Cochiteños and the Santo Domingueños. Ribera's interventions were such that they eventually caused Bandelier to shift his ethnographic focus from Pecos to the middle Río Grande Pueblos.

It seems that Bandelier's "insatiable curiosity" was particularly evident at Santo Domingo, where he became intrusive and overbearing. His initial anthropological forays into the Pueblos were amplified by a "lack of experience and background and partly from linguistic handicaps" (Bandelier [1880–82] 1966, 29). As dealings with the people of Santo Domingo soured to the point of becoming antagonistic, Bandelier looked to Ribera for additional help: "Finally, Bandelier went to Peña Blanca for consultation with Padre Ribera, relations with the Santo Domingans, in general, having worsened" (ibid., 30). The priest, who was closer to the Cochiteños, suggested Bandelier transfer his efforts to neighboring Cochití, the site that would serve as the base for the most extensive of the anthropologist's ethnographic studies in the region.

There is no further mention of Ribera until a decade and a half later, when Ribera began his submissions to *El Boletín Popular*. By this time he was living at Wallace, New Mexico, a railway stopover halfway between Albuquerque and Santa Fe on the Atchison, Topeka, and Santa Fe railroad line, just across from Santo Domingo Pueblo. The change of residence coincided with Ribera leaving the priesthood to marry and raise a family.

During the five years Ribera was at Wallace, he submitted a dozen or more poems to *El Boletín Popular*, material of more than sufficient quality and quantity to fill a small collection. Ribera's poetry, like José Escobar's, falls within the aesthetic dicta of poetry modeled after the fashion of late romanticism in Latin America. But, unlike Escobar, whose early literary formation in Mexico explains his cultivation of such forms, Ribera's influences are harder to locate.

Ribera's sophistication in poetry remains incongruous to his place of residence. At Wallace, José Rómulo was a merchant and his business may have constituted the greater part of the town's primary enterprise of trading post.

Ribera's poems make little concession to the improvisational poetics of the New Mexican *trovo* tradition and display the full spectrum of the Latin American literary arts. This is easily observable in both the content and subject of Ribera's poem, "Al inmortal Acuña,"[46] written on the twentieth anniversary of the Mexican romantic poet's death,

Hoy los amantes del arte	[Today the devotees of art
Ante tu losa agrupados	huddle around your gravestone
Sollozan acongojados	They weep with anguish
Y vienen á saludarte;	They come to pay their regards;
Por lo que toca á mi parte	As for myself
Aunque humilde es mi cantar	Even though my song is humble
Voy á ponerme á labrar	I begin to fashion the work
Lo que te vengo á ofrecer,	I come to offer you
Pues "tambien quiero poner	Since "I too which to place
Mi ofrenda sobre tu altar.	My offering upon your altar],[47]

The titles of Ribera's submissions to *El Boletín Popular* resonate with the emotive subjectivity embraced by the poets of the Latin American anarchist group. These include "Sombras son" (These are Shadows), "La patria y el hogar" (Country and Home, December 8, 1892), "A mi madre" (To My Mother, January 19, 1893), "Epitalamio" (Poem for a Wedding, January 19, 1892), "Una tumba" (A Tomb, March 3, 1893), "A Manuel Acuña: poema en honor a Manuel Acuña (en su vegésimo aniversario)" (To Manuel Acuña: A Poem in Honor of Manuel Acuña [On his Twentieth Anniversary], January 4, 1894), and "En la sentida muerte de la hermana Clara" (On the Occasion of the Heartfelt Death of Sister Clara, June 25, 1895).

The work of biographical reconstruction on Ribera should begin by considering as significant the very appearance of his poems in print. For this act stands in opposition to sociodescriptive characterizations that consigns the territorial period to cultural vacuum unequal in human experience. Church historian Thomas Steele has found that José Rómulo Ribera was among a small group of young men in New Mexico recruited to the priesthood by Archbishop Jean Baptiste Lamy. According to Steele, Ribera's formal education included study in French-speaking Canada and later in France (Steele, 104).

As with other *Neo-Mexicano* writers at the turn-of-the-century, Ribera's poetics are manifold in purpose. Three facets of Ribera's work command attention: his erudite stance, his work as a popular poet, and his work as a commissioned or solicited poet. First, there is in Ribera the need to stake out an erudite stance derived from knowledge of the classics, literary formalism, and the strictures of meter and rhyme. Ribera's image as a "learned poet" reflects the role of authorship as reinforcing the sense of ascendancy that prevailed in the self-concept of his generation. This guise of erudition and worldliness is nonetheless continually modulated against regional exigency that frequently called upon the organic poet to write for needs of his community. For how in fact can the indigenous poet continue to live with his community should he chose to ignore such needs?

Ribera responds to this exigency as had the *bardos* and *trovadores* before him by offering occasional verse tied thematically to local culture. The death of family and personal friends are recorded in the poems, "A mi madre" (To My Mother) or "En memoria de Teresita Padilla" (En Memory of Teresa Padilla). These poems are similar in tone and imagery to the countless tributes published in local papers on the occasion of the death of a community member. Despite the limitations imposed by a formal aesthetic, Ribera's attachment to the local community surfaces to produce original poetry as in "El fandango." "El fandango" calls forth the humor, color, and tradition of a *Neo-Mexicano* wedding dance. Ribera paints the *fandango* as an evening of gaiety and celebration that ends in a fist fight and an emptying of the dance hall. Present are the newlyweds, an odd assortment of rowdy townspeople, and the ever-present *bastonero,* or master of ceremonies. Poet Ribera views the scene from atop a balcony as he writes,

Para de allí presenciar	[From there to witness
El singular panorama	The singular scene
De gente que va a pelear	Of people ready to fight
De plebe que grita y brama.	Of folk who shout and snort.]

Donning the guise of the *trovador* or *corridista,* Rivera holds up a mirror to reflect the carnivalesque atmosphere of the local event for the entertainment of his readers.

A third view of Ribera is that of the poet whose work is commissioned by fellow *Neo-Mexicanos.* It is in this guise that Ribera produced the ambitious poem, "En la llegada de su señoría ilustrísima don Juan Bautista Lamy á Santa Fe," (Upon the Arrival of His Eminence Jean Baptiste Lamy in Santa Fe).

Ribera's talent as a poet was called upon when wealthy Santa Fe scion Miguel Chaves donated a bronze statute of Bishop Lamy to grace the Cathedral in Santa Fe. The formal dedication of the statue included an address by Nestor Montoya, a U.S. representative and the editor of *La Bandera Americana.*[48] Montoya's talk included a recitation of Ribera's "La llegada de Lamy."

"La Llegada de Lamy" is built on biblical and liturgical allusions of the kind that would have been second nature to Ribera, the former priest. Historicity in "La Llegada de Lamy" is derived from accounts of the 1851 event and from the testimonies offered to Ribera by Santa Feans who had witnessed the change in ecclesiastical see from Durango, Mexico, and the installation of Lamy as representative of the American church.

In some recent work, Thomas Steele assesses the poem as the collective acknowledgment on the part of *Nuevomexicanos* of Lamy "as a transcendent hero." Steele contends that the act is proof that the *Neo-Mexicanos* unabashedly deferred to the installation of Lamy as their bishop. Steele insists, "The poem 'En la llegada' allegorically codifies, on behalf of New Mexican Hispanics at the end of the nineteenth century and beginning of the twentieth, their cultural acquiescence in a new way of life which acknowledged Lamy as its anointed emissary." Steele is pointed in his contention that "the New Mexican creole and *mestizo* culture, using Ribera as its spokesman, abases itself before the dominance of European-American "Anglo" culture in general and before French clerical culture in particular" (Steele, 115).

Interpretations along these lines would benefit by mentioning that the poem was solicited from Ribera twenty-seven years after Lamy's death, thirty years after Ribera left the priesthood, and more than sixty years after the event the poem seeks to narrate. A circumstance that leaves far in the past the need for any form of public abasement. Ribera's poem, like the bronze statue commissioned by Miguel Chaves and the speech delivered by Nestor Montoya, forms a part of the obligatory trappings that accompany the posthumous public anointing of Lamy as cleric-hero. An act, one should add, apotheosizing the role of the American Catholic church in the Southwest in the heady days of Americanization in the post-statehood era.

Ribera's poem certainly adds to the *alboroto,* the public stirrings of the day set aside to honor Lamy. Ribera succeeds in enhancing public *admirato* by the use of tropes that are keyed not to a historical Lamy, but to a Lamy purged of socially or personally unacceptable impulses. In Ribera's verses, Lamy becomes a fitting cleric-hero and an apt symbol for the staged event:

Las campanas, imitando	[The bells, emulate
el júbilo popular,	The people's joy
en fiesta tan singular	At this singular feast,
todas están repicando,	All are ringing,
melodiosas anunciando,	sounding sweet in proclamation
que un prelado muy virtuoso	That a most virtuous prelate
humilde, santo, ejemploso	Humble, holy, exemplary,
a la diócesis venía:	comes to the diocese:
!ya llegó su Señoría!	His Eminence has arrived!
-ya vino el pastor piadoso!	The pious pastor is here!]

"La Llegada de Lamy," like the bronze statue of Lamy that stands in front of St. Francis Cathedral, is very much a cultural construction. It matters little that one is in verse, and the other in bronze because their primary function is to shield the real Lamy, the complex Lamy, from public scrutiny. Both works of art leave the good bishop frozen in the apotheosized adipose from which he continues to look out toward the plaza of Santa Fe and in the only form by which he has come to be known by the residents and visitors to that city. It is this reification that prescribes Ribera's description of Lamy as, "humilde, santo, exemploso" (humble, holy, exemplary).

My point here is to underscore the fact that "La llegada de Lamy" was a solicited work, a poem to be recited by Nestor Montoya, Ribera's friend and the publisher of his poems at *La Bandera Americana.* The politics of such solicitation explains the abeyance of Ribera's subjectivity, the absence of his personal views on Lamy as cleric and church administrator. Whatever Ribera's personal opinions, whatever his private thoughts and views (after all, it was Lamy who excommunicated Ribera and dismissed him from the priesthood), he did not speak them on this day set aside to honor the life of the first archbishop of New Mexico after American rule. In short, it was not the occasion for Ribera or any other *Neo-Mexicano* to "air the dirty laundry" of Lamy's tenure as bishop.[49] The stakes simply were too high, what with the criticism of non-Catholics scrutinizing the day's events. Whatever his faults, José Rómulo Ribera, the defrocked *Neo-Mexicano* priest, behaves on the day of Lamy's memorial in the tradition of his *mestizo antepasados,* whose religious loyalty and allegiance to Christlike service had throughout their history been employed to transcend the absolutism of both secular and clerical *extranjeros.*

Isidoro Armijo's "Sixty Minutes in Hades"

Isidoro Armijo authored a number of poems and short prose pieces that he contributed to Spanish-language newspapers in Las Cruces, Santa Fe, and Taos, towns in which he worked as a journalist. His short story "Sesenta minutos en los infiernos" was first published as part of a special edition of the Las Cruces paper *El Eco del Valle* on September 23, 1911. Like other fiction of the times the story is draped by sentimentality and indulges in pathos and melodrama. The story takes as its subject the marital woes of a recently wed couple. Its theme centers on the couples' reconciliation and recommitment to their marriage just at the point they are about to break up.[50]

Isidoro Armijo was a colorful figure and portraits of him show his predilection for stylish dress and attire. A stove-pipe hat, bow tie, and wire-rimmed glasses became his trademarks. These outward signs of erudition and learning were also found among other *periodiqueros* and became the trappings of the social authority and literary agency ascribed to *Neo-Mexicano* literates. Although such stylish accoutrements were late in coming to the Southwest, their function was the same as that described by book historian Rhys Issac in speaking of eighteenth- century Virginia: "There, appropriate demeanor, dress, manner and conversational style were essential. These might confer a presumption of gentility, especially if accompanied by a familiarity with the sources of sacred, classical or legal learning" (Issac, 1983, 245).

Like his contemporaries formed in the contentious territorial period, Armijo could not help but have some knowledge of politics and the law. As a delegate to New Mexico's Constitutional Convention he earned the label of being "the man who wished to annex Texas." Although historical, geographic, and cultural ties all tended to support his views on annexation, the English-language press often referred to the idea of incorporating El Paso into New Mexico as Armijo's folly and political cartoonists ran caricatures of Armijo in his stove-pipe hat, bow-tie, and glasses, straddling the New Mexico-Texas border.

In Armijo's first version of "Sesenta minutos en los infiernos," Eduardo Green returns home one evening to find a letter penned to him by his wife, Florencia. The letter tells of Florencia's decision to leave Eduardo. She has left to run away with a man at the train station. She cites Eduardo's neglect and indifference as the reasons for her leaving. After rereading the letter a dumbfounded Eduardo concludes that all is lost and he must now accept the painful realization that Florencia has left him for another man and another life. Her destination, the letter reveals, is Chicago. Eduardo immediately sits down to pen a response to Florencia in which he repents for his lack of consideration for her. His remorse is great, his only alternative, he writes, is to end his life as he cannot live with the shame of having lost his wife and having ruined a marriage. Eduardo seals the letter in an envelope and addresses it to his wife in care of General Delivery, Chicago, Illinois. Resolute, he removes a revolver from the top drawer of his desk and prepares to end his life.

El Chairman Board Education
County Clerk
Land Agent
Student
Shadow
Good Roads
Colony Land Grant
Dona Ana
La Cruces
THE MAN WHO PROPOSED TO ANNEX TEXAS
Todos dicen que es amigo
Muy derecho y sin reves,
Si comprenden lo que digo.
¿Adivinenme quien es?

At that moment, however, the door of the family home opens. Florencia, it seems, has had a change of heart. She tells Eduardo her hope was that she might return before Eduardo had a chance to read her letter. Her plan was to destroy the letter and go on with her life as before. Eduardo, contrite and tearful, accepts his part in the near collapse of the marriage and shows Florencia his own letter. The couple, now aware of the how close they have come to ending their marriage, vow to renew their commitment to one another.

"Sesenta minutos en los infiernos" was translated and republished in 1924 in *Laughing Horse Magazine*, a literary journal published in Santa Fe by Willard "Spud" Johnson. In the English version, the essential plot elements of the story remain intact, while other changes are introduced. Eduardo Green is rebaptized Xicotencatl Castro and his wife becomes Daniela Castro. Daniela's plan in the English version is to run away with her lover to Santa Fe. The change in destination and other alterations provides the story with a Southwestern setting that was lacking in the Spanish version. These attempts to localize the setting and the ethnicity of characters are curious changes, and there is no clear answer as to whether it was Armijo who authorized them.[51]

In the 1920s and early 1930s *Laughing Horse* often featured literature and arts that exoticized the Southwest. The magazine's promotion of New Mexico as exotic and remote seems to suggest that some degree of orientalization figured into the magazine's publication of Southwestern subjects.

Armijo's "Sixty Minutes in Hades" is significant in other ways as well. Its republication in *Laughing Horse* represents the lone instance of a *Neo-Mexicano* writer crossing over to English publication before 1930. The question of the edification of canon and literary sensibilities in the 1920s seems to have been at work. For Armijo the publication of his story in an Anglo-American literary context represented a kind of validation and access to a readership few other *Neo-Mexicanos* of his generation had experienced. That this event had an impact on Armijo can be seen in the delight Armijo took in later years in describing himself as the "author" of "Sixty Minutes in Hades."

As an experiment in "cross-over," however, Armijo's case proved to have little impact in redirecting the reading sensibilities of his Anglo-American contemporaries. Literary fashion and taste continued to be set by a steady stream of Anglo-American writers and editors arriving in New Mexico from the East. Armijo's story seems oddly misplaced, an ill-fitting example of *Neo-Mexicano* literature among submissions from the Southwest and across the country. Armijo's story, written a decade and a half before, is cast in a romantic genre that was plainly out of fashion with *Laughing Horse* readers. This, in itself, seems to underscore the widely accepted view among Anglo-

---

Fig. 19. Caricature of Isidoro Armijo straddling Texas–New Mexico border. *La Estrella del Valle*, Las Cruces, New Mexico, February 11, 1911.

Americans that *Neo-Mexicanos* were out of step with modern (read Anglo) artistic sensibilities. Anglo-Americans during the period seemed bent on importing modalities in the arts that were rooted in the cultural milieu to which they were accustomed. Sensibilities in English and American letters were thus transplanted whole to the Southwest. Although Anglo-American writers and artists were hungry to experience the region's Indian and *Mexicano* cultures, they were interested in objectifying these cultures, not in letting native cultures voice their reality and certainly not in providing them a platform to stage imaginative flights "across the ethereal heights."

The translation of Armijo's story from Spanish to English is literal in the extreme, a fact apparent even in the epigraph taken from a line in the story that reads: "Of man, love is a thing apart from life, it is woman's whole existence." Other passages throughout the narrative are equally difficult to decipher. The poor translation combined with a poor job of editing complicates the pleasure of reading a story whose romantic discourse would have already taxed the patience of most readers of *Laughing Horse.* One example shows the inadequate translation of Armijo's tale in English:

> My heart was hungry for love. Fate! If I could only have it!
> But no, never, you was [sic] always too bussy [sic], you was [sic] unconditionally bent on your club, to politics, to any other thing that kept you always away from home, to be able to pay any attention to your poor wife.[52]

If Armijo did the translation, such work flies in the face of earlier reports about his proficiency as an interpreter. An English-language newspaper described Armijo in 1908 as "appointed interpreter of the Third judicial district as he is thoroughly conversant with English and Spanish and is a fine scholar in both languages."[53]

Be this as it may, the responsibility of editing the text is much easier to determine. The English version, prepared for publication in a literary venue that touted the editorial talents of Spud "La Papa" Johnson, is an abysmal reflection on whatever editorial prowess *Laughing Horse* wished to promote and maintain. The original Spanish version was prepared with the haste and under the imperatives of newspaper publication, and yet one is struck by the fact that its editing and presentation is of a much higher quality than that of the English version in *Laughing Horse.*

Questions of cultural representation naturally arise from the Armijo example. Most important is how *Laughing Horse,* a first- rate regional magazine for the arts and literature that featured authors such as Mable Dodge Lujan, Alice Corbin Herderson, D. H. Lawerence, and others allowed such editorial oversight. "Sixty Minutes in Hades," filled with editorial flaws points to a double standard in the treatment of contributions by *Neo-Mexicanos.* In no uncertain terms such treatment looms as a cruel joke played upon the unwitting literary aspirations of Isidoro Armijo and other *Neo-Mexicano* writers of the time.

Friend and fellow publicist Camilo Padilla once observed the following of Armijo in *Revista Ilustrada:*

> Each time this good friend passes by my office, I ask myself:
> Why is fate so cruel to the greater part of our brilliant young people? What fault is there in this talented young man that keeps him from occupying the office of Governor or Senator of this state? He possesses all the qualities that could be desired in those offices, and at that, he possesses—education, talent, energy—in abundance. I have come to understand that people easily forget their own . . . but, for their own sake they should not do so, quite so quickly![54]

The distress Camilo Padilla points to in Armijo's life relates to *destino,* that is, to destiny in the Mexican sense of the word, where the consequence of life choices weave a pattern of personal character built over myriad acts and situationalized decisions. Armijo wrote of *destino* in figurative terms as well. For example, he submitted the short narrative "Un palmadita," (A Soft Pat) to the Las Cruces paper *La Estrella.* "Una palmadita" recounts the story of a reigning world boxing champion (an anecdote from newspaper accounts of the day) who retires to private life to take up farming only quickly to face the offers of "agents who tempted him to fight one more man." The boxer returns to the ring "graceful and full of laughter," but to the surprise of those who believe the champ's experience will make for an easy comeback, he is knocked down in the opening round of his come-back fight. From a ringside seat, Armijo tells his readers, "It was a soft pat on the jaw. It was a light blow." Describing himself as, "algo escuchador de discursos y algo lector de libros [something of a listener of speeches and something of a reader of books]," Armijo mulls over the unexpected loss with a fan seated next to him. Armijo listens attentively to his neighbor's summation of the fight: "The athlete cannot separate himself for years from the arena of battle and not expect the punishment of a well-trained boxing opponent."[55] From this Armijo deduces philosophical axioms about boxing and about life in general, "One can say to one's self: 'I'm, going to retire to improve life.' But *destiny* replies, 'Retire if you will but the suffering that today may seem insignificant because you are in the midst of struggle, will emerge and grows greater when you have nothing else to think about'" [emphasis added].[56]

Armijo, knowing only too well the hazards of journalism and politics, occupations that had become his own "arena(s) of battle," advises his readers to persevere and be prepared in all things. Armijo concludes his anecdote with a philosophical resolve reminiscent of Amado Nervo's classic poem *Vida,* a text reproduced frequently in border papers. Armijo writes, "And the prayer of the wise man is, I believe: "Lord make me useful," not "Lord make me secure." "Place some drawbacks in my path, among the delights and the good fortune,—some loss and some gain, one or another stone." These are the soft pats to the jaw that a man will not resist if he has not received them each day."[57] *Mexicano* stoicism as displayed here is present in other of Armijo's writings, the result, perhaps, of the not too few *palmaditas* Armijo had experienced in his personal and public life.

Nine years after the death of Armijo's father, *El Tiempo* of Las Cruces recalled the circumstances of Jacinto Armijo's long illness and a history of misfortune that beset the Armijo family. The elder Armijo had suffered an accident on a buggy trip when returning to Las Cruces from the nearby village of Doña Ana. Jacinto Armijo was forced to suffer a long convalescence and series of operations, that last of which resulted in the amputation of his injured leg. About the same time *virhuela* (small pox) took hold in the household and resulted in the death of the youngest daughter, Jennie. Distraught, Isidoro's father slit his throat with a razor left at his beside.[58]

In the political arena Isidoro Armijo experienced professional setbacks as well. As a delegate to the Constitutional Convention of 1910, Armijo seems to have understood the historic moment represented by the move to statehood, vowing as a delegate to defend the interests of the *Neo-Mexicano* community. Writing in *El Eco del Valle*, Armijo says:

> Every New Mexican should show his interest in conserving the prerogatives and rights that we enjoy up to the present, and we should all be concerned that we are represented by individuals that watch over the well-being of the populace in general [especially] at this time when the most transcendent issue in our history,—the one that will decide our happiness or our ruin—is being publicly aired.
>
> So too, we men of brown skin have been born under the flag of stars and stripes, we also are citizens of Washington and Abraham Lincoln's country and we have the right to demand our personal well-being and a future of happiness for our children and our descendants.[59]

But Armijo's political hopes failed to materialize even with statehood. Perhaps Camilo Padilla had seen Armijo's defeats as representative of the condition of all *Neo-Mexicanos.* Here was one of the best-prepared and ablest individuals among the New Mexican *periodiqueros.* Yet a lifetime of struggle in service to the interests of *nativos* promised little public reward or recognition. By 1926, Armijo struggled on with one newspaper venture after another as *periodiqueros* began to die off and newspaper activity and readership dramatically abated.

Memory of Armijo's accomplishments and achievements had become a faint and distant echo by the time of his death in 1949. Santa Fe's only remaining Spanish-language newspaper carried the following brief obituary, leaving us the only clue as to the last years of Armijo's life:

> Albuquerque
> Armijo, Isidoro: Seventy nine years of age died in his home in Albuquerque on the 22nd of August. The deceased was very active in state politics, having been well known as interpreter for the courts and also as a prominent orator.[60]

Um Totum Revoltijum: Adelfa, Espiridión, and El Pachuco Vacilón

Mis Ultimos Versos
(Para *La Voz del Pueblo*)
Así principiaban:
Idolotrada Esperanza
A quien amo con frensí
Nunca olvidarte pudín . . .
Tampoco podía yo continuar los versos
pues, como soy bruto de nacimiento
estúpido desde joven, e ignorante por
no haber ido a la escuela, no encontraba
otras palabras que rimar con Esperanza
mas que lanza, bonanza y panza. ¿Como
hablar de lanza a mi futura esposa?
Menos de panza. Me decidí por bonanza
aunque tanto ella como yo estábamos más
pobres que el Toro cuando salío de Albuquerque,
vendiendo hasta la cama para
acabalar el precio de su pasaje á Washington.
Puse, pues, descomponiendo lo que
yo (en mi estulticia) creía eran versos:
A pesar de mi bonanza
Y tu grande frenesí
Nunca olvidarte pudín
Idolotrada Esperanza.

[My Latest Poem
(For *La Voz del Pueblo*)
Here's how they began:
"Idolotrada Esperanza
A quien amo con frensí
Nunca olvidarte pudín . . ."
Nor could I complete the verses

since from birth I have been a brute,
stupid since childhood, and ignorant for
not having gone to school, I could not find
any other words to rhyme with
Esperanza other than *lanza, bonanza*, and *panza*.
How could I speak to my future
wife of a lance, least of all, of a
belly. I decided on bonanza, even though she
and I were even poorer than the Bull, who left
Albuquerque selling even his bed to make up
the price of a ticket to Washington. I wrote
down—undoing what I (in my foolishness)
believed were verses:
"A pesar de mi bonanza
Y tu grande frenesí
Nunca olvidarte pudín
Idolotrada Esperanza."

—Espiridión, Las Vegas, New Mexico, 1907

Across the Southwest *Mexicanos* with access to the press often used pseudonyms and aliases when submitting their work for publication. The use of pseudonyms and the idea of masking identity through the use of an invented persona has a long history in literature, but the practice held particular appeal for nineteenth-century romantic and neoclassical writers. *Neo-Mexicanos* well-read in Latin American romanticism and neoclassicism seemed to relish the use of such literary artifice. The pseudonym offered the possibility of controlling authorial disclosure, an advantage to any author wishing to deflect responsibility and engage in scathing verbal attacks on politicians or rival *periodiqueros.* But such anonymity could not be guarded for very long in a community where the talents and inclinations of most *periodiqueros* where easily recognizable. The use of aliases and pseudonyms also had a diversionary purpose; it provided a way to engage in a discursive game of hidden messages, double-entendre, and mistaken identity. As in the *trovos* of rural New Mexico, the object of this literary game was to create an imaginary foil as well as an omniscient and godlike commentator behind which the talent, verbal dexterity, and creativity of the writer might surface unencumbered by scrutiny as to authorship. In this way writers and editors could be as humorous, sarcastic, bitter, or truthful as they liked. Journalists were apt to find the disguise a particularly sane approach whenever unmediated truth was uttered under circumstances that might easily lead to retribution or physical attack.

El Boletín Popular and other newspapers often reprinted such items signed with pseudonyms. The work of two individuals, known to the *Neo-Mexicano* readership only as Adelfa (Rosebay) and Bonafé (Good Faith), stand out in particular. Adelfa was the official correspondent in Trinidad to Santa Fe's *El*

Boletín Popular, and Bonafé, who wrote from Santa Fe, held the same distinction at *El Independiente.* Several submissions by Adelfa appear in Denver's *Las Dos Repúblicas* in 1896 and several others are to be found in *El Boletín Popular* around the same time.

Aldelfa's communiqués are sketches of people, places, and events. These humorous and entertaining pieces contain biographical sketches of notables in the *Mexicano* community, descriptions of towns and regions in New Mexico and Colorado, and summaries of newsworthy events affecting *Nuevomexicanos.* Adelfa's writings are characterized by allusions to classical and world literature and are filled with biting satire, humor, and vivid imagery. These elements, coupled with the fact that Adelfa's communiqués all originated in Trinidad, point to Eusebio Chacón as the likely author of these texts.

In the following communiqué quoted here at length, Adelfa utilized the familiar trope of the procrastinating reporter to explain the circumstances of a lapsed correspondence with her editor:

> We shall make of this correspondence a *totum revoltijum,* as my classmates at the Jesuit College of Las Vegas would say. But before doing so, let us ask a thousand pardons of Don José Segura for the long delay in our letter. Judging our silence, he must have convinced himself, that on this occasion we would send him a great article on politics like those that grace the pages of *La Voz del Pueblo;* he no doubt suspected as much, or that we would give my very worthy Lord a dissertation on New Mexico and her people, like the one being done at *El Independiente;* he must have hoped for a pyrotechnic display with lots of rhetoric and delights, [one consisting] of many verses and irreverent anecdotes mixed in with a bit of advise for the farmers as it often done at *El Nuevo Mundo.*
>
> No, Senor Segura, we cannot promise you anything so grandiose. In its race across the Zodiac, the July Sun failed to see the rabid Dog Star and by accident its [Zeus'] possessed horses have stepped on the animal's tail. And at the very moment, there you have the dog howling so out of control that it has frightened the Sun's horses and that blessed Star now has us all prostrate under its rays.
>
> From the moment we awaken to the time we once more retire to soft bed sheets, we pass the hours sweating thick drops of perspiration like the beads of a conquering Rosary. And here is the truth of the matter, Señor Segura; poor Adelfa has been at the point of suffering a *sunstroke,* and therefore, has not, not even by chance, scribbled you a note. And so things go, how could you have hope that we would sing with stirring inspiration as do the colleagues I have mentioned?[61]

Known only as Bonafé, *El Independiente*'s correspondent in Santa Fe kept readers in Las Vegas, some sixty miles to the northeast, apprised of happenings in the capital city throughout many years. Acting as a kind of cultural reporter, Bonafé reports the details of graduations, fiestas, and feast days held in Santa Fe, while summarizing the proceedings of public meetings of interest to *Nuevomexicanos.* In a tone reminiscent of *El Independiente*'s editorials, Bonafé's correspondence of October 5, 1895, provides a distillation of the *Neo-Mexicano* viewpoint regarding the imminent Americanization of Santa Fe, the ancient New Mexican capital. Bonafé points out the discomforting trends in the larger towns of New Mexico, where the tendency to imitate the manner and ways of Anglo Americans has taken firm hold. Bonafé observes with obvious chagrin:

> Any observer who is the least bit interested cannot but notice the change that has occurred in Santa Fe and in some other towns of the Territory in recent years; a change which clearly indicates that we are becoming Americanized. There are many signs that indicate the trend and make us aware that the customs and ways of earlier years are slowly disappearing and giving way to new practices in imitation of those that are in fashion in the "States." Almost all the youth twenty years of age or younger speak English with more or less fluency, and they have forgotten and or do not show much appreciation for the games and diversions that were the rule in earlier years, and some, the more rash or pretentious among them, imitate the tone and manners of recent arrivals showing themselves to be "more Catholic than the Pope" in the matter of palavering English, and discounting the speaking of their own language.[62]

Adelfa and Bonafé are but two of a number of *Neo-Mexicanos* who made use of invented literary personas and alter egos to express their *sentimiento* in newsprint. The educational formation with the Jesuits of certain *Neo-Mexicano* editors is often revealed in their selection of pseudonyms, which alluded to figures from Greco-Roman tradition and world literature. Camilo Padilla was fond of submitting texts in which he signed as Ignotus or Dimas, while others signed with such intriguing pen names as, Mefistófeles, Fin de Siccle, Ki Ki Ri Ki, El Pensador Mexicano, Meliton, Diógenes, and scores of others.

Often times submissions from readers or untrained poets and writers in the *Nuevomexicano* community were also published with pen names. These *poetas* and *corridistas* were not in the habit of alluding to classical literature or mythology, but took as their inspiration from the local environment. Their verbal disguises allude to occupation, religious or political affiliations, biblical allusions, physical attributes, and above all, to an identification with the village or region where they resided. Interestingly these cultural practices continue to be a part of contemporary Chicano popular culture. Such persona and their contributions in verse and prose are found scattered throughout *Neo-Mexicano* newspapers with names both serious and jocular. Take, for example, the following: Un Moreño (One from Mora), Juan del Jarro (Juan of the Mug), Don Repito (Sir Repetition), Un Caballero de Labor (A Knight of Labor), El Ranchero de la Sierra (The Rancher of the Mountains), El Coloradeño (The One From Colorado), Porfirio, Moises (Moses), and late in the period, El Pachuco Vacilón (The *Pachuco* Joker).

In this way, readers, would-be poets, and *trovadores* in the *Nuevomexicano* community-at-large entered into a discourse of verbal exchange built on innuendo, satire, and the effacement of rival and less able contributors, as is the case set forth in the epigraph at the start of this section. The submission to *La Voz del Pueblo* by Espiridión (possibly from *espirar;* that is, "spirited") offers a self-effacing parody of the policy of local newspapers to publish any and all submissions by local poets. Espiridión, chastises the local editor even to the point of offering his own clumsy attempt at the improvisation of verses as an example of what not to publish. Espiridión describes how the publication of his "ode to Esperanza" caused him to be arrested and brought before a magistrate having been accused by Esperanza's parents of issuing "threats and insults." The judge imposes a fine, takes Espiridión to one side and has the following talk with him:

> Espiridión not only did you threaten and insult your future spouse, you did something even worse, you trampled on the Grammar, the rules of meter and common sense. Don't do it again. . .
>
> —But Sir, I replied, almost no one studies those things and yet we all write poems.
>
> —They are not poems son, they are not poems!

They are stupidities
written by certain gaga people
who, blinded by love,
think themselves inspired
but who should be tranquilized.[63]

Crest-fallen, Espiridión returns to his job as a shoemaker and vows never to write poems again, even when he must resist the pressure of certain political office seekers at election time who Espiridión describes as "alguna bestia me invita a que le haga alguna composición [some ox who invites me to write a composition]." Each time this happens Espiridión gives his standard reply,

Aunque pocos, tengo sesos	[While just a few, I do have brains
No me venga con razones	So don't come to me with reasons
Ya yo no pienso en los versos	Since I don't put my mind on verses
Si no en suelas y tacones	I keep to my business of soles and heels.]

The truth of Espiridión's sarcasm is that the popular press had fueled a tremendous explosion of "literariness" among all classes and sectors of the *Neo-Mexicano* community. Local newspapers were filled with anonymous texts in the folk tradition. Generally referred to as *versos,* these occasional texts by men and women round out the dialogic episteme by which the "masses of *nativos*" are represented in print culture. No doubt there were some *Neo-Mexicano* literates, schooled and studied in the literary arts, who took Espiridión words literally, feeling themselves insulted by the inelegant *versos* of the folk. But, by in large, these did not sway the untutored *bardos* from submitting their verses to their local paper, nor did it keep local editors from publishing them. *Bardos, trovadores,* and *corridistas* sent on their *versos* to local papers as they needed to, when these were required, not by literary convention or taste, but as called for in *nativo* cultural practice. Thus, *memorias* (verse-memorials) continued to be inserted among the week's *defunciones* (obituaries); *corridos* appeared in print the week after tragedy or disaster struck; and spurned lovers sent on their *cuandos* and *desdichas* (verse of unrequited love) as a way "to salve their aching souls." *Los periodiqueros* for their part felt little compulsion to censure their readership and readily gave space to these cultural manifestations of which they were an integral part. In many ways the high aspirations of the learned were bound to the peculiarities of *Neo-Mexicano* cultural practices, with each segment of the populace in its way reaffirming *Mexicano* self-worth in acts of daily living.

The contemporary Chicano literary critic Juan Bruce-Novoa asks, "What then are we to do with the discovery of the pervasiveness in some Chicano urban and rural communities of newspapers like *La Prensa, La Opinión,* or *La Gaceta,* which published a continual stream of literary writing? Is it enough to dismiss them by claiming they have no influence on the writing of today; we must begin to question what significance they had, and why despite their presence and efforts, do they seem to have had so little influence" (1990, 129). As difficult and taxing as the work of such archival reconstruction is, it must precede questions of signification brought forth in assessing what can now be seen as a precursive moment in Chicano literature. That early Mexican-American literary texts were embedded in discourse of Spanish-language newspapers across the Southwest makes them no less worthy of attention. Still Bruce-Novoa's "why despite their presence and efforts, do they seem to have had so little influence" is an intriguing and vexing interrogation of *Mexicano* cultural representations, both at present and in the past. The short answer, of course, is that newspapers and the texts embedded in them, have had "so little influence" on contemporary discussions, simply because we have not read them. The extended and more meaningful answer to Bruce-Novoa's question necessitates a discussion of the politics of cultural arbitration and the social authority of learning that was imposed on the Spanish-speaking residents of the borderlands during the first half of the twentieth century. Here, I believe are answers which may help us see to the heart of the *Neo-Mexicano* situation during the formative period of a Chicano cultural episteme. These are matters I wish to take up in the next and last chapter of this study.

6

The *Neo-Mexicano* Cultural Movement After Statehood

Nuevo México

No ha vivido, ha vegetado	[It has not lived, it has vegetated
Por sesenta años y más	For sixty years and more,
Quedandose siempre atras	Always lagging behind
En su camino cansado;	Upon its labored road
Hoy que le ofrecen estado	Today, when they offered it statehood
Podrá hallar redención	Perhaps it will find its salvation
Si buscan con afición	If they seek; in earnest
Libertad y soberania	Liberty and sovereignty,
Y podrá en cercano día	And perhaps in a not too distant day
Ser estado de la Union.	It will be a state of the Union.]

—*El Independiente,* Las Vegas, New Mexico, November 28, 1907

> One needs to be convinced that if the American people, essentially the Saxon, have managed to become an intelligent and civilized people, it is due to the fact that from the beginning they have protected those newspapers published in English, and not only have they protected them, they read them assiduously, so much so that they have caused the major magazines published in this great country to have weekly circulations in the millions of copies; this suggests that the *Americanos* have shown us that only through buying and reading will newspapers—of whatever kind—instruct, and be protected.
>
> —Camilo Padilla, president of the Hispano Press Association, Santa Fe, 1928

Camilo Padilla above exhorts *Neo-Mexicanos* to "protect" their culture through the buying and reading of newspapers published in Spanish, but his words belie the frustration of years of struggle in resisting the constriction of the social space within which *Neo-Mexicanos* might exercise that very prerogative. Limited to the idea that "we have papers, they have papers, let's support ours as they do theirs," Padilla's call ignores the workings of a hegemonic force far more determinant than mere "Saxon" virtue; nor does it impute the material and economic base of publication, the terms which contemporary book historians employ to interrogate the idea of literacy sublimated to the role of social emancipator.

In fairness to Padilla only recently have literary historians, armed with theories of postcolonial subjectivity, begun to consider the sociohistorical complexity that undergirds the production of printed materials, and the power these have to authenticate representations of self and of the "other." The displacement of power through print discourse brings forth Robert Darnton's equation, "Questions about who reads what, in what conditions and at what time and with what effect, links reading studies to sociology" (1989, 46). Despite Padilla's insistence that *Neo-Mexicanos* should exercise control over their own newspapers (over their own culture), it is clear that the larger sociohistorical project of Americanizing the native people of the Southwest—a tendency that crystallizes in the context of statehood for New Mexico and Arizona—triggered the social implosion that dismantled *Neo-Mexicano* print culture during the first half of the twentieth century. According to Darnton, circuits of communication "operate in consistent patterns, however complex they may be" (Darnton, 1989, 46). Complexity in the *Neo-Mexicano* case includes the containment of print discourse within an Anglo-American cultural paradigm built on an ideology of cultural homogenization.

This condition speaks to Bruce-Novoa's incisive interrogation of historical newspapers and their lack of influence on contemporary Chicano cultural representations. The question of why these newspapers and their literary texts have not been read is nuanced by sociohistorical and sociolinguistic factors. Two major considerations, however, must be kept in mind. One is the nature of this production (that is, as "fugitive works like almanacs and newspapers") (Darnton, 45), and the other is Anglo domination of the arts and cultural production in New Mexico's post-statehood period. Added to this is the matter of the consolidation of an English-dominant circuit of communication—Padilla's weekly circulations "in the millions of copies"—that was oblivious to *nativo* cultural contributions. Padilla himself was already aware that in some circles the mere taking of Spanish-language newspapers brought about accusations of separatism and anti-Americanism, a charge he felt obliged to refute by declaring, "The reading or buying of newspapers in Spanish does not mean that the official language of this great nation will be injured in the slightest way."[1]

Despite the constriction of the social space within which Spanish-language journalism was forced to operate in this period, it continued to influence *Neo-Mexicano* youth in the post-statehood era. In fact, during these years efforts set in motion two decades before were completed. Key are the following developments: 1) *Neo-Mexicana* women writers gained a measure of recognition in the press, 2) *Obras de Felipe Maximiliano Chacón: Prosa y poesía* (Works by Felipe Maximiliano Chacón: Prose and Poetry) was published, 3) *Revista Ilustrada*, a *Neo-Mexicano* magazine for the arts was successfully published for some twenty-six years, and 4) El Centro de Cultura, a statewide center for *Neo-Mexicano* arts, was launched in Santa Fe by Camilo Padilla. But it is also clear that dislocations in the cultural matrix of the region signaled a repositioning of *Neo-Mexicano* cultural and political subjectivity. Among the most visible alterations remains the widespread use of the term "Spanish-American" among *nativos* as both a political and ethnic identifier throughout the period.

New Mexico's and Arizona's *nativos*, who technically had been citizens since 1848, believed statehood would guarantee their status as fully participating citizens of the nation. It should not come as a surprise that this political event, not shared by other Mexican-origin groups in the Southwest, would have great impact on the collective self-image and self-representation of *Neo-Mexicanos.*

La Nueva Generación: The Daughters of Editors

> Why, then, should the most enlightened nation prevent the study of the Spanish language in the schools of New Mexico, where that language is even now the language of the majority of the people?
>
> —Aurora Lucero, Las Vegas, New Mexico, 1911

Aurora Lucero (1893–1964)

Aurora Lucero, born in 1893, came of age with the newspapers established by the pioneer editors of her father's generation. Her father, Antonio, an associate editor at *La Voz del Pueblo,* had distinguished himself in journalism, politics, and education. Aurora Lucero was educated in the public schools in Las Vegas, New Mexico, and from these beginnings her life evolved as a series of important firsts for Spanish-speaking women of her day. As a young girl, Lucero was aware of the public debate and much talked about social and political changes during New Mexico's transitional years to statehood. Central to that debate was the prospect for the survival of the Spanish language and *Nuevomexicano* village arts and traditions.

Lucero became active in politics and campaigned for Democratic party candidates in several statewide elections during the early days of statehood. In 1912 Governor George MacDonald, whose administration her father served as secretary of state, appointed her, then only nineteen, to assist with the preparations for the New Mexico exhibit at the San Diego Exposition. In 1915, while still a student at New Mexico Normal University in Las Vegas (today New Mexico Highlands University), she was asked to serve as interpreter for William Jennings Bryan while he was on a speaking tour through the West. Her participation in the political arena was rewarded with honorary posts in successive administrations of the state government (*Santa Fe Mirror,* 1961, 209). Active in the movement to secure the right to vote for women in New Mexico, Lucero was among the most influential of the *Nuevomexicana* suffragists (Whaley 1994, 84).

In 1915 she received a degree in teacher education from the New Mexico Normal University and two years later began a lifelong teaching career. Her first teaching position took her to Tucumcari, New Mexico, a ranching community located on the Llano Estacado of eastern New Mexico. Later Lucero taught at Santa Rosa, Pojoaque, Madrid, Santa Fe, Santa Cruz, and the Springer Home for Boys. After her marriage to George D. White of Santa Fe, the couple moved to Los Angeles. Lucero's first daughter, Dolores was born while she was enrolled in the graduate program at the University of Southern California. Lucero withdrew from the university after only a semester to return to New Mexico with her family and completed her bachelor of arts degree in 1925 at New Mexico Highlands University (*Santa Fe Mirror,* 1961, 210).

Lucero was the first *Nuevomexicana* to serve as superintendent of schools for San Miguel County, a post she held from 1925 to 1927. At the end of her term she was appointed assistant professor of Spanish at New Mexico Highlands University. She completed requirements for her master's degree in 1929. Her thesis, "El coloquio de los pastores" (The Dialogue of the Shepherds) took as its subject a traditional Christmas folk play enacted yearly in the villages of northern New Mexico. Aurora taught at Highlands until 1934 when she accepted an appointment by first lady, Georgia Lusk, to be assistant superintendent of instruction for the New Mexico Public Schools. Aurora accepted the job and relocated to Santa Fe where she lived for the rest of life (*Santa Fe Mirror*, 1961, 210).

Lucero gained public recognition as a writer while she was still a student. She submitted an essay titled "Should the Spanish Language Be Taught in the Public Schools?" for competition in the yearly oratorical contest at New Mexico Normal University. Her essay was judged the best among entries from colleges across New Mexico and was published in the *Normal University Bulletin* in January 1911.

The essay came in response to the Enabling Act of 1910, which stipulated the speaking, reading, and writing of English with fluency as requisite for any one wishing to hold office or obtain employment in state government. The act was seen as discriminatory by *Nuevomexicanos* whose first language was Spanish. The debate over language rights generated by this punitive legislation brought to the forefront latent issues regarding the education of native *Nuevomexicanos.* It once again raised the specter of racial bias that had conditioned uneasy Anglo-*Mexicano* relationships throughout the territorial period.[2] Lucero, like other *Neo-Mexicanos,* was disturbed by the ill will

Fig. 20. "Miss Aurora Lucero, 1911," Lucero having won the Oratorical Contest for 1911. *New Mexico Normal University Bulletin* (January, 1911).

that had inspired the act, and by the fact that the legislation was being held up as a prerequisite to statehood for New Mexico.

Aurora Lucero's essay cites the cultural and historical rights of New Mexico's Spanish-speaking residents as guaranteed by the Treaty of Guadalupe-Hidalgo, "as contracted most solemnly before the world" and argues that the Enabling Act would disenfranchise *Nuevomexicanos* from their civic and constitutional rights by limiting their participation in education, politics, and employment. Despite substantiating her argument in large measure with a colonial narrative referenced to a litany of historical and literary antecedents that link Spanish in New Mexico to "the language of the Corteses, the De Sotos, and the Coronados." Aurora Lucero did not ignore contemporary reasons for studying Spanish, citing both "the great commercial importance of the language" and its potential to improve cross-cultural relations in New Mexico and the hemisphere. Lucero advised lawmakers to take into account the historical precedent and the cultural background of *Nuevomexicanos*. She writes,

> It is true that we are American citizens, [and] our conduct raises our loyalty and patriotism beyond all reproach. We need to learn the language of our nation [English] and we are doing so; nevertheless, in order to do this, we do not need to deny our origin, our race, our language, our traditions, our ancestral past. For we are not ashamed of these, nor will we ever be ashamed of them, to the contrary, these make us proud.[3]

Aurora Lucero-White emerges as a transitional figure among *Neo-Mexicana* writers, and her essay on language registers the participation of women in the struggle for cultural and civil rights. She is among the earliest women writers published in the Spanish weeklies to break from the anonymity of pseudonyms and see her work recognized for its own intellectual merits. In February 1911, *La Estrella* of Las Cruces ran a front page article on the young writer with the headline, "Honor al mérito," (Honor where honor is due). The caption so often reserved for the achievements of males now took on special meaning in the context of Lucero's work. In the months that followed, New Mexico's *periodiqueros* reprinted Lucero's essay up and down the Río Grande on several occasions.

Womens' Voices in Print

Prior to Lucero's work, the voice of women in Spanish-language journalism in New Mexico seldom emerged beyond the socially conditioned role of the nineteenth-century woman. Although *Neo-Mexicano* journalists featured the works of "consecrated" women writers such as Sor Juana Inés de la Cruz (Mexico), Gertrudis Gómez de Avellaneda (Cuba), Clarinda Matto de Turner (Peru), Emilia Pardo Bazán and Amalia Puga (Spain), and others, *Neo-Mexicanas,* for the most part, were not extended the same publishing opportunities.

Most often *Nuevomexicanas* spoke from the margins of their own society. Their work appeared in print only under very selective criteria. Submissions by women were published if they were in the form of anonymous verse or carried a pseudonym,[4] two avenues of expression that were much more common than is generally known. Works in poetry and verse by *Nuevomexicanas*, like that of scores of unnamed folk poets, were also were published by local editors as occasional verse. Circumscribed by social convention, *Nuevomexicanas* most often spoke from behind the veil of the mourning widow, or in the sorrow of the bereaved mother grieving the loss of a son or daughter. Somewhat rarer was the voice of the woman poet abandoned by her lover, the victim of a man's betrayal.

One example of occasional verse is an elegy by Severina Esquibel, a resident of Las Vegas, New Mexico, written on the occasion of her mother's death. The tribute is a patterned poem in the form of an acrostic where the mother's name, Valentina López de Esquibel, is spelled by the first letter of each verse:

A mi Madre

V oló tu alma al Imperio, ¡Madre mía!
A gozar de celestial mansión
L ápida eterna venero cada día
E n tu retrato que estrecho al corazón
N ada hay más digno de contemplación
T odo en el mundo en tu retrato acaba...
I mpaciente y llorando llamaba
N o respondes Madre mía al corazón?
A l contemplar tu Imágen retratada
¡Oh! Dios... no siento su palpitación.
L os recuerdos que llegan á mi alma
O primen sí; ... mi pecho cada día
P orque al ver tu retrato ¡Madre mía!
E s cuando encuentra la tranquila calma
Z alema humildad y cortecía [sic.]
d o pido al ángel que con celeste Banda
e ntone un canto; dulce melodía
E s verdad... ¡Si estás en el Etér
S i tu dicha es eterna... ¿Porqué lloro?
Q uedó mi padre á quien también adoro
U n padre bondadoso como es él.
I nmortales aquí no hemos de ser,
B uscamos el consuelo, no lo hallamos,
E ntonces ambos dos nos conformamos
L uchando en la angustia y el placer.
—Las Vegas, N.M. Octubre 15, 1892

[For My Mother
V Your soul flew to the Kingdom,—Oh Mother!
A To enjoy the celestial mansion
L I venerate this eternal stone each day
E By drawing your portrait to my heart
N There is nothing greater to behold
T Every thing in this world ends with your image
I Filled with haste and tears I called to you
N Will you not, Mother, answer the longing of my heart?
A As I contemplate your painted image
Oh God, I cannot feel her heart beat!
L The memories that enter my soul
O Afflict my breast each day
P Upon seeing your picture each day, Oh Mother!
E I find peaceful calm
Z Bowing [with] humility and courtesy
d I ask an angel to take up with the heavenly music
e a sweet melodious song
E It is true... If you are in the heavens
S If your joy is eternal, why do I lament?
Q I have my father who I also love
U A generous father like no other
I We were not meant to be immortal here
V We look for comfort and do not find it
E And so the two of us resign ourselves
L Struggling in anguish and in joy.
Las Vegas, New Mexico, October 15, 1892, Severina Esquibel][5]

Submissions like this abound in local papers, but it is Lucero-White's essay on language rights that provides one of the earliest examples of intellectual agency for *Nuevomexicanas* in print. To what degree Lucero's work opened up possibilities for other women writers in New Mexico requires further study but certainly she remains a precursor to the work of other women writers who follow. Beginning in 1920s the names of other *Neo-Mexicana* writers began to appear regularly in print. These first instances of a *Nuevomexicana's* work often came about through a familial or personal relationship with the editor or owner of a newspaper. An early example of a woman as editor of a Spanish-language newspaper is that of Frances Montoya. From 1916 to 1923 Frances was the associate editor of *La Bandera Americana* and did the work of getting the paper out when her father, Nestor Montoya, a U.S. Congressmen, was in Washington during sessions of Congress. A few years later, Herminia Chacón, Felipe Maximiliano Chacón's daughter, published poetry and short stories during the time her father was editor of the same paper.

Publisher Camilo Padilla lead efforts to publish women authors in the 1930s. His *Revista Ilustrada* frequently included the work of women from the El Paso-Juárez border area. Also featured in *Revista Ilustrada* were writings by Santa Fe resident Luz Elena Ortiz. Little is know of Ortiz, but the appearance of her work is novel, since it represents an early example of a *Neo-Mexicana* submitting works for publication that were not prescribed by social conventions and which reflect the agency and instinct of the writer.

Santa Fe's *El Nuevo Mexicano* ran columns by Cleofas Jaramillo and Fabiola C. de Baca on *Nuevomexicano* social customs. Fabiola C. de Baca, the author of the celebrated work, *We Fed Them Cactus* (1954), was also related to well-known *periodiqueros.* Her uncle, Manuel C. de Baca, had founded *El Sol de Mayo* in Las Vegas and was the author of two regional novels. In *We Fed Them Cactus,* Fabiola acknowledges Manuel's influence on her as a writer, but writes that it was her uncle Ezequiel C. de Baca, who as the Associate Editor of *La Voz de Pueblo* brought her in contact with the working of print culture. Fabiola's recollection provides one of the few descriptions available of a New Mexican woman's involvement in the day-to-day work of writing and publication: " I believe I was his favorite niece, at least he trusted me with some of his most important business affairs. I kept books for him, signed checks and measured type in his newspaper establishment when I was fourteen years old and only in high school" (C. de Baca, [1954] 1993, 163).

The Unfinished Work of "Bringing Honor to the Homeland": Felipe Maximiliano Chacón (1873–1949)

> The mere fact that *El Cantor Neo-Mexicano,* as our poet has been titled, is a native son of this earth which his ancestors have made immortal with their great feats of conquest and colonization, is reason enough for the people of New Mexico to give this book a most cordial and generous welcoming. Not a single household should be left without this book. Everyone should get a copy and cherish it like a holy object of one who has found the way to bring honor to his homeland and to his people through the beautiful creations of his clear thought.
>
> —Isidoro Armijo, *La Bandera Americana,* Albuquerque, New Mexico, June 1924

An early reference to Felipe Maximiliano Chacón in the Spanish-language press comes by way of advise given to him by the editor-in-chief of Santa Fe's *La Aurora.* The counsel forms part of the editor's farcical "Last Will and Testament," a text meant to entertain the paper's readers. *La Aurora's* editor, Dr. Pietre Balducci, an Italian immigrant to Santa Fe, offered his *testamento* (last will) in response to a *gacetillero's* (copyboy's) request that the editor make his bequests to staff public. Balducci's "Last Will" builds on the metaphor of the editor-in-chief as absolute monarch who lords over the operation of the copy room.

At the time of Balducci's last will, Felipe Maximiliano's father was employed as an editor in the offices of *La Aurora.* Felipe, a boy of eleven, often visited Urbano at the offices of *La Aurora,* where he spent time learning the business of the newspaper. Felipe, it seems, had already demonstrated an inclination to "hacer versos" (to invent verses) in the style of the *trovadores* of earlier times. Noting promise in the boy, Balducci wills him the following:

> To *La Aurora's* poet, so young, so valiant, so courteous a young man, to him I pass on the recommendation that he open and unfold his wings and that he guide his imagination, more and more toward the world of ideas, [toward that world] fertile in fantasy where the poet can forget the realm of reality, that of today, tomorrow and the future. I urge him to not to abandon the dreams that enchant, widen, please, and console the heart. As proof of my love I leave him my bow and arrows (though not the poisoned arrows) so that he can complete the conquest of the one who is today the aurora of his thoughts.[6]

Historian Benjamín M. Read, confirms reports that Felipe had his first poems published, in *La Aurora* at age fourteen.[7] Felipe Maximiliano's early involvement in newspaper publication acquainted him with many of the *periodiqueros* and in time sparked his desire to become a journalist and a writer.

Felipe Maximiliano Chacón was born in Santa Fe in 1873; his first cousin was the poet and novelist, Eusebio Chacón. Felipe Maximiliano attended public schools in Santa Fe and later, as was the established practice in his family, graduated from St. Michael's College. His father died suddenly in 1886 while serving a second term as superintendent of the Santa Fe public schools. Years later Felipe remarked that this loss was the single most devastating of his misfortunes.

Felipe Maximiliano spent a number of years working in mercantile stores in Santa Fe and pursuing a part-time career in journalism. During this time he was also becoming known in *Neo-Mexicano* circles an orator and writer. Adelfa, *El Boletín Popular*'s correspondent in Trinidad, for example, heaped praise on Felipe Maximiliano on the occasion of a speech he delivered at the Fourth of July celebration in 1897 in the mining town of Hillsboro (Sierra County).

Coming into his own, Chacón became the associate editor of *La Voz del Pueblo* in Las Vegas in 1911 and later founded *El Faro del Río Grande*, a paper he published in Bernalillo, New Mexico, for about a year before moving the press to Albuquerque in the spring of 1915. Selling his interest in *El Faro del Río Grande,* he returned to the Las Vegas-Mora area. In 1916, Chacón began editing *El Independiente* for Enrique H. Salazar and later, with the death of Enrique Sosa, he assumed the editorship of *El Eco del Norte* in Mora, New Mexico.

Absent for a time from Spanish-language newspapers, it is only after he assumed the job of editor and general manager of *La Bandera Americana* in Albuquerque in 1922 that *Neo-Mexicano* readers again benefitted from his work. Felipe Maximiliano would remain at *La Bandera Americana* for the next seven years.

Soon after his arrival, *La Bandera Americana* began to receive praise from other *Nuevomexicano* journalists throughout the state. Felipe Maximiliano had begun to make submissions to *La Bandera* as early as December 1917, the date of publication of a poem titled simply, "La Navidad" (Christmas). "La Navidad," which served to mark the Christmas season, proved to be a favorite with *La Bandera's* readership, and was reprinted yearly. Chacón's work as a journalist had begun in the territorial period and he continued to devote his energies to developing a corpus of writing that would register the experience of his community. After December 1922 he made exhaustive use of *La Bandera's* literary section to publish many of his more serious poems and those that would become the basis of his collection *Obras de Felipe Maximiliano Chacón, El Cantor Neo-Mexicano: Prosa y poesía* (Works by Felipe Maximiliano Chacón, The New Mexican Troubadour: Poetry and Prose). Along with Eusebio Chacón, Felipe Maximiliano is among editors and writers from this period who are viewed by contemporary Chicano literary historians as precursors to Chicano writers.[8]

The publication venues available to *Nuevomexicanos* at the turn of the century shaped *Prosa y poesía* as much as Felipe Maximiliano's love of poetry. The fact that *nativos* could at last point with pride to Felipe Maximiliano's work as a textual vessel of *Nuevomexicano* authorship should not be underestimated.

Prosa y poesía was published in a limited edition on the presses of *La Bandera Americana* in June 1924. Much anticipation surrounded the publication of Felipe Maximiliano's work. Prior to its publication, *La Bandera Americana* ran a photograph of the author along with a description of his work as a writer. Readers were asked to remit a small coupon to *La Bandera* along with $3.50 to cover postage and the price of the book. The actual number of copies printed is not known, though it must have been a fairly short run of a few hundred copies.[9]

The preface to *Prosa y poesía* is an apologia conforming to the literary fashion of the day and in which the poet expresses excessive modesty to drive the point that he serves at the indulgence of his readership. Chacón, declares that he hopes his works will add to books written for pleasure and pastime, what he calls, "lectura recreativa para las masas populares [reading of a pleasurable kind for the masses]."

A prologue by Benjamín M. Read introduces the work to the reading public. Read viewed Chacón's book as the culmination of years of struggle by *Neo-Mexicano* literates to be recognized in the field of letters. Encouraged by such promise Read writes: "I have no doubt that in time, the works of Felipe Maximiliano Chacón are destined to mark a distinct epoch in the literary

Fig. 21. Felipe Maximiliano Chacón, author of *Prosa y Poesía. La Bandera Americana,* Albuquerque, New Mexico, December 21, 1923.

history of the United States" (Chacón 1924, 5). Clearly this kind of hyperbole characterized the times, but Read's assertion also reflected an abiding belief in the efficacy of literacy to overcome all manner of social stratification. Read's remark, premised on his own enthusiasm at seeing the work in publication, makes clear that he was blind to the reality of the interethnic antagonism and misunderstanding that continued to mar Anglo-*Mexicano* relations. For Read, publication alone represented a "triumph" of sufficient magnitude to set new literary directions. From this singular act Read believed other *Neo-Mexicano* literary works would continue to spring forth.

Read, like others in the post-statehood period, had come to believe that *Nuevomexicanos* had finally managed to penetrate Anglo-American hegemony on matters of language, writing, and cultural validation. But, in truth, recognition of Chacón's work would be limited to the Spanish-speaking readers. Even while the literary canon of Southwest letters was in its formative stage, not an iota of mention would go to Chacón or any other *Neo-Mexicano* work during this period. Acceptance by the dominant society was still only a vague and ennobling notion that had little or no tangible result.

Read's prologue does offer a telling assessment of Chacón's decision to write in Spanish. For ironic as it seems, Chacón was compelled to educate himself in Spanish, his native tongue. By the time Chacón attended St. Michael's College, the educational aims of that institution had turned toward proficiency and mastery in the English rather than in Spanish. For Chacón, as for other *Neo-Mexicanos*, it would become necessary to supplement his studies of Hispanic literary traditions.[10] For Read overcoming this cultural dislocation only furthered his respect for Chacón: "Proof of just how well our poet has taken advantage of his time is the way by which he has managed to learn and cultivate the Spanish language, without the benefit of direction in a nation whose language is English and where there are few or no opportunities whatsoever to learn Spanish with proper instruction."[11]

Prosa y poesía consists of fifty-six poems and three short stories. The work is divided into the sections "Cantos patrios y misceláneos" (Patriotic Songs and Others), "Cantos del Hogar y Traducciones" (Songs of Home and Translations), and "Saetas Políticas y Prosas (Prose and Political Verses). Erlinda Gonzales-Berry writes that the poems in the book deal with "six broad categories: love, personal misfortune, philosophical musings, patriotism and homage, commemoration of special occasions and humor" (1989, 190). Each group of poems marks a shift in the voice of the poet. The poems of "Cantos patrios" are inflected with the tenor of public oratory, while those of "Cantos de hogar" are tinged by a softness of expression that conforms to the exploration of self in the context of family and community. This aesthetic may seem disingenuous to contemporary readers who have become accustomed to the ethic of the personal as political, but in fact a conceptualization of this sort remained outside the consciousness of these early writers who held that the public and private person occupied distinct and separate spheres.

The poems comprising "Cantos patrios," speak, as their title suggests, to the attendant meanings of patriotism in the context of the struggle for statehood. Chacón, for example, pays homage to the exploits and service of *Neo-Mexicanos* in the United States military in the poem "Odas a los héroes," (Ode to the Heroes), in which he praises the valor of *Neo-Mexicano* doughboys recently returned from the World War:

Pero altivos seguís neomexicanos
En Chateau Thierry y San Miguel luchando
Y en alianza de hermanos
Laureles de victoria conquistando.

[But you go on, proud New Mexicans,
Fighting in Chateau Thierry and San Miguel County
in alliance with your brothers
and winning the laurels of Victory.]
(Chacón 1924, 21)

"Oda a los héroes" retains the function of the *corrido* in its work of historicizing events that effected the collective experience of Mexican Americans in this period. Thus it provides validation for *Neo-Mexicano* sacrifice in the wars of the nation and is a text that specifically counters the short shrift given to the record of service by *Neo-Mexicanos* soldiers in the English-language press at the time.[12]

New Mexico's admission to statehood is in many ways the subtext to all the poems in "Cantos patrios." Chacón addresses this directly in "A Nuevo México" (Poem to New Mexico). Here Chacón is unrestrained in his poetic exuberance, though his stance has been misconstrued as the sycophantic flattery of a colonized subject, the poem must be read against the barriers to enfranchisement that had kept New Mexico a territory for some sixty-four years. "A Nuevo México" ultimately is a homage to the homeland; to *Nuevo México,* the step-child of the American conquest. For Chacón, *Nuevomexicanos* had every reason to be proud as they triumphed over de facto discriminatory and racial oppression. The poem, laudatory in tone and infused with the cadence and triumphal stride of an inaugural march, does not, however, salute Congress or the president, rather it pays tribute to the men and women of New Mexico in their struggle to fully participate in society. In the verses that follow, Chacón creates ethnopolitical commentary as he personifies collective struggle in a direct address to New Mexico as homeland:

Luchaste contra el hado endurecido Batiendo del Congreso la injusticia Y con ella el insulto proferido Del perjuicio racial por la malicia.	[You battled against unyielding fate Defeating the injustice of Congress, And so too insults and insinuations of ill-spirited racial prejudice.] (1924, 43)

Chacón intersperses a number of philosophical and lyrical poems throughout the "Cantos patrios" section that are inspired by the romantic and modernist poets in Mexico and Latin America. In these poems Chacón adheres to the formalist canons of these literary schools. However, their content is inspired by a *Nuevomexicano* cultural milieu. Among the best realized poems in this vein are "A Santa Fe" (Poem to Santa Fe) and "Al Enviudar Mi Madre" (Upon My Mother Becoming a Widow).

The first of these poems is dedicated to the city of Chacón's birth. The poem casts the city as a symbol for all *Nuevomexicanos.* In the opening strophe Chacón paints an image of the New Mexican capital as a desert garden and oasis that rejuvenates the spirit of all *Neo-Mexicanos*:

Suelo bendito de la antigua villa, Histórico verjel donde las flores Abren gustosas ante el sol que brilla	[Holy Earth of the ancient city History-filled garden where flowers gladly open to the bright sun

Sus broches de perfumes y colores;	as swatches of fragrance and color.
Allá donde florecen de tu arcilla	From earthen pots
Frutas y mieses, entre mil amores,	grains and fruit bud amid great love
Bajo tu azul repleto de fragancia	There under your blue aroma-filled sky
Se ha mecido la cuna de mi infancia.	The bed of my infancy has been cradled.]
	(ibid, 25)

Personal tragedy also shapes the subject matter of several of Chacón's poems. The death of his father, Urbano Chacón, when Felipe Maximiliano was a boy of thirteen, left a deep and enduring psychological mark that may have pushed Felipe Maximiliano toward poetic reflection and introspection. As Felipe turned inward he acquired a reputation among those who knew him as a brooding thinker. In "Al Enviudar Mi Madre" Chacón senses his mother's pain upon the loss of her spouse.

The poems of "Cantos de Hogar" are dedicated to family members, loved ones, and close friends. Included here are poems written for Chacón's children: Herminia, Felipe, Josefina, Elvira, Buenaventura, and Melba. The section closes with Spanish translations of works by the North American and English poets Longfellow, Dryden, Byron, and others.

Felipe Maximiliano's short fiction speaks more directly to the ordinary experience of life in the Southwest. "Un baile de caretas," for example, is set in "a medium size town in the state of Colorado,"—in all likelihood the town is Trinidad. It is the tale of how a certain Pancho Morales is duped by the narrator of the story—Chacón's alter ego—into believing that a masked stranger at a *fandango* is a beautiful and alluring woman named Carmen Hinojosa. Morales, who fancies himself a lady's man and whose pompous mannerisms irk his acquaintances, is easily fooled. Pancho is beside himself upon hearing the prospect of a new romantic conquest. As the evening progresses Morales invites the stranger to dance and does not leave her side for hours. The pretense is brought to an end when Pancho Morales escorts the woman home. Anxious to know the identity of his alluring companion he asks her to remove the mask, only to find that the impostor is a male friend named José Olivas. Olivas, the narrator and his friends, we are told, have all been in on the prank. The story ends with Pancho Morales, wounded in his ego and pride, making a hasty departure on the next train out of town. The story, along with "Don Julio Berlanga" that follows it, is meant to be humorous and light hearted, and takes its inspiration from local anecdotage that mocks the idea of male prowess common in stereotypical narratives of the "Latin Lover" ilk.

"Don Julio Berlanga" centers on the tragicomic situation of a *Nuevomexicano borreguero,* or sheep herder, whom the narrator has met at the train station in Las Vegas, New Mexico. The sheep herder, Julio Berlanga, relates the experience he had on an earlier visit to Las Vegas, which he tells the narrator he will never forget. Don Julio recounts that after a sojourn herding the flocks of Anglo ranchers in the grasslands of Wyoming he had accumulated enough savings to allow himself to a few days of leisure in Las Vegas.

The day of his arrival he treats himself to a bath and shave, and buys new clothes. That evening he makes his way across town and ends up at a community *fandango*. At the dance he meets a beautiful woman who recently has been abandoned by her husband. Don Julio leads the woman on, giving her every indication of being a generous gentlemen of means. He convinces the young woman to leave behind the life she knows and return with him to Wyoming. In Wyoming, Don Julio provides the woman with a rented house, food, and furniture before trudging off to the barren expanses to continue his work as sheep herder. Six weeks later, Don Julio, who has agreed to marry the woman, returns only to discover that the woman has left him for an "Americano." Adding misery to insult, Don Julio learns that she has sold off all his furniture and taken everything of value with her, leaving a cuckolded Don Julio to stew in the realization of his own folly.

"Don Julio Berlanga" is informed by the very common experience of a generation of *Nuevomexicano* villagers drawn to employment outside New Mexico at the turn-of-the-century. The story is taken directly from a cycle of anecdotage known in northern New Mexico as *cuentos de la borrega* (tales of sheep herding). These personal narrations often abound with references to illicit love affairs or the transgression of social mores within *Nuevomexicano* village society. Chacón is careful to employ the Spanish spoken in northern New Mexico to add realism to his narrative.

Felipe Maximiliano's most ambitious prose narrative is the novelette "Eustacio y Carlota." The story takes unexpected turns the result of accidents, coincidence, mistaken identity, and other contrivances commonplace in romantic literature. It is clear that Chacón adapted the story from newspaper accounts of the day. On more than one occasion the narrator comments that the travails of his protagonists Eustacio and Carlota were widely publicized and much commented on in many parts of the county.

The popular press was not above running stories that toyed with strange and seemingly unreal events. *La Estrella* of Las Cruces ran one such story in April 1924 with the headline "Cuando iban a casarse supieron que eran hermanos [When They Were To Wed They Found Out They Were Brother and Sister]." The article reports the case of James and Josephine Buckly of Boston, who discovered that they were brother and sister just as they were to be married. In the real-life situation, a parish priest researches church and baptismal records, because neither James nor Josephine had any knowledge of the circumstances of their birth. The priest finds that they were twins placed in an orphanage at birth eighteen years earlier. Separated at age three, the pair was reunited later in life unaware of their true identity. The twist of fate ends simply. James and Josephine do not marry, but simply expressed their good fortune at reestablishing their sibling relationship.[13]

Chacón distends the basic elements of the newspaper account by adding a turgid and convoluted panoply of chance meetings and fateful circumstances to the story of a brother and sister orphaned and separated as children. Eustacio Quintanilla is taken by the Collins family to Toronto. Carlota, two years younger, is adopted by a wealthy family and grows up in Denver. Nineteen years after they are separated a tragic accident brings them together. Eustacio, who now goes by the name Henry Collins, happens to be among the rescuers who are aiding the victims of a derailed train. Through shear coincidence, Eustacio pulls the foster parents of Amanda Freeman (Carlota) from the rubble of their private coach, "the Anaconda." Henry is rewarded with Amanda's gratitude. Eventually the two marry, unaware that they are brother and sister. On their wedding night, just as they are about to consummate the marriage, Henry notices that the medal Amanda is wearing is similar to one given to Eustacio by his mother as a child. A birthmark above Amanda's elbow confirms Henry's suspicion that Amanda is actually his sister. Confronted with the revelation, Amanda's parents disclose that indeed they are not Amanda's biological parents. This realization triggers a catharsis in the protagonists. The narrator reports: "All cried tears of joy and pain; joy because the two had finally been reunited; pain because of the unexpected failure through which the marriage had come undone, since by divine and natural law they were null and void" (ibid., 179). The story's resolution comes when Amanda marries Orlando Havens, a friend of Henry's who had been Amanda's suitor prior to the train accident. The reader learns in the epilogue that Amanda and Orlando are happily married and live in Los Angeles. The couple, we are told, have two children, ages nine and seven, appropriately named Eustacio and Carlota.

"Eustacio y Carlota" plays heavily on nineteenth-century ideas of destiny and fate dictating individual choice and circumstance.[14] The story, set in cities like Los Angeles, Chicago, Toronto, and New York, evinces little affinity to New Mexican concerns. Chacón attempts to introduce a New Mexican touch in the person of Don Melitón Gonzales, a friend and army buddy of Orlando Havens, who is also a misogynous and surly veteran of the Spanish-American War.

From an allegorical point of view, the story's use of the tropes of orphanhood, abandonment, and the recovery of lost identity, nags at readers who see in such material a tie to the political circumstance of Mexican-Americans in the Southwest. Erlinda Gonzales-Berry inquires, "Despite the melodramatic tone of this romance, might it be possible to read it as a parable for the *rico* class of New Mexico? Loss of natural parents (Mexico); 'legal' adoption by Anglo parents (United States) and subsequent assimilation; discovery and acceptance of true identities" (1989, 196). Yet the connection to *Mexicanos* in the Southwest is overridden by the fact the Eustacio and Carlota are born to a Spanish immigrant family in a New York borough. The circumstances in which they live apparently reflect a downward social slide: "This family lived in middle of a labyrinthine crowd of common people, which characterizes one aspect of life, of the life of the slums of that prodigious orb" (Chacón, 1924, 152). An allegorical reading does emerge, but only when the basic story is transposed to an immigrant experience. It is also possible to draw some incidental parallels between Chacón and the "Latin" origins of his characters, but ultimately the story moves away from the specificity of the *Neo-Mexicano* experience, a consequence of the fact that its themes and motifs are drawn from newspaper headlines that garnered the attention of the nation. Curiously, "Eustacio and Carlota" is among the more intriguing (and among last) exemplars of "una literatura nacional" in the sense that Chacón's narrative embellishment provides evidence of the creativity and originality that tie it to the poetics of that movement. The story's elaboration of the immigrant trope reflects Chacón's desire to engage in a national discourse (that is, the "nation of immigrants" idea) that includes the Southwestern motifs (New Mexico veterans of the Spanish-American War). Like many of Chacón's poems, "Eustacio y Carlota" is a literary offering to cultural pluralism and regional diversity, a tenet clearly in line with the poetics of *Neo-Mexicano* literates.

Chacón's association with *La Bandera Americana* advanced one of the principle objectives of the *Neo-Mexicano* cultural movement—the publishing of entire collections of work by *Nuevomexicano* authors, writers, and poets. It is also telling that Chacón was among the very few writers of his day to find a measure of confirmation for his efforts within his own lifetime. *La Bandera Americana* published a review of Chacón's work in June 1925. The item, penned by the editors of *La Victoria* of Raton, New Mexico, leaves no doubt that *Neo-Mexicanos* shared a collective sense of accomplishment. As in other examples, *La Victoria*'s review tied the progress of a people to progress in literacy and educational attainment, and focused on the idea that such attainment was highly racialized in U.S. society:

> As we have said in past editions, in each *Hispano* home should be found one of the works of Señor Chacón; this should be the case for several important reasons. One [of his works] is an instructive and inspiring work; the other will of itself make us conscious of the intellectual worth of our people, and it will forge among us a new spirit that will have us aspire to a respectable norm that peoples of the white race occupy rather they continue sliding to the level of peonage and slavery toward which our community slowly but surely has moved toward in the past few years.[15]

Felipe Maximiliano Chacón, celebrated in life by his fellow *periodiqueros*, died in relative obscurity on July 10, 1949, in El Paso, Texas.

Revista Ilustrada: Time Capsule of *Neo-Mexicano/a* Representations

Camilo Padilla published his "magazine" *Revista Ilustrada* for twenty-six years. *Revista Ilustrada,* a contemporary of *El Palacio,* the New Mexico Historical Society's publication, was born out of the need *Nuevomexicanos* had for an analogous publication of art and literature in their own language.

Camilo Padilla, a member of the New Mexico Anthropological Society, maintained an association with such leading figures in the cultural life of New Mexico as L. Bradford Prince, ex-governor and founding member of the New Mexico Historical Society. Padilla had made the acquaintance of the historian Colonel Ralph E. Twitchell, and in later years those of Senator Bronson Cutting and publisher Willard Johnson, the editor of *Laughing Horse Magazine. Revista Ilustrada* was launched at the exact time that Anglo-American specialized publications on art, history, archeology, and literature made their first appearance in New Mexico.[16] Camilo Padilla's resolve as a publisher was sharpened by this kind of development. He conceived of *Revista Ilustrada* as a specialized venue specifically tailored to *Nuevomexicano* needs. Padilla described his magazine in its early titles as "Publicación mensual de industria, comercio, literatura y arte" (A monthly publication of industry, business, literature and art). Later, with the magazine's permanent relocation to Santa Fe, Padilla subtitled it "Magazine de hogar," (Home magazine) and described its purpose to be, "Crear interés por el idioma de nuestros padres [To create interest in the language of our forebears]."

With its inaugural issue published in El Paso, *Revista Ilustrada* opened up a heretofore unknown space for representing the creative work of the Mexican-American community in art and literature, and its format was that of a literary magazine. The poems, short stories, and historical articles featured in each issue were enhanced with photographs, wood block prints, and other graphics. The magazine's columns and features promoted leading figures from all walks of life in the Spanish-speaking community of the Southwest. Padilla's collaborations with editors in El Paso and Mexico lent the magazine a dynamic and transnational outlook. Its inclusiveness reduced the tendency to view issues and concerns in New Mexico as unrelated or disconnected to realities in other areas of the Southwest, making patent a cultural affinity to the El Paso border area, to Mexico, and other to parts of the Hispanic world.

Spanish-language newspapers of earlier days, arbitrarily divided as they were between news, announcements, editorial commentary, poems, and other writings, were subject to the immediate concerns of daily life. The poems, essays, or other writings supplied by local editors and writers were filled with an urgency that took precedence over more formal refinements of the texts. *Revista Ilustrada* was removed from the immediate context of social and political happenings, thus it encouraged a process of distillation in the thought and writing of *Nuevomexicanos* that had not been possible earlier.

Fig. 22. Cover page of *La Revista Ilustrada,* Santa Fe, New Mexico, February–March, 1928.

The magazine's mission benefitted from several established voices in the community who were concerned with the fate of *Neo-Mexicano* culture and arts. *Revista Ilustrada* published the works of Benjamín M. Read, Eusebio Chacón, noted Hispano philologist Aurelio M. Espinosa, Luz Elena Ortiz, and Isidoro Armijo. Camilo Padilla offered his commentaries in a column titled, "A traves de mis cristales" (From My Point of View).

In its format and presentation, *Revista Ilustrada* rivaled the work of its contemporaries in the local English-language press. Far from being parochial and provincial—a charge often directed at the Spanish-language press—it displayed the works of Mexican and Latin American authors, and opened its venue to include *Mexicana* writers. Padilla supplied his readership with a list of books available for purchase from "La librería de la Revista" (The Review Book Shop). The list included a number of works of world literature (among them, Hugo, Dumas, Verne, Cervantes), works from the national literature of Latin America (*María* by Jorge Isaacs, *El perriquillo sarniento* by Fernández de Lizardí, and others), and a number of works of a regional and local nature such as "La llorona" (The Weeping Woman), "Cuento: Pedro de Urdimalas" (The Story of Pedro de Urdimalas), and "Chucho el roto" (Chucho, the Bum). Presumably, Padilla authored some of the latter works, which he sold for fifteen to thirty cents a copy.

All in all, its typical sixteen-page issues were carefully edited and executed. At the time of Padilla's death, the *Santa Fe New Mexican* noted of *Revista Ilustrada*, "It was well edited, attractively illustrated and was full of literary gems. It did much to stimulate interest in the Spanish language throughout the Southwest."[17]

After 1925, when *Revista Ilustrada* was permanently moved to Santa Fe, Padilla began to use the magazine as a vehicle to discuss two important causes to which he was particularly committed. The first was the founding of El Centro de Cultura in Santa Fe. Padilla envisioned the creation of a cultural center to unite the more loosely organized *Nuevomexicano* literary and debate societies that already existed in Santa Fe and other New Mexican towns. A cultural center, in Padilla's mind, would serve as a focus and center for cultural, literary, and social events sponsored by its membership. Padilla first announced the opening of El Centro de Cultura in January 1926. In giving notice of its inaugural activities in *Revista Ilustrada* Padilla also expressed his pleasure at realizing his dream of according a public presence and providing a public forum for the expression of *nativo* art and literature. Padilla's descriptions of El Centro de Cultura's first evening program are enthusiastic: "We are overjoyed. Our beautiful dream has been fulfilled. Finally we have established a cultural center in this lovely capital city." In the same issue, Padilla outlined the goals of the *centro*. For Padilla the cultural work of the center was an extension of the work carried on by *Revista Ilustrada:*

> The major goal of the Centro will be to support and create interest in the language of our elders and in Spanish literature; to hold conferences on subjects of general interest, History, etc., and to host musical and literary evenings each month and to create reading rooms where our people will locate periodicals, magazines and books in the Spanish language, and, if possible, a place to keep a library of works in Spanish for the use of its members.[18]

The work of El Centro de Cultura began in earnest within the first month after it opened. The February-March issue of *Revista Ilustrada* for 1926 carried notice of the success of the centro's first "velada literario-musical." The evening's program of musical and literary offerings was held in the auditorium of the Lorreto Academy. Many distinguished Santa Feans were in attendance. The program for the evening included musical performances by the *centro*'s "orquesta," which was followed by readings, recitations, and speeches by noted members of the *centro.* The highlight of the evening was a choral recital of well-loved songs from Mexican and New Mexican folk traditions. "A la ciudad de Santa Fe," a song-poem written by El Paso native Zeferino M. Mares, published some years before in *Revista Ilustrada,* was sung by a choir of young women as a tribute to the city. Padilla ended his description of the evening by expressing his gratitude for the support the event had generated among Santa Feans. As he summed it up, "Por haber puesto en práctica su idea de establecer este Centro [for having put into action the idea to establish a Centro]."

The February-March issue of *Revista Ilustrada* also carried full-page portraits of the *centro*'s officers. Senator Bronson Cutting, a strong supporter of Padilla's efforts, was given appropriate recognition with his photo heading those of the *centro*'s officers: Camilo Padilla, president; R. L. Baca, vice president; the honorable David Chávez, Jr., second vice president; and Isidoro Armijo, treasurer.

Padilla's other interest at this time was his involvement with El Club Político Independiente (The Independent Political Club). El Club began as a third-party movement to organize the *Nuevomexicano* electoral power in the state by creating a voting block among *nativos* that could influence the outcome of elections. The club's purpose was straightforward. Padilla maintained that El Club Político allowed *Nuevomexicanos* to exercise political clout by insuring that their vote would not be taken for granted by the major political parties.

Following its inception *La Bandera Americana* reported that El Club was capable of mustering some thirty thousand votes that it would throw in behind candidates who could be counted on to support a *Nuevomexicano* political agenda. Padilla lent only occasional space in *Revista Ilustrada* to Club Político matters and was careful to not allow politics to change the literary and cultural focus of the magazine. Padilla did take time to report on the club's convention, held in Albuquerque in 1927. In a short item Padilla noted that the work of the convention had been to lay down a constitution and agenda for the party. Also at that convention, Padilla emerged as the club's vice president.

Esteem was often voiced by Padilla's contemporaries, many of whom had worked with equal fervor in the cause of a *Neo-Mexicano* cultural movement. That praise should come from Eusebio Chacón is especially telling. In October 1914, Chacón responded to Padilla's request for the submission of an article on the history of New Mexico to *Revista Ilustrada*. Writing that he was much honored by the solicitation, Chacón ended his note with praise for Padilla's long career in journalism and for the noble, albeit, difficult task Padilla had set for himself in attempting to bring literature and art to the masses of *Nuevomexicanos*. Chacón writes that he found the idea of having a submission published in *Revista* as fanciful a notion as Padilla's dream to bring high-quality literary journalism to the state:

> I have read this letter several times; I have pinched myself to make sure that I am not dreaming. . . . Oh yes, dreaming one of my friend Padilla's rose-colored dreams, my friend who so heroically dedicates himself to elegant and refined journalism in New Mexico, as one would say, sacrificing his life by "tossing marigolds" . . . to a citizenry who does not appreciate as it should such sacrifice.[19]

Eusebio Chacón's words reflect the somber, perhaps unconscious realization, that the ideology of literacy, once held out to be the great social enabler had not transcended structures of unequal educational and social attainment. While at Padilla's death in 1933, praise for his work as editor, educator, civic and political figure continued to be voiced in many quarters, with the *Santa Fe New Mexican* lamenting the loss of "a pioneer educator, a trenchant publicist, pioneer printer, editor and publisher,"[20] such lamentations would prove to be fleeting accolades.

The value of Camilo Padilla's work as a writer, journalist, and publisher is immeasurable, though regrettably even copies of his successful *Revista Ilustrada* are for the most part unknown in libraries and archival repositories across the Southwest. Like the work of other members of his generation, Padilla's efforts passed into obscurity and neglect within a very few years after his death in 1933. Tragically, Eusebio Chacón's words "sacrificing his life by 'tossing marigolds' to a citizenry who does not appreciate as it should such sacrifice"—while meant as a tribute to Camilo Padilla's selfless endeavor in literary journalism, ring prophetic from a contemporary vantage point. Padilla spent a lifetime attempting to ameliorate the neglect in education and the arts that typified life for most *Nuevomexicanos*. But in a few short years after his death, Padilla's name and the record of his achievements dropped from public memory. With Padilla's death the most dynamic period in the *periodiquero* movement drew to a close.

Fig. 23. Sketch of Camilo Padilla by a Local Artist. *Santa Fe New Mexican*, Santa Fe, New Mexico, November 23, 1933.

Padilla was seventy-three years old at the time of his death and despite his ill health had managed to produce, even into his waning years, some of the best work in journalism by any *Nuevomexicano* of his day. Padilla's lifelong friend and fellow *periodiquero,* Benigno Muñiz, the editor of *El Nuevo Mexicano,* paid final tribute to Padilla with the publication of his photo, to which he added a terse and unadorned line: "Las penas y mortificaciones de este mundo han terminado para nuestro buen amigo y compañero, Camilo Padilla . . . Descanse en paz [The sufferings and mortifications of this world have ended for our good friend and companion, Camilo Padilla . . . May he rest in peace]."

Containment Within and Without: Arbitrating the Authority of *Neo-Mexicano* Cultural Representations

By the 1930s the social authority to determine what was suitable and appropriate learning for both native and nonnative peoples in New Mexico (that is, Darnton's "who reads what, in what conditions and at what time and with what effect?") had passed into the hands of a growing community of recently emigrated Anglo-American educators, authors, historians, ethnographers, editors, and a sundry group of cultural do-gooders, who, for all their love of Southwestern subjects, remained tied to the print culture of the eastern United States, that is to say, they operated as agents of a "circuit of communication" that privileged Euro-American observations and ideas over those of regional and ethnic communities. This change in the social validation of learning meant that English would become the prerequisite for the publication of anything resembling "high literacy."

The social authority of learning vested in Anglo-American discursive practice continued to undermine *Neo-Mexicano* self-representations in print while severely prescribing the parameters of representations drawn from the oral tradition. Genaro Padilla points out the effects of the installation of Anglo-American discursivity: "This system of exclusion, I contend, was so powerful that the literary activity of an entire generation of Nuevomexicanos was at once selected, organized, and controlled by a powerful nonnative discursive network that divided their ability to see straight to the heart of their own historical and material condition, or the extent that they did, muted their capacity to speak without fear of nullification or erasure" (Padilla 1993, 207).[21] Most insidious, however, was that such obfuscation caused *Neo-Mexicanos* to doubt the validity of their cultural knowledge and pressed them to recast their cultural episteme to fit a hegemonic construction that Padilla terms "the lore of the Southwest *san* unpleasant political complications" (ibid., 205).

The case of Aurora Lucero-White and of her father Antonio, whose academic careers are linked, illustrates the predicament *Neo-Mexicano* literates faced in the years following statehood. Like her father, Aurora Lucero assumed a position to teach Spanish literature at New Mexico Highlands University but her docent differed from her father's.

During his tenure at Highlands, Antonio Lucero adopted the expected norm of his time and taught the consecrated texts of the Spanish Golden Age literature to his students. In other words, Antonio's mission as an educator was circumscribed by the canonical restraints of his profession. Ironically, such constraints negated the very agency of Antonio's years in cultural journalism. It is doubtful that the elder Lucero ever had occasion to formally lecture his students on work he and so many others of his generation had undertaken to promote *nativo* literary aspirations. In all likelihood, the works of Eusebio Chacón, Benjamin M. Read, Severino Trujillo, or Luz Elena Ortiz were never incorporated into courses he offered his students.[22] One explanation for this is that Lucero may have felt himself too close to the source to be able to critically judge the worth of texts published in the Spanish-language press. Another is that Lucero was awed by the literary edifice—texts of criticism, literary biographies, histories—that were accoutrements to the study of Spanish Golden Age literature and was daunted by this reification of the literary text at a time when the authority of the literary canon was beyond question.

To complicate matters, nineteenth-century views of art and culture held that literature was high art that existed in opposition to folk or oral traditions. Such views precluded the possibility of the kind of analysis that contemporary book historians see as a more accurate assessment of interactions with residually oral cultures. An affect that limits "the place of books in folklore, and of folk motifs in books, [which shows] that influences ran both ways when oral traditions came into contact with printed texts, and that books need to be studied in relation to other media" (Darnton, 1989, 47).

Unable or unwilling to recognize a symbiosis between literature and the ethnopoetics of his region, Antonio, it seems, was hesitant to venture forth the names and works of his fellow *Neo-Mexicano* writers as worthy and deserving of study. Against the accoutrements of high culture, the print ephemera of newspapers, magazines, and periodicals in which *Neo-Mexicano* literates published garnered little attention. Given this pedagogical straight-jacketing, it is not surprising that the episteme of *Neo-Mexicano* literary journalism was not carried over to subsequent generations of *Nuevomexicano* youth via formal study in the university setting.

If Antonio Lucero's search for cultural identification and continuity lead him toward things Ibero-American and to the study of traditions often times removed from his own cultural inheritance, Aurora Lucero-White's odyssey would be different. Her interest was centered squarely in the cultural milieu of her own community and people. Aurora Lucero saw in the study of folklore a genuine expression of the sensibilities and worldview of *Nuevomexicano* communities. The oral poetics and ritual cycle of *Nuevomexicano* pastoral and agrarian traditions provided her with an immediate and direct cultural discourse that was infused with a heightened sense of communal identity reinforced by *nativo* social values. Describing Lucero-White's dedication to the folkways of her community her biographer notes:

> It was during her San Miguel County superintendency that Aurora's interest in folklore really became engrossing. As roads were bad and distances great, she stayed in the field from Monday to Friday, visiting the remote villages. At one, she would happen upon a wedding, at another a baptism or a baile, or at still another, a fiesta. Around Easter there were preparations connected with Los Hermanos; during the cold months, rehearsals were going on for the holiday presentation of Los Pastores, Nuestra Señora de Guadalupe, or Los Matachines. (*Santa Fe Mirror*, 1961, 210)

By the early 1930s Aurora had turned her interest entirely toward recording and compiling materials drawn from the folk culture of northern New Mexico village life. Over the next few years Lucero-White would publish a series of pamphlets on *Nuevomexicano* folklore intended for use in the public schools. The series consisted of monographs such as "Folk Dance Book" (1936), "Los Pastores" (in English and Spanish, 1940), and other items that later became the basis of Lucero's two books of folklore. Aurora Lucero-White's countless hours of field work in towns throughout New Mexico resulted in the publication of *The Folklore of New Mexico* (Seton Village Press, 1941) and *Literary Folklore of the Hispanic Southwest* (Seton Village Press 1948). In 1962, she published an adaptation of the folk tale "Bertoldo." The tale, which was still being told in many rural communities, was recast in Lucero-White's voice and was issued by Vintage Press with the title *Juan Bobo*.

Fetishing Folkness

While it would be unfair to question Aurora Lucero's sincerity in taking up the study of folk life in support of cultural preservation, Genaro Padilla has shown us how even such work was too a kind of cultural dismembering. As Padilla puts it, "Should a *Nuevomexicana* wish to write during the first half of the twentieth century, she would be coerced (perhaps not verbally or otherwise directly coerced) into composing a text—ethnographic, fictive or autobiographical—determined by the overwhelmingly nonnative discursive terrain that tightly controlled the gird of articulation" (1993, 203). At the time that Aurora Lucero-White and others were recording and transcribing the oral traditions and celebrations in village communities across New Mexico, only a handful of New Mexico's *periodiqueros* were still active and the number of Spanish-language newspapers in publication dwindled. The accomplishments of Eusebio Chacón, José Escobar, and Camilo Padilla, like those of Antonio Lucero, began to recede from public consciousness. Public education in New Mexico accelerated the displacement of Spanish as a public language, precluding its use as a language of instruction in the schools. While Spanish continued to be the mother tongue for most *Nuevomexicanos* in the generations prior to World War II, it nonetheless had been effectively decentered from the public domains it had once occupied and was reduced to the sphere of the home or those of intimate social and religious gatherings.

As native and nonnative ethnographers turned their sight and attention to village celebrations, rituals, and reenactments, that is, to those areas of social life in New Mexico where the use of Spanish was considered most pristine and unadulterated, they unwittingly made the study of folklore and folk life synonymous with study of the *Nuevomexicano* past. Aurora Lucero-White was by no means alone in work that Genaro Padilla labels a "mass romanticizing project" (1993, 203). Aurora Lucero-White, Cleofas Jaramillo, Juan Rael, and Arturo L. Campa joined in the trend to record the quaint and colorful aspects of a vanishing culture, a trend that reached a fevered pitch in anticipation of New Mexico's Coronado Cuatro Centennial celebration of 1940.

The noted folklorist Arturo León Campa was busy compiling ballad compositions in New Mexican villages, and through this work met Severino Trujillo, by this time a man in his seventies. Campa's interest in Trujillo was as a village bard in the *trovador* tradition. Campa's book *Spanish Folk Poetry in New Mexico* (1946) is enriched by Trujillo's poetic compositions styled in the traditional poetics of the region. Campa failed to query, or if he did ask, he failed to record as significant Trujillo's life as a seminarian in France or his participation in the newspaper movement of the 1890s. To Campa, Trujillo was just one more informant whose recitation of *décimas* and *memorias* served to reconfirm the primacy of orality enclaved in a people he deemed the possessor of a pure folk culture. Isidoro Armijo, another of Campa's informants suffered the same fate. Neither his outlandish dress nor his public recognition managed to get a rise out of Campa in this regard. The *décimas* recited by the "man who wished to annex Texas" are noted in Campa's compilation with the name Isidoro Armijo and his place of residence: Santa Fe.

In Campa's view the poet-singer who had memorized his repertoire was a notch above the poet-scribe who "with a less retentive memory wrote them [songs] down in order not to forget them" (ibid., 20). This did not keep Campa from lifting the "poetic gems" from Trujillo's large repertoire of *décimas, corridos, inditas,* and other popular forms, which he kept in several handwritten notebooks. Like other folklorists of the day Campa was tragically incapable of viewing Trujillo as a social subject.

The degree to which a decontextualized interpretation of the oral culture set in motion a selective (highly idealized) recuperation of the New Mexican past operates, for example, in Campa's disparagement of the content of the remaining Spanish-language newspapers of his day: "The *décima* as it appears today in the Spanish newspapers in New Mexico is nothing but a mold in which to cast political diatribes. For real folkness we must go back to the traditional *décimas* composed by the troubadours of a generation past" (Campa 1946, 129).

Increasingly by the 1930s, if *Neo-Mexicanos* and *Neo-Mexicanas* wished to remain a part of the public discourse that expanded around them, they were obliged to write in English, and within a modality of expression that precluded references to a social history of conquest and subordination. *Nuevomexicano/a* writers of the period almost without exception opted to present their cultural practices in a manner innocuous and inoffensive to outsiders. To accomplish this it became necessary to operate within the fiction that print culture had never contaminated the episteme of the folk, and that *Neo-Mexicano* native practices offered unadulterated exemplars of what Padilla calls, "a harmonious and ahistoric plane of edenic cultural experience" (ibid., 214). But the truth of the *Neo-Mexicano* sociohistorical situation, as the existence of print culture demonstrates, is far more nuanced and complex, such that it follows the universal dynamic observable whenever print and orality overlap in any society. Walter Ong's statement that there is "hardly an oral or predominantly oral culture left in the world today" (Ong 1982, 15), already applied to the Southwest a hundred years ago. Had native and nonnative ethnographers in the 1930s managed to avoid the " 'presumption' that elites and lower orders automatically think differently and express themselves in different modes" (Scott, 1983, 279), and had they bothered to read the pages of Spanish-language newspapers, they would have found that alongside the texts authored by *Neo-Mexicanos* and *Neo-Mexicanas* was much of the oral epistemology of *corridos, décimas, crónicas,* and other oral forms, and what is significant about this is not that such material was neatly transcribed in print, but that it had been reintroduced into a subsequent generation of readers, the very dynamic that established the central role of print in extending *nativo* cultural practices well into the twentieth century.

But questions of literacy and reading are always tied to sociological developments. So too the fetishizing of "folkness" that began in the 1930s also served political and ideological ends. For this vision of New Mexico as an enclave of folk culture was also a way to erase the greater part of *Neo-Mexicano* social and historical agency. Such an approach made it much easier to ignore the sociomaterial conditions of a people held in poverty and provided a reason for students of the culture to fret over the authenticity of courtly ballads and folksy *dichos,* when to do otherwise might authorize the work of say someone like, Luz Elena Ortiz. Ortiz's submission to *Revista Ilustrada* is quoted at length below, if only to indicate that in her scathing critique, the romance of the Southwest crumbles faster than an unplastered adobe:

> With so many fine newspapers of large circulation; with so many writers of Spanish with clear talent and able pen who could present in a clear manner the regrettable situation of the poor who hold on to a few acres of land. Now, with the crisis in which New Mexico is found; as never before, unity and harmony is desirable among the editors. Dispossessed of their lands and homes what can they do? Obligated to pave the roads, even the public roads are [destined] for the transit of others, since they never use them, unless it is the poorest among them that go by on a dispirited donkey loaded down with wood. The motorist and the foreign tourist expect the roads to be financed for him. Immigrate to other places?
>
> Why and where? Allow the foreigner to acquire by unjust means lands which have been their ancestors for over two hundred years, lands upon which, with swords in hand, they opened paths through woodlands, forests and among uncivilized peoples.
>
> Dear editors, your work should not be about beginning our defense, but about finding a way to halt the pen once it has begun to write. The cause you are dedicated to is great, sacred and magnificent. Go live among them [the poor] in the small villages as I have done. Interact with the people of humble origin, as they are referred to in this world. Speak to the "ignorant," as they are categorized by the educated from the East. Act as their guide and teach their children. [23]

As Sarah Deutsch suggests, it is the sanitized version of the Southwest that continues to distract us even into the present: "Few historians have written of the Spanish Americans of northern New Mexico, and fewer about Colorado, but since at least the 1930s sociologists and anthropologists from eastern universities, as well as from the Southwest, have studied them as the 'peasant' within our borders. Their reflections, relatively unchallenged, have gained a remarkably tenacious hold on public opinion, for they loaned their authority to older stereotypes echoing those that dominators held about subordinates elsewhere" (Deutsch 1987, 5). Here then is another element that has blocked our view of a *nativo* past in the Southwest and diverted our scholarly attention from unraveling the sociocultural significance of *Neo-Mexicano* cultural representations in print.

"Fighting the Good Fight": La Prensa Asociada in Post-Statehood New Mexico

La Prensa Asociada brought together a diverse cadre of journalists, editors, poets, and writers who were united by a common language and culture, and whose literary agency was keyed to the social, educational, and cultural progress of the Spanish-speaking residents of the Southwest. *Los periodiqueros,* many of whom had entered journalism with the surge of Spanish-language publication in the 1890s, continued to publish well beyond statehood. The long standing associations and years of shared commitment to the betterment of their community and society created strong and lasting bonds of fraternalism and camaraderie among *periodiqueros* across the Southwest. The politics of the statehood movement, however, would represent a far more serious challenge to cultural unity than had the ethnic animosities and political cleavages of the territorial period.

After statehood La Prensa Asociada began to experience waning membership, reorganization, inactivity, disunity, and dissolution of purpose. All, however, was not lost. Newspaper historian Porter Stratton affirms that new efforts to revive La Prensa Asociada surfaced on the eve of statehood: "Such efforts were renewed in 1911, and an association was formed at Albuquerque. Nestor Montoya of *La Bandera Americana* of Albuquerque was elected president, and Elfego Baca of the Albuquerque *Opinion Pública* became treasurer" (Stratton 1967, 66). The reorganization of La Prensa Asociada laid the foundation for the establishment of the present-day press organization in New Mexico: "In 1912 this association in cooperation with eastern New Mexico weekly editors organized a newsmen's organization which later became the present New Mexico Press Association" (ibid., 66). Conversely, the ideological restraint implicit in the organization's realignment signaled a departure from La Prensa Asociada's original mission to bring to an end "the repeated injuries that are commonly committed against [the Spanish-speaking community]." Members where split along ideological and political lines that pitted cultural guardians against assimilationists.

A conciliatory gesture to include eastern New Mexico [Anglo] weeklies in the organization was lead by Nestor Montoya of Old Albuquerque. Montoya's paper, *La Bandera Americana,* took a more accommodationist policy with regard to ethnicity, and the absorption of *Nuevomexicanos* into what one editor labeled "el gran mole que es la ciudadanía de los Estados Unidos americanos," or the U.S. melting pot.

A salutation in the first issue of *La Bandera Americana* left no doubt that Montoya espoused the progressive absorption and assimilation of *Neo-Mexicanos* into the body politic of the United States, an idea echoed in the emblematic patriotism of the paper's name. *La Bandera Americana* promised to continue to advocate for the education of greater numbers of New Mexicans, "to bolster as much as possible, as our feeble efforts permit, the education of the masses of the people,"[24] but in saying so Montoya also placed the onus of responsibility for progress on the community itself, interjecting, "to prepare our future citizens to firmly take in hand the reins and sovereignty of a state within the American Union and to discharge and enjoy our privileges as citizens of this great Republic."[25]

Montoya's stand signaled a change from the generally accepted view espoused by La Prensa Asociada regarding the maintenance of the Spanish language and the manner in which *Nuevomexicano* culture might be situated within plural New Mexico in the decisive years after statehood. While earlier journalists and writers never discounted the importance of learning and using English, they nevertheless held to the view that Spanish should have an equal place in the institutions of society and, particularly, in public education. In Montoya's mind, the language issue had become "un asunto delicado [a delicate matter]" because "this item merits very careful attention in view of our American citizenship."[26] *La Bandera Americana* encouraged the use of English in the public schools, and among all classes of *Nuevomexicanos*, suggesting to its largely monolingual Spanish readership, "We believe that there is not a single man in the Territory that will oppose our assertion to generalize that language."[27] Likewise, Montoya's pledge to advocate for statehood and seek greater educational advantages for *Nuevomexicanos* appears more tempered than assertions voiced by La Prensa Asociada in the past. In prior decades, editors had seen the establishment of a vigorous press as the means to "educate the populace," but Montoya, noting *La Bandera Americana*'s own "feeble efforts," seemed to substantiate the idea that the press alone could not, in and of itself, enlighten, educate, and inform the society at large. In Montoya's mind, political pragmatism and economic development were the keys to *Nuevomexicano* opportunity and prosperity in the coming years of the new century. Evoking a kind of economic determinism, Montoya downplayed ethnic and cultural identification, arguing instead for the development of New Mexico's natural resources, "since it is accepted that our riches in the three areas mentioned are immeasurable and that all that is required to exploit them is the investment of capital which will change the face and future of our land and make its inhabitants happy."[28]

By the decade of the 1920s, *Nuevomexicano* editors registered pessimism concerning the future of the Spanish-language press in New Mexico and how it might assist in maintaining the sociocultural standing of the community in whose name it spoke. In early 1928, José Montaner, editor of *La Revista de Taos,* acted to counter the apathy and discord among *Nuevomexicano* publishers. Montaner called for a meeting of editors. Representatives from ten of the thirteen remaining Spanish-language newspapers in the state attended an organizational meeting held on February 23, 1928, in Santa Fe. Reorganized as La Asociación de la Prensa Hispana en Nuevo México (the Hispano Press Association) the group elected Montaner as the group's interim president and A. J. Martínez of Las Vegas as interim secretary.[29]

Given the tenor of the late twenties, and accumulated frustration at improving the prospects for Spanish-language journalism in the post-statehood period, it is no wonder that the remaining Spanish-language editors in New Mexico continued to express a growing uneasiness and pessimism about the future. In June 1928, Camilo Padilla was elected the new president of La Asociación de la Prensa Hispana. Assuming office, he noted several pernicious trends announcing the decline of Spanish-language journalism, but nonetheless, offered a spirited appeal to bilingualism in the state:

> I have seen with sadness that many Hispanos, for reasons that I don't want to investigate but which are known to all, lean toward newspapers written in English, surely because they are "the latest," as is commonly said or because they have not realized the need to maintain the language of our parents, our customs and traditions, which because these are so much [a part of] who we are, we should never forget them.[30]

Becoming editor of *La Bandera Americana,* Felipe Maximiliano Chacón warned that the Spanish-language press needed to assert its worth or it would disappear. Chacón pointed to *El Independiente* of Las Vegas as an example of the press in decline. Spanish-language newspapers, he cautioned, had become exceedingly reliant on political affiliations for support and advertisement. In Chacón's view the lofty ideals of nonalignment once espoused by the paper's founder, Enrique H. Salazar, were compromised. According to Chacón, *El Independiente*'s columns had become filled with political diatribe: "It would seem that Hispano journalism is a means to exploit fools, well, they are satisfied to use the columns of the paper to play local politics and, regrettably, this is out of line and out of time."[31]

In assessing the legacy of a *Neo-Mexicano* culture of print and the cultural movement *Neo-Mexicano* newspapers fostered, it is important to keep in mind the observations of book historian Cathy Davidson: "The ideology of an empowering 'cultural literacy' works only insofar as the possessors of that advanced literacy can negotiate a society's power structures." Davidson adds, "For most nonwhite citizens in the past century, that transaction was simply not allowed, and the rhetoric of literacy ultimately failed to bring the social and material rewards that the rhetoric promised" (1989, 13).

In the New Mexican case several factors had begun to limit the success of Spanish-language publication in post-statehood New Mexico. Anglo Americans reached numerical parity just as New Mexico entered the Union as a state. Their presence in business, politics, and education became more determinant than at any previous time. Towns such as Las Vegas and Santa Fe, which had large Spanish-speaking populations, and which had enjoyed the support of prosperous *Neo-Mexicano* businesses, began to experience large population shifts. Advertisement in Spanish-language newspapers shrank in an era in which *Nuevomexicano* business ventures closed their doors at an alarming rate and *Nuevomexicano* laborers out-migrated to other states in search of employment. The Public Education Law of 1890 had made English the language of instruction in the public schools. In time, the legislative privileging of Anglo social mores would effect a language shift that reversed whatever gains Spanish-language journalism had made in its attempt to retain Spanish at the center of public life in New Mexico. The Spanish-language press began to show the effects of the hegemonic constriction of *Nuevomexicano* language and culture by Anglo-dominated social institutions. Felipe M. Chacón, growing uneasy at seeing Spanish-language publication in disarray and decline, concluded that *Nuevomexicanos* were losing ownership and agency of the newspapers they had founded. Citing the example of *La Voz del Pueblo*, Chacón observed caustically, "It is in the hands of a Texan who is barely able to write in the language of the nation [English], and who, not even out of courtesy, speaks, however mangled, the language of the Hispano, and yet he publishes a few columns in Spanish for the 'Mexicans' who are unfortunate enough to receive his rag."[32]

Statehood for New Mexico led to a hardening of political borders, which in turn disrupted *periodiquero* cultural ties to southern Colorado, southern Arizona, and West Texas. A reorganized Prensa Asociada now found itself divested of the bold and decisive regional agenda it once proclaimed would "benefit the Latin race more than any other, this is, the association of the Spanish press in New Mexico, Arizona, California, Texas, and part of Mexico."[33] By 1930 the association had been reduced to a dwindling membership at the statewide level.

Spanish-language newspapers continued to be published in several communities in New Mexico into the forties and fifties, but the early trends adversely affecting such publication that had begun in the late 1920s became more pronounced and evident after World War II. By the late 1950s, *El Nuevo Mexicano* was the only Spanish-language newspaper established in the 1890s that remained in publication. After sixty-seven years of continuous publication, *El Nuevo Mexicano* ceased publication on April 30, 1958. Pedro R. Ortega, the paper's last editor, was of the opinion that the amalgamation of Spanish and English had obsolesced *El Nuevo Mexicano*'s raison d'etre:

> Now in 1958 when *Raza* heads of household are in most instances as proficient in English as in Spanish, since the younger generations can only read in English, moves toward majority rule have caused many households to receive the paper in English [in place of Spanish]. For this reason, this spring, *El Nuevo Mexicano* will become the bride of the *Santa Fe New Mexican* and will even take its name.[34]

The discontinuance of *El Nuevo Mexicano* was a signal to many that ethnic depurations in New Mexico, at least at the level of public culture, were complete. The region's social history as it regarded *Nuevomexicanos* could now be commuted to nonthreatening tricultural motifs that bolstered existing political and economic alignments in the state. But issues of historical redress and inequity would not go unvoiced for long. Less than a decade later, a new movement would spring from the distress of *Nuevomexicanos*, who continued to struggle with social, educational, and political disparity in the land of their *antepasados*. By 1965, grassroots Chicano leaders were employing a bilingual activist press to recast in vibrant articulations many of the same issues that had preoccupied earlier generations of *Neo-Mexicanos*, and in doing so, continued to contest the very same forces that encouraged the social and historical erasure of a Mexican-American presence in the Southwest.

Epilogue

Herminia Chacón González

El cielo nos la preste	[May heaven entrust her to us
con alma pura y bella,	with a pure and radiant soul
Estímulo de dicha	(she is) the cause of our ideal,
sin límite, ideal;	unending joy,
Que brillen sus virtudes	May her virtues shine
constantes como estrella,	constant like a star
Que fluyan a raudales	May her good fortunes flow
las venturanzas de ella,	in torrents
Y Dios la guarde ilesa,	And may God keep
—Perlita angelical!	this pearl angel, from all harm!]

—"A Mi Hija, Herminia," *Prosa y poesía,* Felipe Maximiliano Chacón, 1924

In a recent letter Doña Herminia Chacón González, the subject of the poem above, responded to a query about her father, Felipe Maximiliano Chacón, by writing "Right off, I can't give the exact date of my father's death. It is perhaps careless of me but it has been nearly 50 years ago."[1] As one of the last links to the generation of *periodiqueros* discussed in the preceding chapters and as a writer herself, my hope in contacting Señora Chacón González had been to expand on information about Spanish-language journalism, not in 1949, the year of her father's death (later confirmed in family papers), but in the decades prior to the publication of Felipe Maximiliano Chacón's *Prosa y Poesía* in 1924. Her reply, nonetheless puts certain things in perspective concerning the receding public awareness of Spanish-language publication and the ephemeral nature of this type of cultural work.

As I drove to El Paso to meet with Doña Herminia for the first time, I wondered if anything at all might come of the interview: Would she be able to remember events that had transpired nearly three decades or more before her father's death?

Señora Herminia Chacón González greets us at the door of her tidy apartment at the Jewish Housing Federation in El Paso. Assisted by a walker she remains remarkably strong and active. She is *muy gente* [welcoming] and takes time to show us the rooms of her apartment and pauses before her *Sagrado Corazón* [statue of the Sacred Heart of Jesus] and the array of family photos on her bookshelves before asking us to sit down. Whatever reservations I had about Señora Herminia's memory evaporate at the outset of an interview conducted both in English and Spanish and lasting nearly two hours. At ninety-two, Doña Herminia is clear in her thinking: "her virtues," continue to "shine constant like a star." She remains steadfast in her commitment to assist the work of "finally recognizing our old Spanish language newspapers and their editors."[2]

Our interview ranges over a number of topics and individuals. She is able to confirm certain relationships I suspected to have existed among the editors and owners of certain papers. Recalling Felix Martínez's relocation to El Paso, for example, Señora Herminia corroborates his decisive influence on a group of *Nuevomexicano* editors and business people who picked up and moved with Martínez to El Paso at the turn-of-the-century (see chapter 3). Her father, Felipe Maximiliano, was among them: "They came to El Paso because Felix Martínez brought a group of people from New Mexico to establish businesses here."[3] While working at an uncle's store in El Paso, Felipe Maximiliano Chacón met Herminia's mother, Otilia Cristina Domínguez, a native of Rosales, Chihuahua. The couple met at a dance cosponsored by the Mexican, British, German, and American consulates in Ciudad Juárez in 1902 and the two married soon after.

Later in the interview, my wife, who accompanies me, encourages Doña Herminia to speak in detail about Aurora Lucero-White. She recounts having worked with Aurora Lucero-White, Olibama López, and Lorin Brown,[4] in the Press Section of the United States Bureau of Censorship during World War II. Doña Herminia summarizes their contribution to the war effort saying, "We had to report Nazi propaganda and the opinion of Mexican newspapers whether in favor of or against the United States."[5] Of Aurora Lucero-White she remembers, "Well, she was a very independent. She was White then and she had a daughter. They came here, and . . . I don't know how to say this but . . . she was not pretentious and she cared little about what people might say. She did whatever she felt she wanted to do."[6] Aurora Lucero-White didn't remain in El Paso; she resigned her job and returned to Santa Fe before the end of the war, but not before confiding to Herminia, "The war will end and we'll still be here writing out little scraps of paper that don't amount to much."[7]

When the matter of working for her father's paper, *La Bandera Ameri-*

cana in Albuquerque, comes up, Doña Herminia resists the idea of being considered a writer in her own right. I have brought copies of a number of short stories and news items she contributed to the newspaper to share with her, but she says, "Well, I would go to the paper just to help him [her father] so that he wouldn't be left by himself." I ask, "But isn't it true you also wrote?"

"Well," she answers, "From time to time some things occurred to me."[8]

As I am interested in knowing about the public's reaction to the diminishing publication of Spanish-language newspapers in the Southwest, I return on several occasions to the causes of their dissolution. Señora Herminia adds personal insight on what I have labeled in my work "the hegemonic constriction" of the use of Spanish in the public domain. Asked to discuss the closure of Spanish-language papers, Doña Herminia suggests it came about "Because people, the New Mexicans, have forgotten Spanish, they've forgotten the language and *we were encouraged to forget it*" (emphasis added).

When I ask if the language-shift made it difficult for her father to keep publishing, she remarks, "I don't think he noticed. Nobody did at the time. He thought it was a pity afterwards. Because I think it was by 1930 that people were speaking English and I remember they used to tell us they weren't going to teach their children Spanish." Indeed, by 1954, the year Fabiola Cabeza de Baca published *We Fed Them Cactus*, the repression of Spanish and *Nuevomexicano* culture was so generalized that it had been internalized, especially by urban residents. "At that time," Doña Herminia recalls, "people were beginning to use more English than Spanish. I remember that some of the people in Albuquerque, they'd tell me, they'd brag about it. They'd say, 'My children don't speak Spanish.' They thought that it was below them to speak Spanish when we never did feel that way."[9]

Doña Herminia's memories of the social shift in Spanish-language use speak to the xenophobic requirements for linguistic conformity that operated in the Southwest. Linguistic intimidation ("we were encouraged to forget it [Spanish]") proved corrosive and resulted in a "discouragement of Spanish" that regrettably surfaced in certain *Nuevomexicano* families who in the 1940s prided themselves on the fact that their children (if not themselves) had negotiated the new social expectations. The cultural disclaimer, "My children don't speak Spanish," heard all too often during these years was loaded with self-effacement. Such sycophancy certainly held no promise for nurturing the readership of Spanish-language newspapers. Quite opposite acts tended to follow such thinking as old newspapers and other documents penned in Spanish were, literally, burned on pyres (a scene I saw repeated in various households in my own childhood) ushering out "old ways" and heralding in the "new [or was it Anglo] ways."

Pedro Ribera-Ortega

> Next week, "the blessed race" in their ancestral homes on both sides of the Rio Grande and the Pecos River—and in their new residences spread across the states of Colorado, Wyoming, Montana, and California—will begin to read the news of the world, personals about their families and friends, and of the Spanish-speaking community in all of New Mexico, in the *Sunday New Mexican.* Even though it is published in English.
>
> —Pedro Ribera-Ortega, April 10, 1958, Santa Fe, New Mexico

In the recollections of Pedro Ribera-Ortega, the last editor to issue *El Nuevo Mexicano,* subtle questions regarding the impact of the "language-shift" on Spanish-language publication breech and give way to a particularly acerbic mixture of bigotry, "bottom-line" demands, and a disinterest in the needs of Spanish-speaking of the region. These factors, Ribera-Ortega recalls, were invoked to "darle muerte prematura," (deliver the death blow) (Ribera-Ortega, 1992) to the last Spanish newspaper operating in New Mexico with roots in the nineteenth century.

In December 1956, with the death of *El Nuevo Mexicano's* editor, Juan Medina, Pedro Ribera-Ortega stepped-in to "pinch hit" as an interim editor of *El Nuevo Mexicano.* Finding the paper in disarray he went to work getting *El Nuevo Mexicano* on track. To his surprise he would not leave the paper until forced to do so some two and a half years later.

In April 1958, Don Pedro received a memo from the owner and operator of the Santa Fe New Mexican Publishing Company, the parent company of *El Nuevo Mexicano.* In simple, terse, and unflattering terms the memo ordered the discontinuance of *El Nuevo Mexicano.* Citing diminishing circulation, the directive was also laced with a good dose of anti-New Mexican feeling that, it seems, was not tempered in any appreciable way by Santa Fe's claim to the public relations image of being "a tricultural Mecca." Dispensing with such formalities, the owner of the *Santa Fe New Mexican,* recalls *Don* Pedro, went to the heart of the matter, saying closure was required "because you Mexicans have finally learned English, therefore you don't need the Spanish newspaper."[10]

Don Pedro's last official act as editor was to mediate between management and several thousand subscribers in California, New Mexico, Texas, Arizona, Utah, Nevada, and Wyoming. In a last editorial, he glossed over his boss's incivility, saying only that *El Nuevo Mexicano* would cease publication "por la amalgación del idioma inglés [because of the amalgamation of English]"[11] in the region, then he channeled whatever indignation he felt personally into a call to subscribers to write and demand a return of the unused price of their subscriptions rather than take management's offer to continue on with the English *Sunday New Mexican.* For Don Pedro this was an expression of resistance and discontent with a structure of power that had harbored ill will toward the manifestation of his culture in print.

Sentimiento

I include the testimony of Herminia Chacón González and Pedro Ribera-Ortega in closing because each represents a vital link to the world of editors and writers that created and sustained *Neo-Mexicano* print culture in the Southwest. In their recollections Doña Herminia and Don Pedro voice the agency of journalists long silenced by accident, neglect, and suppression. In many ways, the interviews I conducted with them as my book neared completion served to reconfirm the need for the recovery of the multiple aspects of this cultural legacy in print.

In the moments before completing our interview in El Paso Señora Herminia asked, "Do you have my father's book?" Before I can answer, she continued, "Well you can have that copy, I still have some left."[12] She is still concerned with disseminating the work of *Neo-Mexicano* print culture. Today we would say she is working at the task of cultural representation. At my last meeting with Pedro Ribera-Ortega in Santa Fe, he handed me a file folder filled with correspondence, memos, news clippings, and other items related to his work at *El Nuevo Mexicano*. These documents represent the only records known to exist of day-to-day management of the paper in its final years of publication. The file contains poems, announcements, editorials, and historical documents offered by subscribers for publication in *El Nuevo Mexicano*, items which never saw the light of day in print. "Look these over," Don Pedro says. Though I am overjoyed at having acquired the documents and an original copy of Chacón's *Prosa y Poesía*, I return to the realization that if I am to keep faith with the work of recovering the poetics of print in *Neo-Mexicano* communities—"so all is not lost,"—I shall be pouring over newly uncovered materials for a good time to come.

In 1992 the *Santa Fe New Mexican* assented to publish one page a week in Spanish. Carmela Padilla, the reporter assigned to the page, returned to the name "El Nuevo Mexicano." Asked to contribute an article for the first installment, Pedro Ribera-Ortega exclaimed, "Que viva nuestra cultura por medio de nuestro idioma impreso! [Long may our culture live by way of our language in print!]." In light of such developments, I shall forgo the matter of final conclusions for the moment.

Notes

Introduction

1. The quote is taken from a series of interviews with Mr. Miguel Casías of San Juan, New Mexico, recorded in the summer of 1987 and 1988. Mr. Casías described himself as a poet-troubadour in the *Nuevomexicano* tradition and punctuated his responses to questions on *Nuevomexicano* culture of his youth with recitations of poems, *corridos*, and the like. Mr. Casías was eighty-two years old at the time of the interviews. The original quote reads, "Yo estas historias las agarraba porque en esos tiempos mi padre agarraba, agarraba él . . . periódicos, ve. Agarraba *El Faro*, agarraba de Juárez, agarraba de aquí . . . *El Nuevo Mexicano*. Cada vez que salía una historia la cortaba y la guardaba, la cortaba y la guardaba. . . . Y mi mente la guardaba y parece que no se me olvidan, ¿quién sabe?"

Chapter 1

1. I have provided my own translations to English of original documents throughout, except in cases where previous published translations exist and where items are noted as such. In regard to the original texts in Spanish that accompany notes, it is important to keep in mind that variations in punctuation, accentuation, and orthography routinely appear in texts taken from Spanish-language newspapers and other nineteenth sources. Most often such discrepancies are the result of the informality of the medium and the haste with which these materials were prepared for publication. Often the original citations reflect both the orthographic conventions for the Spanish of the period and variability in the use of accents and a regional lexicon. In citing these materials, I have elected to quote them in their original form, and to note only those instances where the usage, grammatical form, or lexicon obstruct the meaning or intent of the writer.

2. Taken from a facsimile of the title page of *Cuaderno de Cuentas* in Henry Wagner's "New Mexico Spanish Press," (1937).

3. "La provincia no cuenta, ni ha podido contar hasta ahora, lo que otras de España sobre establecimientos públicos; tan atrasada se halla en este ramo, que aun ignora sus nombres. El de escuelas de primeras letras está reducido á los que tienen facultades

para contribuir al maestro, pueden enseñar á sus hijos; en la misma capital no se ha podido dotar un maestro para hacer comun la enseñanza.

Por supuesto que tampoco hay colegio alguno de estudios: de aquí proviene el desconsuelo que manifiestan muchas personas que advierten la buena disposición de los hijos de la provincia para las ciencias, y en mas de docientos años de la conquista no cuenta uno colocado en ninguna carrera literaria, ni aun de sacerdote; cosa tan comun en las demás provincias de América." (*Noticias históricas* 1849, 61)

4. "*Libertad de Imprenta.* La libertad de imprenta es el vehículo que comunica las luces á todas las clases de la sociedad, particularmente a la infima del pueblo. Este don precioso que nos ha regalado la sabiduria de los grandes legisladores de la república, es el más firme apoyo de las instituciones liberales, porque estas se conservan mas que por la fuerza física, por la moral: obra de la ilustracion de los ciudadanos; mas este bien inestimable está como muerto para el territorio, pues no se conoce una imprenta, ni circulan papeles que proporcionan aquel espíritu público, única arma de la libertad republicana.

La escasez de libros, particularmente de aquellos elementales que tanto contribuyen para generalizar las ideas, es otro obstáculo que se opone á la ilustracion, y no lo es menos la enorme distancia á que se encuentra este lugar, y la ninguna comunicacion que tiene con la interior de la república." (*Noticias históricas* 1849, 62)

5. "Si bien sospechamos que existieron periódicos en español publicados en la Alta California antes de 1848, desafortunadamente no tenemos noticias acerca de ello. . . . Sabemos que el primer documento que se imprimió, en 1834, fue el *Reglamiento provincial para el gobierno de [. . .] la Alta California*, y el primer libro, en 1835, el *Manifiesto a la República Mejicana*, del General José Figueroa. Puede ser que algún periódico haya salido de las prensas de Agustín Zamorano en Monterrey donde se publicó el *Manifesto* de Figueroa." (Leal, unpublished manuscript)

6. "Porque ya es tiempo de exigir del gobierno pleno cumplimento de sus promesas de incorporanos a la hermandad de Estados en la Union Federal y de admitirnos al gozo de verdaderos ciudadanos de los Estados Unidos, segun estipulado en el tratado de Guadalupe Hidalgo, el cual fué el más grande inducimiento que pudiera habersenos ofrecido para abrigar los derechos de ciudadanos de los Estados Unidos y renunciar aquellos de ciudadanos de la república de México. (J. D. Sena, "Veinte y cuatro razones: Porque los nativos de Nuevo México—o sea los Mexicanos como los llaman—Deben votar por la constitucion y eriguirse en Estado," *El Nuevo Mexicano*, Santa Fe, New Mexico, September 27, 1890)

7. "Desde tiempo he estado observando atentamente y examinando con escrupulosidad las circumstancias que rodean nuestro país, el cual á no dudarlo, está muy atrás de las demás naciones en lo que respecta á la cultura del entendimiento, el desarrollo de los poderes mentales del hombre. De aquí esa aciaga miseria que cual contagiosa gangrena ha ido cundiendo por casi todas las clases de la sociedad." ("Prospectus de la *Estrella de Mora*," from *El Anunciador de Nuevo Méjico* Las Vegas, New Mexico, January 12, 1878)

8. "Pues si tales son los hechos que nuestro país yace en miseria, y que esta miseria se origina y mana directamente y principalmente de la falta de instrucción en la masa del pueblo quién no ve en este caso la necesidad que todos tenemos de un medio de instruccion público, el cual iluminando nuestras ideas y operando eficazmente el desarrollo de nuestro espíritu nos conduzca, en fin, digámoslo así como por la mano á

mayor grado de prosperidad, y nos ponga al nivel de todos los pueblos cultos que existen sobre la superficie de la tierra." (ibid.)

Chapter 2

1. In his informative study of Chicano autobiography, Genaro Padilla calls attention to social transformation registered in Rafaél Chacón's *Memorias,* a personal narrative of life in post-1848 New Mexico. Chacón's memoirs form a finely wrought portrait of a nineteenth-century *Nuevomexicano* traversing the unfamiliar ground upon which the new social and political order of the Southwest was being redefined.

2. For more complete accounts on the military mission of the Texan–Sante Fe Expedition, see Anselmo Arellano's *Las Vegas Grandes on the Gallinas: 1835–1985* (Las Vegas: Telaraña Publications, 1985) and Rodolfo Acuña's *Occupied America: A History of Chicanos* (New York: Harper and Row, 1981).

3. In a letter to a Santa Fe newspaper in 1888, Alarid expresses his gratitude and pleasure at the reception he and his wife were given by his students:

> "Concluida la recepcion de los niños se presentó una comisión de tres niñas y felicitándome me invitaron á pasar á su escuela; ofrecimiento que aceptamos con gusto, yo y mi esposa. En seguida fuí tambien invitado por otra comision de niños en nombre de los habitantes de Galisteo á pasar á la casa de escuela. También en esto ofrecí complacerlos. En la noche fué cuando los niños, cerca de veinte que habían preparado discursos análogas á mi arribo se dirigían á mí y á mi esposa con palabras que nos hacían conocer el amor que ellos y sus padres nos profesaban. Cada uno concluía con estas palabras: 'Querido maestro, lo que deseamos es que se venga con nosotros.' y después pedían al público tres vivas por su maestro y familia."
>
> [At the conclusion of the children's welcome a group of three girls arrived on the scene and congratulating me, they invited me into the school, an invitation my wife and I accepted with pleasure. Next I was invited by another group of children who in the name of the residents of Galisteo also invited me to see the school house. Here again I indulged them. That evening the children, some twenty of them, who had prepared speeches on the occasion of my arrival, presented their talks to my wife and I. Their talks were filled with words that let us know the love they and their parents expressed for us. Each talk ended with these words: 'Dear teacher, what we would like most is for you to come and be with us.' Then, they would ask the assemblage for a round of three *vivas* for their teacher and his family.]
>
> ("Remitido, J. M. H. Alarid," *El Boletín Popular,* Santa Fe, New Mexico, March 22, 1888)

4. "En Wagon Mound, nuestros paisanos hicieron un bailecito en donde las principales familias asistieron, con tanto gusto que hasta un sesenteño como yo le daban ganas de bailar. Lo más agradable de todo fué el día de hoy que afortunadamente hubo misa en el lugar celebrada por el hábil sacerdote el Rev. P. Rivera. Durante la misa mi orquesta tocó solemnes marchas y los cánticos que acompañaba al pueblo devoto." ("Comunicado, Wagon Mound, N. M., Enero 27 de 1895," *El Independiente,* Las Vegas, New Mexico, February 2, 1895)

5. "Despues de misa hubo varios bautismos los que fueron hechos con toda la pompa, entre ellos, el del infante Romualdo, presente que hizo la señora Roibal. Los padrinos fueron nuestro apaciable y joven amigo Don Serapio Romero y la Sra. Juanita B. de Romero.Desde la iglesia una marcha acompañaba al recien nacido, pero como no todo en el mundo es alegría, al llegar a la casa tuvimos noticia de la muerte de nuestro amigo y honesto ciudadano el Hon. Felipe Delgado, que en paz descanse; aquí cesó el regocijo y se convirtió en pesar recordando el pesar de la inconsolable familia." (ibid.)

6. The complete text of the *décima* as it appeared in *El Independiente*, June 29, 1895 is:

Décima
-Ay viene el ferrocarril!
Estos versos el cantaba
¿Quien pudiera presumir
Que ese ferrocarril lo matará?
Una vez que fui a su casa
lleno de satisfacción
Alegre su corazón
De alegrarme daba traza
Y como en el mundo pasa
La alegría y el placer
Al lado de su mujer
Trataba de divertir
Y cantaba con placer
Ay viene el ferrocarril
Todo era huato y placer
Regocijo y alegría
Pasa la noche y el día
En festín sin entender
Que más tarde había de haber
—Un pesar!—Un sentimiento!
—Una desgracia!—Un tormento!
Cuando menos se pensaba
y ponerlos como un cuento
Esos versos el cantaba
Lamento tu triste muerte
Y de ti jamás me olvido
Pues el lazo que está unido
De amistad siempre estará
Y jamás se cambiará
Y me será hasta el morir
Pero en la casualidad
¿quién pudiera presumir?
Adios mi amigo querido
Adios mi amigo leal
Siempre fuiste distinguido
en tu amistad muy formal
Y tu fuiste a descansar

A la mansión celestial
Más. . . . quién pudiera esperar
Tal cosa imaginara
Qué un día triste y fatal
Ese ferrocarril te matara.

(J. M. H. Alarid, Trinidad, Colorado, Junio 19 1895; "Ay viene el ferrocarril," *El Independiente,* Las Vegas, New Mexico, June 29, 1895)

7. "Viva el estado de Nuevo México," *El Independiente,* Las Vegas, New Mexico, January 12, 1895.

8. "El idioma español," in *Los pobladores nuevo mexicanos y su poesía, 1889–1950,* 37.

9. "Se retira de la política activa, y solo se dedicará á conservar la amistad de todos en general, especialmente de aquellos nobles corazones que durante su infortunio no lo han olvidado y le han brindado consuelo y ayuda material, . . . El profesor Alarid vive quietamente con su amable esposa en la aldea de Galisteo, donde estaba de maestro cuando fué atacado por la fatal enfermedad de la vista." ("El Hon. Jesús M. H. Alarid de Galisteo, N. M., se retira de la política activa," *La Bandera Americana,* Albuquerque, New Mexico, March 20, 1913)

10. "El Profesor Alarid fué prominente en su vida en el estado de Nuevo México y en el de Colorado, como educador, orador y filarmónico, fue preceptor en muchas épocas, un orador magnético y un artista en la música." (*La Bandera Americana,* Albuquerque, New Mexico, Friday, January 11, 1918)

11. "Debemos siempre recordar que es una mengua para nuestro pueblo ser goberando por advenidizos y extraños cuando entre nosotros tenemos hombres competentes y buenos para llenar todas las posiciones desde la primera hasta la última." ("Nuevo México para los Neo-Mexicanos," *La Voz del Pueblo,* Las Vegas, New Mexico, March 9, 1889)

12. "Esta institución bajo la dirección de los Hermanos de las Escuelas Cristianas fue establecida en 1859. El curso de estudios comprende los ramos elementales y comerciales en Inglés; Lecciones de francés, español y alemán, fonología y escritura tipográfica. El estudio de química, ensayo de minerales y música instrumental." ("El Colegio de San Miguel," (advertisment) *El Independiente,* Las Vegas, New Mexico, August 18, 1894)

13. Ibid.

14. Eleuterio Baca, personal correspondence, September 26, 1871, St. Louis, Missouri.

15. *Jubilee,* p. 161.

16. "Don Eleuterio Baca Fiel y digno Discípulo de Calderón y Lope de Vega, el primero de los poetas Neo-Mexicanos estuvo en la Cuidad esta semana, de su residencia en el Sapelló." (*La Voz del Pueblo,* Las Vegas, New Mexico, September 9, 1891)

17. "Don Francisco N. Baca (Obituario,)" *El Independiente,* Las Vegas, New Mexico, November 22, 1918.

18. Many of the works issued by the Jesuit College, and which assuredly were used in the education of New Mexicans, are known only through Hubert Howe Bancroft's enticing reference to them in his *History of Arizona and New Mexico* (1889). Referring to the Jesuit College of New Mexico, Bancroft lists a mix of secular and religious material published by its press:

This latter institution has published *Spelling Book for the Use of Public Schools of N. Mex.*, Albuquerque, 1874, 16 mo, 47 p.; *Elementos de Aritmética*, Las Vegas, 1876, 16mo, 146 p.; *Herrainz y Quiroz, Elementos de Gramática Castellana*, Las V., 1877 16mo, 124, p.; and besides these educational works, the following of a religious and general character: *Balmes, La Religión Demostrada*, Alb., 1873, 16mo, 110 p.; *Los protectores de Juventud*, Alb., 1874, 16mo, 151 p.; *Lamy, Constituciones Eclesiásticas para la Diócesis de Sta Fé*, Alb., 1874, 8vo, 37 p.; *Franco y Benajmina, Novela Contemporánea*, Las V., 1877, 12mo, 140 p.; Id., *Los Corazones Populares, Novela*, Las V., 1878, 12mo, 140 p.; Id., *La Pobrecilla de Casamiri, Novela Histórica*, Las V., 1879, 12mo. 293 p.; *Centelas, Diálagos y cartas*, Las V., 1883, 12mo, 156 p.; *Ambert, El Heroísmo en Sotana*, Las V., 1883, 12mo, 128 p.; *Los Jesuitas*, n.p., n.d. 16mo, 51 p.; *Colección de Cánticos Espirituales*, Las V., 1884, 16mo, 198 p.; *Ripalda Catecismo*, Las V., 1884, 16mo, 87 p.; and *Classic English Poetry*, Las V. (college press), 1884, 12mo, 139 p. All with one exception, bear the mark of 'Imprenta del Rio Grande,' from which press is also issued the *Revista Católica.* (1889, 775 n. 11).

19. "El jóven Casimiro se fué al lado del Padre Salpointe á prestar sus servicios para el aseo y quehaceres interiores de la casa, para ayudar como *monacillo* en el sacrificio de la misa y para acompañar al sacerdote cuando saliera á los partidos á cumplir con su ministerio. En compensación de sus servicios tendría con el padre, habitación, ropa, comida y la instruccion que el sacerdote le impartiera." (ibid.,17).

20. "Vemos todas las escuelas de los filósofos, todas las sectas heréticas, afuera de la Iglesia y de su autoridad, estraviarse, contradecirse, dudar y desesperar de poder encontrar la verdad." "La Iglesia Católica: Discurso pronunciado ante el Ilmo. Chapelle en su visita á la capilla de Guadalupita, Condado de Mora, NM," (*Revista Católica*, Las Vegas, New Mexico, August 13, 1892)

21. Ibid.

22. For a discussion of the political construction of the term "Spanish-American," see Phillip B. Gonzales's "The Political Construction of Latino Nomenclatures in Twentieth-Century New Mexico."

23. "Celebremos la virilidad que caracteriza a esos jovenes intrepidos de la vecina republica mexicana. Y a proposito de esto, nosotros llenos de entusiasmo y patriotismo exclamamos: por que la juventud neo-mexicana no puede hacer lo mismo? ¿Qué no será posible para la juventud neo-mexicana—esa juventud que no ha nacido para que se le dicte por uno que otro político corrumpido—unirse y organizarse, y así hacerse conocer y respetar." ("A la juventud neo-mexicana," *El Mosquito*, Mora, New Mexico, May 5, 1892)

24. For a thorough discussion of this idea, see David Montejano's comprehensive study, *Anglos and Mexicans in the Making of Texas, 1836–1986.*

25. "Ninguno puede entender mejor los asuntos de una casa como el que la habita. Esto aplica a nuestro territorio. Por lo tanto repetimos y repetiremos siempre, Nuevo México para los Neo-Mexicanos." ("Nuevo México para los Neo-Mexicanos," *La Voz del Pueblo*, Las Vegas, New Mexico, March 9, 1889)

Chapter 3

1. "Se asociará como debe la prensa Hispano-Americana; y cuando esto se haya verificado será por cierto una inauguración que beneficiará primeramente a la raza latina en lo general, y segundo, facilitará grandes ventajas á los periodistas que

representan la misma." ("La asociación de la Prensa Asociada Hispano-Americana," *La Voz del Pueblo,* Las Vegas, New Mexico, February 27, 1892)

2. "Compañeros en la prensa Las Dos Repúblicas os invita á trabajar con ella, donde quiera que haya una brecha que defender, donde haya un muro que tambalee y amenace desplomarse; donde el enemigo concentre sus fuerzas para atacar con más ardor nuestro frente; allá tendréis siempre esta redacción defendiendo a su pueblo, no desdeñéis seguirla. Pero si hay entre vosotros alguno que todavía se obstine en sus caprichos necios bueno será que deje su bufete editorial que arroje al fuego la pluma y no deshonre más con su presencia á los nobles huestes del periodismo." ("La Prensa Unida," *Las Dos Repúblicas,* Denver, Colorado, May 16, 1896)

3. "Convenir en los medios y medidas que sean más propios y necesarios adoptar para el adelanto y mejoramiento del pueblo á quien ella representa." ("La Prensa Asociada," *El Sol de Mayo,* Las Vegas, New Mexico, March 31, 1892)

4. "Nuestra raza lo verá que la prensa asociada neo-mexicana tomará el escudo en sus manos para hacer su deber sin necesidad de maltratar ni injuriar á nadie pero si aseguramos que el tiempo esta muy oportuno cuando los hispano-americanos pondran fin á las repetidas injurias que muy comunmente se le cometen." ("La Prensa Asociada," *El Sol de Mayo,* Las Vegas, New Mexico, March 31, 1892)

5. "La prensa hispano-americana es naturalmente y por consecuencia debe ser el fideicomisario y defensor del linaje que representa." (ibid.)

6. "No necesita más recomendación que decir que está redactada por los literatos mexicanos Sres. Gutiérrez Nájera, Carlos Díaz Dufoo, Luis G. Urbina y otros. Los amantes de la buena literatura en nuestro territorio en donde mucho se necesita la lectura de buenos autores, no deberian dejar de suscribirse a tan interesante publicacion." (*El Boletín Popular,* Santa Fe, New Mexico, May 31, 1894)

7. *El Boletín Popular* began publication in 1885. Absent from existing library collections are issues of the paper for the first two years of its publication. Benjamín M. Read, (*Historia Ilustrada,* 1911) did, however, record the visit of General Riva Palacio to Santa Fe, indicating in a note that the source of his information was an article in *El Boletín Popular* for July 10, 1886.

8. Francisco Lomelí and other Chicano literary critics have identified Eusebio Chacón as an early exponent of Mexican-American literature. Lomelí suggests that Chacón worked to "create the authentic New Mexican novel" (Lomelí 1989, 134).

9. In noting this dynamic, I take the view of Cathy Davidson, who explains that "varying levels of literacy" operate in situations of uneven literacy. Davidson further notes "the term 'literate' as applied to either individuals or society, can be elastic." (1989, 9)

10. "Por cuanto el dogma de la sociedad y negocios prevalente en los Estados Unidos de América, en la presente época no ha satisfecho que á fin de guardar el rango que los derechos de la constitución americana nos garantiza se nos hace incumbente formar asociaciones para que nuestras fuerzas medren á la par de los demas de nuestros conciudadanos y con el objeto de que la dignidad de nuestra antecendencia y decendencia sea debidamente respetada." ("La Prensa Asociada," *El Sol de Mayo,* Las Vegas, New Mexico, March 31, 1892)

11. "Cuando lejos de nuestra patria adorada nos encontrábamos y pensábamos sobre este suelo que está hoy, como un arado viejo, en el mercado; cuando en compañía del joven patriota Maximiliano Luna, contemplabamos lo que aguardaba á nuestro pacífico y buen pueblo, lo que ha llegado como una plaga aquí, la discordia entre nuestros compatriotas." ("Nuestro patrio suelo," *El Mosquito,* Mora, New Mexico, December 10, 1892)

12. "El suelo neo-mexicano, el cual está rociado y comprado con la sangre de nuestros padres, debería ser para nosotros tan sagrado como es el patrio suelo para el buen patriota y ciudadano. . . . Así es que cuando se vé á un novo-mexicano vender un terreno á un extranjero, aquello le parece profano, porque el vendedor demuestra lo poco que aprecia aquella herencia legada por sus antepasados." (ibid.)

13. "La necesidad de concordia," *El Boletín Popular,* Santa Fe, New Mexico, May 31, 1894.

14. "El tiempo transcurrido entre estas dos fechas—1874 y 1894—significa mucho para nosotros. Ahí encontramos la llave de nuestra situación. . . . Durante ese lapso se ha operado en nuestras conciencias una marcada tendencia al apartamiento, un movimiento de desunión que de día en día aumenta en progresión verdaderamente aterradora. En nada existe verdadera comunión de ideas; los grandes principios que daban unidad á nuestras acciones y que establecían entre los hombres de una misma raza una especie de confraternidad ó se han desmoronado ó amenazan ruina.

Consecuencia fatal de esta disgregación es la envidia, la ambición y la mala voluntad que nos tenemos, que han venido á suplantar y á empequeñecer no sólo los grandes principios de confraternidad que heredamos de nuestros padres sino hasta nuestra fé. La intriga y la mentira—esos mónstros (sic) que acompañan la política del día—han venido á suceder á la sinceridad y la verdad. El sentimiento particular ha tomado el lugar del sentimiento colectivo; el último hoy no existe, ó si existe, avergonzado de ver tanta perfidia, se oculta en el pecho de uno que otro de nosotros." ("Nuestra única salvación," *El Boletín Popular,* Santa Fe, New Mexico, April 12, 1894)

15. "Aplaudo desde aquí desde los márgenes del Potamac tus patrióticos esfuerzos." ("Carta de un amigo," *El Independiente,* Las Vegas, New Mexico, August 4, 1894)

16. "Acabamos con la ficción de inferioridad de raza con que nos motejan nuestros amigos." ("Nuestro provenir," *El Independiente,* Las Vegas, New Mexico, November 9, 1895)

17. "Muchas son las personas observadoras que notan y comentan de la anómala posición que actualmente guarda la población hispano-americana de este Territorio, y con sobrada razón se admira de las cosas que están pasando. Esta admiración proviene de hecho que aunque los hispanoamericanos forman la mayoría é incluyen las cuatro quintas partes de la población de Nuevo México, sin embargo, su importancia social y política en la mayoría de los casos no es en nada equivalente a su superioridad numérica, y preciso es confesar que cada día va disminuyendo." ("Decadencia de nuestro pueblo," *El Independiente,* Las Vegas, New Mexico, March 16, 1895)

18. "Debemos decir que el nuevo colega, sobre estar elegantemente impreso, está escrito en buen castellano, circunstancia que no ha caracterisado [sic] al periodismo político de ese condado en muchos años." ("El Independiente," *El Boletín Popular,* Santa Fe, New Mexico, March 29, 1894)

19. "A nuestros patrones," *La Voz del Pueblo,* Santa Fe, New Mexico, August 24, 1890.

20. For more on this matter, see Rosenbaum's chapter "El Partido del Pueblo Unido."

21. "Nuestro periódico, con la excepción de locacion, velará continuamente por los intereses, honor, y adelanto de todas las secciones de nuestro gran Territorio. El bienestar del pueblo Neo-Mexicano y principalmente del pueblo nativo, será en toda ocasion el poderoso móvil que impulsará nuestros esfuerzos á mayor energía en la publicacion de nuestro semanario. Somos soldados del pueblo que velamos por sus derechos, de esta manera, creyendo que la lucha se acerca, deseamos plantar nuestras baterías donde tengan mas efecto y hagan mas daño al enemigo. Este es, en fin la razón por la cual nos trasladamos á Las Vegas." (Despedida," *La Voz del Pueblo,* Santa Fe, New Mexico, June 7, 1890)

22. "Este periódico se dedicará al adelanto é ilustración del pueblo y a la defensa de los verdaderos y legítimos intereses del condado de San Miguel y del Territorio de Nuevo México." (ibid.).

23. "Llevan por tema regular con tino primeramente la defensa de nuestro pueblo y nuestro pais, nuestro linage (sic) debe por supuesto depender de buenas armas para su propia defensa y nuestra raza lo verá." ("La Prensa Asociada," *El Sol de Mayo,* Las Vegas, New Mexico, March 31, 1892)

24. "El Sol de Mayo," *El Sol de Mayo,* Las Vegas, New Mexico, May 1, 1891.

25. "Señalando las transgresiones que podamos observar ya sea por particulares ó combinaciones, pues nuestros mayores enemigos á quienes no perderemos de vista son nuestros primos Gorras Blancas y Ruedas y Anillos políticos siendo estos elementos más perniciosos y mayores enemigos al pueblo." (ibid.)

26. "Está presentado un gran servicio á la causa de las leyes y el buen orden, y es acreedor al apoyo y alabanza de los hombres honestos y decentes del territorio." ("Empresa meritosa," *El Sol de Mayo,* Las Vegas, New Mexico, March 31, 1892)

27. "Necrology," *Old Santa Fe Magazine,* 3, no. 10 (July 1916): 286.

28. "Y todos los que no están conmigo, son contra mi; es mi lema pues, mi hermano Ezequiel que es un joven muy inteligente, muy honesto y más juicioso que yo, lo declaro un miembro extraño a mi familia, por el solo delito de ser un colaborador del "La Voz del Pueblo," periódico opuesto á mis intereses." ("Asombrosa convercion [sic]," *El Defensor del Pueblo,* Albuquerque, New Mexico, August 22, 1891)

29. Paul Walter's mention of Lucero in his master's thesis in anthropology at the University of New Mexico remained, until now, the only document to examine Spanish-language newspaper publication and its relationship to community leadership.

30. "Se ilustre y este en conocimiento de todo aquello que atañe en sus derechos de ciudadanos." ("La Prensa Asociada Hispano-Americana," *El Hispano-Americano,* Las Vegas, New Mexico, May 14, 1892)

31. Escobar's letter of reference was penned at the Mexican Consulate on June 1, 1889. It reads: "To whom it may concern: By this I take pleasure in recommending the bearer J. E. Sosa, a Mexican citizen and a painter by profession as a very industrious and honest man worthy of protection in his art. Respectfully J. Escobar."

32. "Los residentes de Mora y lugares circunvecinas no hay duda que han de sentido sobremanera la repentina separación de un hombre que se esforzó por el bienestar de ellos, tanto financiera como moralmente." ("Nuestro cumplido compañero pasa a las mansiones celestiales," *El Eco del Norte,* Mora, New Mexico, January 28, 1918)

33. "Era hombre honesto, positivo en sus ideas y amante de sostener, por medio de su pluma, el caracter y estima del pueblo de Nuevo México y los principios del gobierno Americano con lealtad. El capitan Sosa hará mucha falta en el periodismo del estado y sentimos sobremanera su muerte, y en union con sus numerosos amigos simpatizamos con su afligida esposa é hijos." ("En Mora, N. M.," *La Bandera Americana,* Albuquerque, New Mexico, January 25, 1918)

34. Letter of Reference for Jesús Enrique Sosa by José Escobar, June 1, 1899. (Sosa Family Papers).

35. Escobar worked at the following newspapers: *El Defensor del Pueblo* (Albuquerque, 1891–92), *La Libertad* (Mora, 1892), *El Combate* (Albuquerque, 1892), *El País* (Las Vegas, 1893), *La Voz de Nuevo Mexico* (Albuquerque, 1894–95), *El Progreso* (Trinidad, Colorado, 1890–93), *La Opinión Pública* (Albuquerque, 1894), *Las Dos Repúblicas* (Denver, 1896), *El Independiente* (Walsenburg, Colorado, 1896), *El Amigo del Pueblo* (Raton, New

Mexico, 1896), *El Nuevo Mundo* (Albuquerque, 1897), *El Defensor de Socorro* (Socorro, New Mexico, 1897), *El Combate* (Socorro, 1898), and *Las Dos Américas* (El Paso, Texas, 1898).

36. "En el 1ro de enero del presente año de 1892 estuvo personalmente en mi casa un tal José Escobar, güerito, delgadito, chapucerito, pertardista y lépero." "Román Bermúdez Letter," *El Tiempo,* Las Cruces, New Mexico, May 5, 1892.

37. "Por último, la idea de ilustrar este semanario con magníficos grabados, complemento es, que viene á colocar al mismo, si no al frente, por lo menos en la primera fila de las publicaciones del Oeste de esta gran República Norte Americana." ("Nuestro periódico," *Las Dos Repúblicas,* Denver, Colorado, January 11, 1896)

38. "Hemos procurado hacer de este semanario una hoja de utilidad é interés para todas las clases sociales, y que, en sus columnas, las artes, las ciencias, la literatura y las novedades tienen sus secciones correspondientes." (ibid.)

39. For more on Escobar as a poet, see (Meyer, 1979).

40. "Esa misma prensa, en los últimos años ha mejorado de una manera bien notable, y en sus editoriales y boletines, se observa ya algo más que ese estilo embrionario de la prensa que nace; la argumentación lógica y justa que combate, ya no por una idea de partido; sino por algo mucho más grande todavía: por el mejoramiento de las masas sin diferencias de creencias religiosas y políticas." ("Progreso literario de Nuevo México," *Las Dos Repúblicas,* Denver, Colorado, July 11, 1896)

41. "Fomentad vuestras nobles ambiciones de saber; preservad en vuestra noble lucha." (ibid.)

42. *Who's Who in New Mexico* (1937,14).

43. "Los enemigos de nuestro pueblo no van a conseguir el atropello de nativos, quitandoles el derecho de ciudadania Americana, pues en la Convencion Constitucional, el vocal Hon. Isidoro Armijo, redactó y presentó ante dicha convención una noble ley e idea la cual fué adoptada unanimamente, que incluye el tratado de Guadalupe-Hidalgo como parte de la Constitución." ("Palitoriales," *La Estrella,* Las Cruces, New Mexico, February 6, 1926)

Chapter 4

1. "Menosprecio de que son objeto los Neo-Mexicanos, y que algunos de ellos ayudan a fomentar," *El Independiente,* Las Vegas, New Mexico, April 8, 1897.

2. "Nos hemos encariñado tanto con el papel de secundadores de planes para el provecho de extraños que hemos olvidado del todo la independencia innata que debía ser nuestro norte y guía de nuestros procederes. Si aquellos que nos usan de instrumento nos arrojan a un lado cuando ya no somos útiles y nos desprecian en todo tiempo por nuestro servilismo y subyugamiento, ¿a quién hemos de culpar sino á nosotros mismos?" (ibid.)

3. "Mas ya que ha fracasado por nuestra propia culpa el esfuerzo colectivo para elevarnos al nivel colectivo de las demás comunidades de la nación y para conservar nuestros derechos, al menos hasta la fecha, esto no debe ser motivo para que depongamos el esfuerzo individual y nos dejemos abatir y desterrar en todos los campos de la industria material é intelectual, con gran menosprecio y deterioro de nuestra dignidad como hombres y de nuestros intereses pecuniarios. Tenemos a la vista el espejo donde debemos mirarnos en los actos y procederes de los inmigrantes que de otros estados vienen a resentarse en nuestro medio, los cuales, sean lo que fueren en otros respectos, son dignos

de alabanza por su amor acendrado al trabajo y por el esfuerzo constante que siempre están haciendo para mejorar su suerte. Imitando sus virtudes é ignorando sus defectos es como se abrirá para nosotros la senda del adelanto y progreso que es tan indispensable para que no seamos relegados á la categoría de seres inferiores, sin independencia y sin iniciativa, con el sólo arbitrio de obedecer el mandato y recoger las migajas que caen de la mesa de los amos." ("El Provenir de Nuestro Pueblo: La manera en que deben obrar los hijos del país para no ser relegados a la categoría de raza inferior," *El Independiente,* Las Vegas, New Mexico, November 9, 1899)

4. "Según vayamos adelantando en las artes é industrias de la civilización, lo cual acabará con la ficcion de inferioridad de raza con que tanto nos motejan nuestros enemigos." ("Nuestro Porvenir," *El Independiente,* Las Vegas, New Mexico, November 9, 1895)

5. "Procuremos escribir buenos periodicos para la enseñaza popular." ("Deberes que la prensa tiene para el pueblo, y deberes de este para la prensa," *Las Dos Repúblicas,* Denver, Colorado, February 15, 1895.)

6. "Deberían, repetimos, leer ya que no es posible gruesos volúmnes, por los menos las hojas periodisticas que circulan en su localidad." (ibid.)

7. ". . . satíricas alusiones y mordaces calumnias de los periodistas del Este." (ibid.)

8. "Ellos fueron los verdaderos exploradores de este continente y no les guardan ninguna comparación los Pike, los Clark, los Fremont y otros exploradores americanos cuyos viajes y exploraciones en el presente siglo han sido tan ponderadas por la voz de la fama, y que realmente son juego de niños si se compara con las acciones que llevaron á cabo los españoles más de docientos años antes." ("La necesidad de una historia verídica y exacta de Nuevo México," *El Independiente,* Las Vegas, New Mexico, March 6, 1895)

9. "No intencionadamente sino porque estando ignorantes de todos estos puntos y no teniendo aptitudes para estudiarlos, se han limitado á referir unos cuantos hechos conocidos acerca de los individuos promientes que entraron á este pais desde y despues de la anexión americana." (ibid.)

10. "La vida de Carson empezó a crecer debido principalmente a libros escritos en su elogio, en los que se daba relación muy ardiente de su vida y proezas y aunque estas obras no hicieron ningún ruido y fueron casi totalmente desconocidos en el Territorio, hallaron eco en los estados del oriente y poniente donde quedó establecido el renombre de Carson." ("Las cosas en su punto," *El Independiente,* Las Vegas, New Mexico, July 31, 1897)

11. "La pretension que muchos han tenido de imponerlo sobre nuestro pueblo como el héroe titular de Nuevo México. Semejante atentado constituye una especie de usurpación que falsifica los hechos y la historia y se vale de un falso pretexto para perpetuar y establecer una falsedad que desmienten los anales neo-mexicanos.

Si nuestros conciudadanos abrigan el deseo de inmortalizar las hazañas y hechos de hombres ilustres que se han señalado en su historia tienen á la vista el campo extenso de donde escoger sin necesidad de tributar a extraños los honores que pertenecen á los suyos." Ibid.

12. "Contiene tantísimos errores y ficciones y demuestra en muchas partes tanta parcialidad contra los nativos pobladores del país y sus ascendientes que su valor como historia viene a ser enteramente nulo." ("La necesidad de una historia verídica y exacta de Nuevo México," *El Independiente,* Las Vegas, New Mexico, March 6, 1895)

13. "Esta tarea corresponde legitimamente á un hijo del país penetrada del zelo y patriotismo escenciales á empresa semejante y que al mismo tiempo se halle bien equipado con la laboriosidad, instruccion y criterio que se requieren para poder dar á

luz una historia que no se componga de errores y mentiras y que ponga en evidencia los hechos de nuestros antepasados, los obstaculos que vencieron y los peligros que con gran perserverancia y entereza han arrastrado durante tres siglos." (ibid.)

14. Bandelier notes the collaborations, "The first installment appeared on January 17, 1889, and was entitled "Historia de descubrimiento de Nuevo México por el Monjé Francisco Fray Marcos de Niza en 1539." The item ran with an introduction and translation to Spanish provided by a Dr. L. Zabala of Santa Fe. The Fray Marcos de Niza account would henceforth provided a point of departure for every historiographic narrative produced by *Neo-Mexicanos* in the 1890s. (Bandelier [1889–1892] 1984, 289)

15. "El Hon. Tito Melendez
Candidato para Tesorero y Colector

El Sr. Melendez nació en Mora, sus honrados padres, aunque pobres, lo educaron en el Colegio de los Hermanos de la Doctrina Cristiana, llamado Colegio de Santa María.

Comenzó a trabajar en la máquina de Rajar madera del Sr. Roa, y en poco tiempo ganó la confianza y estimación de su patrón a tal grado, que le vendió todo el negocio a plazo.

El Sr. Melendez, con su actividad y economía pagó en poco tiempo, y con su inteligencia y empeño ha logrado que su máquina sea hoy una de las mejores que existen en el Condado.

Es liberal con sus sirvientes, paga al punto y cumple sus promesas al pie de la letra. Tomó interés en la política y fué uno de los que conquistaron la administración, liberandola de los demócratas que la especulaban, fue electo entonces como Comisionado de Condado y consiguió por sus esfuerzos y buen manejo desvanecer las ideas y mala fama que existía respecto a la fiananzas del Condado: desde entonces convención tras convención fué solicitado con diferentes nominaciones, pero él sedia [sic.] sus derechos en bien del partido, y con su ayuda, influjo y dinero postulaba a otros personas en el lugar que a él ofrecian.

En 1903 a instancias de sus amigos aceptó la nominación de Alguacil Mayor, y fue electó por grande mayoría sobre su competidor, y desempeñó esta posición con crédito para si mismo y para sus constituyentes.

Ahora ha convenido en aceptar la candidatura para Colector y Tesorero: en esta posición se necesita un hombre de talento conocimientos, honradez y confianza. El Sr. Melendez está revestido de todas estas virtudes y el pueblo al darle su sufragio puede confiar que en el Sr. Melendez tendrá un sirviente fiel y una persona honrada y digna de todas su confianza.

No olviden Don Tito es uno de los brillantes hijos del Condado, nada orgullos a pesar de sus méritos, liberal en todos sus negocios y atento y cortés con todos.

Los votantes del condado al votar por el Sr. Melendez, votan por su beneficio y por la honra y buen nombre del Condado." (*El Eco de Norte,* Mora, New Mexico, October 19, 1908)

16. "Con la confianza que acompañan siempre las acciones que tienden al bien y al la proseperidad de una raza esperamos que los amantes á las letras, lean el libro de que venimos hablando en el folletin de 'El Progreso,' para que cuando el mismo esté elegantemente encuadernado, y adornado con finas y bellas ilustraciones que representarán los monumentos antiguos y modernos del suelo de Nuevo México, asi como los retratos de los hijos ilustres del mismo Territorio procuren hacerse de un ejemplar." ("De interés para Neo-Mexicanos," *El Boletín Popular,* Santa Fe, New Mexico, October 12, 1893)

17. "Tal empresa se inició sin consultarme, sin mi conocimiento y sin mi consentimiento. No consiento desde luego que mi nombre se inserte como socio y suplico a V. lo retire cuanto antes, de donde se encuentra. Por lo mismo que la obra de que Vds. se ocupan no es compatible con la que originalmente contemplamos escribir, me he separado del Sr. Escobar, y en lo sucesivo la 'Historia de Nuevo México' se escribirá por cuenta mía individual." ("Historia de Nuevo México," *El Boletín Popular,* Santa Fe, New Mexico, January 11, 1894)

18. Newspaper ads describe "Revista Histórica Quicenal" as "the first and only edition in Spanish, illustrated with *biographical sketches of the ancient rulers and the present day men in public life.* Monuments, buildings, features, and descriptions of its customs and traditions" (emphasis added). The ads stipulated that the price for the work would be three dollars in American gold coin.

19. "Cuyo principal objeto es, ayudar en algo a la literatura nacional al mismo tiempo que proporcionará á la juventud Neo-Mexicana una breve sinópsis de los acontecimientos culminantes de su historia, para que en ellos se enseñe á admirar las virtudes cívicas de sus antepasados." ("Carta abierta: Historia de Nuevo México," *La Opinión Pública,* Albuquerque, New Mexico, February 10, 1894)

20. Despite the attention the "Hombres Ilustres" project garnered in the Spanish-language press, copies of García de la Lama's *La Opinión Pública,* in which it may have been published, have not survived. Escobar began another series titled "Historia Popular de Nuevo México, su pueblo, sus tradiciones y sus costumbres" (Popular History of New Mexico, Its People, Its Traditions and Its Customs). As Doris Meyer has noted the first installment of this work appeared in *El Amigo del Pueblo* at Ratón, New Mexico, on January 8, 1896. (1978, 34, N. 22)

21. "Le deseamos un verdadero éxito y trinufo en lo que Vd. piensa publicar." *La Opinión Pública,* Albuquerque, New Mexico, February 10, 1894.

22. "En los últimos años, escritores tan distinguidos como el muy Ilmo. Arzobispo J. B. Salpointe; el entendido arquélogo, Adolfo Bandelier, y el Sr. Cura J. Defouri, hánse encargado de escribir la historia de la Iglesia Neo-Mexicana; y talentos tan brillantes como los del jóven abogado E. Chacón, han, empeñosamente, comenzado á escribir las primeras disertaciones históricas en español." ("Progreso literario de Nuevo México," *Las Dos Repúblicas,* Denver, Colorado, July 11, 1896)

23. Jacqueline Meketa notes the existence of other important documents in the possession of the Chacón family. (See Meketa, 1986. 356 n. 2)

24. " 'Historia de Nuevo México' por Don Gaspar de Villagrá. Es una obra en verso suelto de 34 cantos publicada en Alcalá de Henares por el librero Luis Martínez Grande en 1610. La única copia que existe en Nuevo México es la propiedad del Lic. Eusebio Chacón y él posee una magnifica coleccion de documentos para la Historia de Nuevo México. Se publicará en las ediciones que siguen." ("Preciosa joya bibliográfica," *El Progreso,* Trinidad, Colorado, July 30, 1898)

25. An original copy of this work formed part of the small library kept by my own family. For years I spied the small volume wedged between our set of encyclopedia and the family Bible, not knowing nor suspecting its significance. I am grateful to my mother and father for guarding and keeping this very valuable cultural heirloom through the many years of their marriage. It is one I have turned to often in doing this study.

26. A biographical profile in Read's *Historia Ilustrada* provides the whole of what is known about Fernández. It reads, "José Emilio Fernández was born at Trinidad, Colo-

rado, April 10, 1882, the son of Jesús María Fernández, a prominent figure in the 70s in Taos County and Mrs. Rosita Martínez. Mr. Fernández was educated in the country schools of Colorado. At the age of 15 he taught a private school at Catskill, New Mexico, and started his first public school at Gulnore, Colorado, December 12, 1898. He taught in the public schools until 1907 when he took charge of *El Progreso* of Trinidad, Colorado. At 14 Mr. Fernández was assistant postmaster at Madrid, Colorado. Since 1907 he has been writing several Spanish works and in May 1911, he wrote in Spanish *Forty Years as a Legislator,* or *Biography of Senator Casimiro Barela.* At present Mr. Fernández is writing Senator Barela's Biography in English. Mr. Fernández has also been prominent in politics in Las Animas County for the last five years" (Read 1911, 750).

27. "Como las persecuciones eran terribles como se recordarán con pavor los sucesos del 19 de enero de 1847 en Fernández de Taos, así fue que la familia de don José María Barela, domiciliada en Mora, tuvo que salir, regufiandose en El Embudo, Condado de Río Arriba, Nuevo México, donde por el Arquitecto Supremo que la Señora María de Jesús Abeyta de Barela, presentara á su esposo, el día 4 de Marzo, de 1847, con el niño que hoy llamamos el Senador Casimiro Barela" (1911, 4).

28. "Por eso yo, que desde años he tenido la honra de contarme entre sus amigos particulares, he sentido un verdadero regocijo en lo de obsequiar los deseos del dicho autor escribiendo, con toda sinceridad de mi corazón, estos apuntamientos en forma de introducción á la obra que ha de perpetuar en los corazones de los hispano-americanos de Colorado, y Nuevo México, los grandes servicios é incontables beneficios que han recibido de uno de los más fieles y más desinteresados de sus compaisanos y consanguíneos—Nosotros los Neo-Mexicanos lo reconocemos y lo apreciamos, como hijo de este suelo, pues que en efecto lo es; y de ello tenemos orgullo." (Fernández 1915, xviii).

29. Book circular, *Cuarenta años de legislador,* Trinidad, Colorado, August, 1911.

30. "Necrology," *New Mexico Historical Review* (1927: 1, 396).

31. One exchange involved Don Rafaél Chacón, whom Read wrote to in June 1911 seeking clarification on matters pertaining to the Chacón family history and events in which Chacón had been a participant. In a series of letters between the two, Don Rafaél took the occasions to widen the historical field by suggesting that Read's history was incorrect on matters related to the Bernal Díaz and Francisco Gómera account of the conquest of Mexico. Not wanting to offend the elder Chacón, whom Read considered an extremely important source of information, he responded to such suggestion with extremely lengthy and detailed explanations regarding the points raised by Chacón and concludes in his letter of June 20, 1911, the following,

> "Conque, buen amigo, ya verá que las correcciones que ud. sugiere, en ese particular, no se deben, ni se pueden hacer. La corrección sobre los nombres de su madre y su abuela se harán con sumo placer."
>
> [So, my good friend, you will see that the corrections you suggest, on that matter, should not, nor can they be, made. The correction regarding the names of your mother and grandmother will be made with great pleasure.]
>
> (Benjamín M. Read Series II, "Rafael Chacón, 1911").

32. "Necrology," *New Mexico Historical Review* (1927: 1, 396).

33. Circular, New Mexico Printing Company, Santa Fe, New Mexico, June, 1911.

34. "Los últimos dos capítulos son de índole diferente de la de los precedentes, de un punto de vista que los hace aparecer como que carecen de unidad y forma, por tratarse en ellos de eventos é incidentes que por haber ocurrido en el Nuevo México (entónces provincia de México) parecerá, á primera vista, que no tienen conneccion [*sic*] con la obra, pero cuando se haya leido con la debida atencion se verá que esos eventos é incidentes no eran otra cosa que un fragmento de los efectos producidos por la misma causa, ó en otras palabras, eran una de las muchas ramificaciones del cáncer original" (Read 1910, 5).

35. Of the one hundred and forty-six *bocetos,* or profiles, included in the book, six are of prominent women in the *Nuevomexicano* community. Read also included group profiles representing the participation of women in development of New Mexico. Included in these descriptions is the work of the Sisters of Charity and the Sisters of Loretto.

36. "Necrology," *New Mexico Historical Review* (1927: 1, 396).

37. The following item published by Manuel C. de Baca in *El Sol de Mayo* reflects the high regard in which Read was held by many *Neo-Mexicanos:*

> Al Señor Read lo quisieramos más bien de residente que de visitante, tales hombres como él de una manera principal y varonil empujan el carro del progreso en una comunidad, y más se llena uno de orgullo al tener que decir, que es un hombre contra quien no hay un solo cargo ni tacha para echarle en la cara. El posee virtudes de un ardiente patriotismo en favor del país donde nació. Estas cualidades necesariamente tiene que exhaltarlo á una escala superior, como premio de esas virtudes. Adelante Sr. Read.
>
> [We would prefer Señor Read as a resident rather than as a visitor, such men as he, in an important and virile way push the cart of progress in a community, and what is more, one is filled with pride upon having to confess that he is a man against whom no charge or fault exists that can be thrown in his face. He possess the virtues of burning patriotism in favor of the homeland where he was born. These qualities will by necessity exalt him to a higher ground; and will be a reward for these virtues. Onward, Señor Read!]
>
> ("Un hombre digno de mencion," *El Sol de Mayo,* Las Vegas, New Mexico, July 30, 1891)

38. While copies of Read's works can be found at the Center for Southwest Research at the University of New Mexico, my own access to this material was through the loan of a copy of *Historia Ilustrada* kept by a long time friend and colleague, Walter Archuleta. Archuleta's father, Don Luis Archuleta, kept a copy of Read's *Historia* in his household in Embudo, New Mexico, for more than seventy years. Walter, to whom the book has been passed, recounts that his father read and consulted the work countless times sharing what he had learned with his *vecinos* and *parientes.*

39. "[El libro] narra la parte que Nuevo México ha tomado en las guerras de los indios, en la Guerra Civil, guerra de España y la guerra mundial." "Libro del historiador Read," *La Bandera Americana,* Albuquerque, New Mexico, November 24, 1922. *La Bandera Americana* noted that Octaviano A. Larrazolo, ex-governor of the state was slated to write the introduction to the book.

40. "Y del año 1846 para acá, ¿cuántos esfuerzos no se han hecho para conseguir el

ideal de nuestra libertad? Grande en verdad es nuestra dicha. Digno de admiracion es el patriotismo que impulsó a nuestros leales ciudadanos á batirse valerosamente con los que tanto esfuerzos hicieron para privarnos de nuestra autonomía. -Magnífico espectacúlo fué el ver durante la dura lucha á los buenos hijos de Nuevo México convertirse en verdaderos patriotas y de patriotas en oradores, hablando todos con una elocuencia posible solamente en los momentos en que la vida ó la libertad de todo un pueblo peligra" (Read 1911, 605).

41. In his study of the *corrido*, Saldívar argues, that nineteenth-century *corridos* in Texas provided an "imaginative seeding ground" for present-day Chicano narratives. Saldívar writes that the *corrido* tradition was not only patently historiographic, but that it produced a kind of substitute for the writing of history, "The very orality of the corrido served as the symbolic function of providing alternative interpretations of empirical events (functioning as a substitue for history writing) and of creating counterfactual worlds of lived experience (functioning as a substitute for fiction writing)" (Saldívar 1990, 48).

Chapter 5

1. "El poeta," *El Eco del Norte*, Mora, New Mexico, December 21, 1908.

2. Chicano historians Rodolfo Acuña and John Chávez have both pointed out the distinctiveness of the New Mexican situation in this regard. Chávez notes, "Command of military power, of course, determined that Anglos would hold the major positions everywhere in the Southwest, but the factor that decisively undermined Mexican political strength was the enormous growth of the Anglo population. We has already seen that the increase of that population in eastern Texas destroyed local Mexican dominance even before the revolution of 1836. *Nuevomexicanos* were more fortunate because they remained a majority in New Mexico well into the twentieth century. In northern California, on the other hand, where the Gold Rush of 1849 resulted in a huge influx of Anglos, *californios* were left powerless almost immediately." (1984, 43)

3. "Con hechos [obras literarias] de este género, puédamos desvanecer los injustos cargos y torpes calumnias de los *touristas*." ("Progreso literario de Nuevo México," *Las Dos Repúblicas*, Denver, Colorado, July 11, 1896)

4. "Las satíricas alusiones y mordaces calumnias de los periodistas del Este." ("Deberes que la prensa tiene para el pueblo," *Las Dos Repúblicas*, Denver, Colorado, February 15, 1896)

5. "Resoluciones pasadas por la primera reunión de editores neo-mexicanos," *El Sol de Mayo*, Las Vegas, New Mexico, March 31, 1892.

6. "El gobierno que tanto alarde hace hoy de educar á los Cubanos, Puertoriqueños y Filipinos, nada ha hecho para diseminar la educacion entre nosotros. Las pocas instituciones de educacion que hay entre nosotros, son obra de nuestro propio trabajo, levantadas con nuestros ahorros, y mantenidas á nuestra costa. Allí no hay ni un solo centavo de nuestro gobierno nacional." ("Elocuente Discurso," *La Voz del Pueblo*, Las Vegas, New Mexico, November 2, 1901)

7. "Es un error . . . querer que un pueblo que por circumstanicas perfectamente anómolas tuvo que dedicarse más al ejercicio de las armas que al aprendizaje de la literatura, pueda mostrar el interés que los pueblos perfectamente civilizados y cultos." ("Progreso literario de Nuevo México," *Las Dos Repúblicas*, Denver, Colorado, July 11, 1896)

8. "Como en la prensa en los círculos literatos de aquel simpático suelo [Nuevo México] hace tiempo han operado un cambio radical, y hoy, mismo en las ciudades que en las pequeñas villas existen sociedades literarias y de debates en las que la juventud va frecuentemente a ensayar." ("Progreso literario de Nuevo México," *Las Dos Repúblicas,* Denver, Colorado, July 11, 1896)

9. "Aunque todavía el nombre de ningun Neo-Mejicano haya llenado el orbe con su fama, no estamos tan dejados de Dios por acá como nos pintan algunos escritores que pasan por entre nosotros como caballeros apocalípticos, con la copa de hiel en una mano y la guadaña del odio en la otra." ("Elocuente discurso," *La Voz del Pueblo,* Las Vegas, New Mexico, November 2, 1901)

10. "Progreso literario de Nuevo México," *Las Dos Repúblicas,* Denver, Colorado, July 11, 1896.

11. "Se vio a nuestra juventud, que hábida de saber, iba desde sus retiradas aldeas á esas instituciones en las que con afán bebía las benditas y dulces aguas de aquellas preciosas fuentes que debían hacer fructificar muy en breve las claras inteligencias de los neo-mexicanos, poseedores en su mayoría de un magnífico talento natural." ("Progreso Literario de Nuevo México," *Las Dos Repúblicas,* Denver, Colorado July 11, 1896)

12. "Los viajeros que á la fecha recorren en cómodos carros dormitorios las altas serranías, fértiles valles y extensas llanuras de este terrritorio, no pueden apreciar en manera alguna el favorable cambio que el genio del progreso ha hecho en ese suelo; pero el que esté familiarizado con la historia de ese heroíco y hospitalario país, no podrá menos que admirar la energía del nativo y del colono extranjero." (ibid.)

13. "Esa misma prensa, en los últimos años ha mejorado de una manera bien notable, y en sus editoriales y boletines, se observa ya algo más que ese estilo embrionario de la prensa que nace; la argumentación lógica y justa que combate, ya no por una idea de partido; sino por algo mucho más grande todavía: por el mejoramiento de las masas sin diferencias de creencias religiosas y políticas!" (ibid.)

14. "Y hoy, lo mismo en las ciudades que en las pequeñas villas, existen sociedades literarias y de debates, en las que la juventud va frecuentemente a ensayar, ya el estro melancólico del bardo; ya el recto juicio del historiador; ó bien la cortante metáfora de la crítica, o la difícil concepción de la novela de costumbres y los sentidos romances nacionales." (ibid.)

15. "Se nota desde luego la facilidad de estilo y asombrosa fecundida [sic] de la imaginacion, del escritor, en tanto que en la segunda [*Tras la tormenta, la calma*] se observa poco después, de la lectura de algunas páginas, la precosidad de un talento superior que desde muy temprano observa y razona." (ibid.)

16. *El Independiente* of Las Vegas published the prologue to *Vicente Silva y sus cuarenta bandidos* on July 4, 1896, the week before Escobar's essay appeared in Denver. The July 4 issue of *El Independiente* also noted that the author, Manuel C. de Baca, was in Denver purchasing the engraving plates for the book.

17. "El libro que acaba de escribir el Lic. Baca, es en nuestro juicio el primero que llena todas las exigencias y reglas de la novela de costumbres, teniendo la peculiaridad de estar escrito en un estilo tipícamente nacional. La verdad histórica de los sucesos ha pasado á las páginas de ese libro con toda su pureza, y la trama es de tanto interés, está tan habilmente tejida por el talento del autor, que una vez leídas las primeras hojas, se sienten vivos deseos de leer, leer y leer, hasta concluir esas páginas en las que además del buen gusto y sencillez de estilo, hay un fondo moral de gran enseñanza para la juventud." (ibid.)

18. "Entre tanto, reciba el Lic. Baca nuestras más calurosas y justa felicitaciones por ese trabajo literario de verdadera utilidad social, y ojalá que su ejemplo estimule á la juventud nativa para que con hechos de ese género, puédamos desvanecer los injustos cargos y torpes calumnias de los *touristas* [sic] que sin conocernos más que *á vuelo de tren,* nos acusan de falta de cultura y escasez absoluta de talento." (ibid.)

19. "Hemos pedido á los agricultores un ramillete de *alfalfa* para cierto *periodiquero* que promete divertirnos mucho con algunas críticas de ciertas *novelas tormentosas.* Como los *clarines de aquí en casa* saben dar buenos trompetazos cuídese bien el Cantor de Popé, no sea que le salga el tiro por la culata. Y así que *au revoir monsieur.*" ("Correspondencia de Trinidad," *El Boletín Popular,* Santa Fe, New Mexico, August 5, 1897)

20. "Desde el destierro," *El Defensor del Pueblo,* Albuquerque, New Mexico, February 20, 1892.

21. When at last Escobar relocated to El Paso/Juárez area in March 1898 he disclosed to his readers the intense feeling generated by his absence from Mexico in the following note:

> Para el proscrito que como yo, por años y años ha estado ausente de la patria, hay emociones tan gratas al volver á pisar el suelo en que se vé la luz primera, que si pueden sentirse, no pueden en cambio ni traducirse, ni expresarse! Después de siete años de ausencia, pude al fin de nuevo ver el bellísimo cielo de mi querida México, y á pesar del duelo inmenso y del luto que envuelve mi alma, sentí algo sublime que llenó mi corazón de inefables consuelos y benditas esperanzas.
>
> [For an exile, like me, who has been absent from the homeland for years and years, there are such pleasant emotions in being able to set upon the earth where one first saw the light of day, emotions which thought can easily be felt, on the other hand, are not easy to translate, nor express. After seven years of absence, I was able once again to see the beautiful sky of my beloved Mexico, and in spite of the immense grief and mourning that surrounds my soul, I felt something sublime that filled my heart with unspeakable comfort and blessed hope.]"
>
> ("A Vuela Pluma," *Las Dos Américas,* El Paso, Texas, March 7, 1898.)

22. Escobar began to publish this work as a series in *Las Dos Repúblicas* in March 1896. He began with an installment titled "Leyendas Neo-Mexicanas: Popé" (New Mexican Legends: Popé), which appeared on March 14, 1896.

23. "Leyendas Neo-Mexicanas: Popé," [Part IV] *Las Dos Repúblicas,* Denver, Colorado, March 16, 1896.

24. "Noticias generales," *Las Dos Repúblicas,* Trinidad, Colorado, October 3, 1896.

25. "Correspondencia," *El Boletín Popular,* Santa Fe, New Mexico, January 27, 1898.

26. "A Vuela Tren," *Las Dos Repúblicas,* El Paso, Texas, July 25, 1898.

27. Oratory and extemporary speaking were extremely common activities in towns across New Mexico and just as the *boceto* summarizes expectations for *Neo-Mexicano* politicians, there too was a template that served to guide the formation of community orators. An indication of the importance of oratory in New Mexico is seen in the inclusion of the profile of Adelino C. Sánchez, a twelve-year-old boy from Tomé who had distinguished himself as "a child orator." The profile of young Adelino among the bio-

graphical sketches compiled by Benjamín M. Read emphasizes the importance given to rhetorical skill as part of the educational formation of youth (Read 1911, 538).

This tradition seems to have been seen quite differently by Anglo obervers of *Neo-Mexicano* cultural practices. Writing in *New Mexico Quarterly* in 1934, S. Omar Baker makes the practice in New Mexican villages of giving every member of the community a chance to speak at public meetings the object of his ridicule. Baker's parody of a precinct meeting in the village of Rociada, opens with the following caricature:

> If all the natural born orators of the native New Mexican villages were laid end to end, they would still rise to rousing climaxes as soon as the next *campaña politica* begins to infiltrate the brisk October air. For politics and political speechmaking come as natural to these American descendants of the *conquistadores* and their colonists as does their taste for *chili.* And they like it hot. Juan, Pedro, Jesús María, Toribio, Melaquias, Fulano y Tal—every *ciudadano,* every *paisano,* be he tie chopper, farmer, *peon, vaquero, borreguero,* teacher, merchant, can and does upon occasion rise in his place at the *junta* and make a speech. Extempore, of course; modestly apologetic at first bud, but blossoming surely into the full flower of ornate and vigorous oratory as he proceeds. (Baker [1934] 1946, 45)

28. "Con gran placer felicita *La Aurora* al jóven Eusebio Chacón, de Trinidad, Colorado por el bonito y elaborado discurso que pronunció el día 6 del corriente ante la Asociación de Mutuo Adelantamiento del condado de las Animas. El jovencito cuenta apenas 13 años de edad, y muestra un talento sorprendente que le abrirá mas tarde un vastísimo campo donde puede recoger los laureles de un feliz y venturoso porvenir." *La Aurora,* Santa Fe, New Mexico, September 27, 1884.

29. "Son creación genuina de mi propia fantasía y no robadas ni prestadas de gabachos ni extranjeros. Sobre el suelo de Nuevo Mexico me atrevo á cimentar la semilla de la literatura recreativa para que si después otros autores de más feliz ingenio que el mío siguen el camino que aquí trazo, puedan volver hacia el pasado la vista y señalarme como el primero que emprendió tan áspero camino." (Chacón 1892)

30. "Se sorprende al talento del jóven literato: unas veces sarcástico y burlesco, y otras, elevado, filosófico y altamente moral. En suma: el librito de Chacón, aunque desconocido de muchos de los nativos, es una verdadera joya en nuestra literature nacional." ("Progreso literario de Nuevo México," *Las Dos Repúblicas,* Denver, Colorado, July 11, 1896)

31. In this I am in disagreement with Francisco Lomelí's characterization of the novelette when he argues that "the storyline functions as a faithful mirror of the prevalent chaos in his region, and its composition gives testimony to actual events witnessed by the author." See Francisco Lomelí, "Eusebio Chacón an Early Pioneer of the New Mexican Novel."

32. "A Enriqueta," *El Boletín Popular,* Santa Fe, New Mexico, May 11, 1893.

33. "A la patria," *El Boletín Popular,* Santa Fe, New Mexico, October 7, 1897.

34. "Cometiendo el grave error de todo escritor superificial, pretende sacar conclusiones generales de premisas particulares. Esta persona no nos conoce; si nos conociera no hablaría así." ("Elocuente Discurso," *La Voz del Pueblo,* Las Vegas, New Mexico, November 2, 1901)

35. "En las casas de campo donde las necesidades de la vida son más sencillas, no hay lámparas de alabastro, ni los sofás de blanco terciopelo que hacen parecer nuestras

casas palacios en miniatura. Pero sí hay mesa abundante, donde la hospitalidad endulza los azares del viajero, donde la caridad cristiana nunca niega un lecho para que el extranjero fatigado pueda reclinar la frente." (ibid.)

36. "Pero si esta Señora, verdaderamente hubiera visto una de nuestras habitaciones en el interior, habría notado que siempre tenemos buenas camas y buenas mesas; que nuestros niños crecen rodeados de todas las amenidades que el cariño puede prodigiar." (ibid.)

37. "Cuando en compañía del joven patriota, Maximiliano Luna, contemplábamos lo que aguardaba á nuestro pacífico y buen pueblo." ("Nuestro Patrio Suelo," *El Mosquito,* Mora, New Mexico, December 10, 1892)

38. "Y en esas ocasiones más de una lágrima llegó a empeñar nuestros ojos—humilde ofrenda de unos jóvenes que tendrán todas las faltas del mundo pero así también arde la antorcha del patriotismo en sus pechos." (ibid.)

39. "Obtuve un cuarto cerca de Emilio y todas las noches nos juntabamos, ya para platicar, ya para tomar un paseo.

—Qué ratos tan memorables aquellos!

Ya platicamos sobre Nuevo México y la raza neo-mexicana, ya sobre aquella hermosa ciudad y sus atractivos.

—O pláticas benditas, que habeis, cual ingratos pájaros, emprendido el vuelo para no volver jamás. Mientras duraban aquellas plácticas, los hermosos ojos negros de mi amigo se hallaban bañados en lágrimas. Me recuerdo de un capítulo de su residencia en ese lugar, y del cual los voy á dar alguna idea al narrar lo siguiente." ("Historia Original Neo-Mexicana: -Pobre Emilio!," *La Gaceta de Mora,* August 14, 1890)

40. "A menudo me decía: 'O no hay en este mundo mujeres tan tiernas apasionadas, sinceras, como las nuestras—las mexicanas. Lo que nuestras primitas son todo lo contrario—frías, metalizadas, especuladoras.-Mexicanas, mujeres nobles, Dios las bendiga mil veces!' Y cuando llegaba á esto afirmaba que realmente sentíalo [sic.] que decía, consagrándolas una lágrima." (ibid.)

41. "Al momento puso el revolver sobre la mesa é hincado y llorando dijo: 'Si no fuese por Vdes.-O mi pátria y querida madre! yo me volaría la tapa de los sesos. Pero como ciendo [sic] que tal vez necesiteis mis humildes servicios, debo de ocultar debajo de una falsa sonrisa mis penas, y defendros con mi voz, pluma y espada. Es contigo,-patria querida! con la que me esposo, y no es sino por ti quien vivo.'" (ibid.)

42. "Aun nos recordamos de los tiempos en que no nos daba vergüenza decir que nuestros hermanos se habian ido a cazar cíbolos ó que habíamos comido empanaditas, y en que nos deleitabamos bailando á cadera suelta *La Indita.*" ("Nuestra única salvación," *El Boletín Popular,* Santa Fe, New Mexico, April 12, 1894)

43. "Mientras que las costumbres del hogar sean respetadas entre nosotros hay esperanza de salvarnos de los elementos que quieren desmembrarnos. Mientras que el hombre respete a su esposa, el hijo obedezca a sus padres, y en cada paisano veamos un hermano,—loado se el niño Dios! no hay que temer por nuestro porvenir." ("La Nochebuena," *El Boletín Popular,* Santa Fe, New Mexico, December 20,1895)

44. *El Boletín Popular,* Santa Fe, New Mexico, July 17, 1892 and June 7, 1894.

45. "[Ribera] se dedicó a la poesía, siendo el bardo y cantor previlegiado de Nuevo México." ("Don José Rómulo Rivera fallece en su residencia en Albuquerque el sábado pasado," *La Bandera Americana,* Albuquerque, NM, September 21, 1917)

46. The popularity and influence of the Mexican romantic poets was widespread in

the Southwest. In the case of Manuel Acuña we also know that it was of long duration. The Las Cruces paper, *El Tiempo*, reported in April 1907 that *El Club Dramático Neo-Mexicano* of that city was about to stage Acuña's play "El Pasado." The annoucement offers notice and commentary on the forthcoming production:

> La Compañía Cómica de aficcionados denominada, "Club Drámatico Neo Mexicano" conforme a lo que anunciamos en nuestro número anterior, pondrá en escena, en el Salón Rink, el sábado 27 del presente el drama social: El Pasado, escrito por el poeta de las hondas tristezas y sublimes sentimientos, ese poeta cuyos cantos conoce y estima todo amante de la belleza, que brilló en el cielo literario, dejando una estela de luz y cuyo nombre es: Manuel Acuña. Los personajes que presenta Manuel Acuña en su drama los encontramos a cada paso, y, ni sabemos complacer á unos ni perservarnos de otros.
> [A comic troupe (made up) of fans and called the "New Mexican Dramatic Club,"—as we announced in our last issue—will stage the social drama *El Pasado* at the Rink House on Saturday the 27th: (The play) written by the poet of profound sadness and sublime sentiment, a poet whose songs are known and held in regard by all lovers of beauty, and who has shone in the literary sky; (and) leaves a wake of light; (and) whose name is Manuel Acuña. We encounter the personages Manuel Acuña presents in his play at every turn not knowing how to take in some nor how to keep ourselves away from others.]

47. "Al Inmortal Acuña," *El Boletín Popular*, Santa Fe, New Mexico, January 4, 1894.

48. Sometime after 1900 Ribera set up a private school offering classes in literature, reading, writing in both Spanish and English at his residence at 1515 South Second in the Barelas neighborhood of Albuquerque. From there he continued to submit poems for publication, most often to Albuquerque's *La Bandera Americana*.

49. Lamy's tenure as bishop and later archbishop of Santa Fe (1851–85) was, in large measure, premised on the need to "modernize" a region considered primitive and backward by European standards. Largely unsympathetic and dismissive of *nativo* religious practices, Lamy's attitude translated into the deligitimization of *Nuevomexicano* cultural ways. The clerical perrogatives of Lamy and the French clergy in New Mexico are summarized by Patricia Clark Smith who notes, "Bishop Lamy, upon whom Cather modelled her hero Latour, is widely viewed as a prelate inclined toward rigidity, unsympathetic to the New Mexican church he was given to oversee, sadly unable to comprehend the aesthetic of native art like *santos* and *retablos*, unable to understand the deep social and religious needs served by the *Penitente* Brotherhood in isolated Hispanic communities, unconscious of the inappropriateness of erecting a Midi Romanesque cathedral in the heart of Santa Fe, and tragically mistaken in his estimation and treatment of Padre Martínez" (1988, 104).

50. Isidoro Armijo was married to Las Cruces native Jeannie Archibald, but little is known of their married life. "Sesenta minutos en los infiernos" offers only the staid views of the period regarding love, marriage, honor and so forth, leaving the reader to speculate as to the degree of autobiographical authority that girths the story.

51. There are antecedents for Xicotencatl or Jicoténcal as a literary and historical figure. According to the Spanish chronicler, Antonio de Solis, Xicotencatl was a young Tlaxcalan noble who figured prominently in the events of the Spanish conquest. He appears as the hero-protagonist of Felix Varela's 1826 novel *Jicoténcal*, published in

Philadelphia and in several nineteenth-century dramatic representations produced in Mexico. For a complete discussion, see Leal and Cortina's introduction to the reedition of *Jicoténcal.*

52. "Sixty Minutes in Hades," *Laughing Horse Magazine,* No. 10 (May 1924), Santa Fe, New Mexico: 6–16.

53. "Men of Honor in New Mexico: Probate Clerk Isidoro Armijo of Doña Ana County," Undated news clipping, Prince Papers "Contemporary New Mexicans," folder 3, New Mexico State Archives Santa Fe, New Mexico.

54. "Cada vez que este buen amigo mio pasa por junto a mi oficina ambulante, me pregunto: ¿Por qué el Destino es tan cruel para con la mayoría de nuestros más brillantes jovenes? ¿Qué pecado ha cometido este talentoso joven para que no ocupe el puesto de Gobernador o Senador de este estado? El posee todas las cualidades que se pudieran desear para esos puestos y hasta eso, él las posee de sobra: educación, talento y energía. Ya comprendo que la gente es olvidadiza de lo suyo. . . . Pero no debería serlo a tan alto grado, por su propio bienestar." ("A traves de mis cristales: Isidoro Armijo," *La Revista Ilustrada,* [January, 1926] Santa Fe, New Mexico, p. 4)

55. "El atleta no puede separarse de la arena del combate por años y no esperar el castigo del contrincante pulgista (sic) adiestrado." ("Una palmadita," *La Estrella,* Las Cruces, New Mexico, December 6, 1924)

56. "Se puede decirse así mismo: 'voy a retirarme a ganar la vida.' Mas el destino contesta: 'Retírese si lo desea, pero las penas que hoy parecen chiquitas porque está en medio de la lucha, surgirán y se aumentarán más cuando no tenga otra cosa que pensar.'" (ibid.)

57. "Y la oración del hombre sabio, creo es: 'Señor tenédme útil,' no, 'Señor [tenédme] en la seguridad.' 'Poned algunos fracasos en mi camino, entre mis delicias y buena suerte,—algunas perdidas y algunas ganancias, una que otra piedra.' Estas son las palmaditas en la quijada que el hombre no puede aguantar si no las recibe todos los días." (ibid.)

58. "Deplorable suicidio," *El Tiempo,* Las Cruces, New Mexico, June 6, 1908.

59. "Todo Nuevo Mexicano debe interesarse porque se nos conserven las perrogativas y derechos que hasta hoy hemos tenido, y todos debemos interesarnos por estar representados por personas que vean por el bienestar del pueblo en general hoy que se ventila el asunto mas trascendental, en nuestra historia, que pueda decidir nuestra felicidad ó nuestra ruina.

Tambien los hombres de color moreno hemos nacido bajo el pabellón de las estrellas y listas, también somos ciudadanos de la patria de Washington y Abraham Lincoln y tenemos derecho a pedir nuestro bien estar personal y un futuro de felicidad para nuestros hijos y descendientes." ("Alerta Pueblo," *El Eco del Valle,* Las Cruces, New Mexico, August 18, 1911)

60. "Albuquerque

Armijo, Isidoro: de 79 años de edad falleció en su domicilio en Albuquerque el 22 de agosto. El finado fue muy activo en la política del estado, siendo muy conocido como interprete en las cortes y tambien como orador de prominencia." ("Armijo, Isidoro," *El Nuevo Mexicano,* Santa Fe, New Mexico, September 1, 1949)

61. Adelfa's letter does give away some information that identifies the author. For example, it indicates that the writer also was a collegian at the Jesuit College and also that he is very familiar with other journalists in New Mexico, singling out

the work of José Escobar as editor of *El Nuevo Mundo*, here and in correspondence of August 5, 1897:

> Haremos de esta correspondencia un *totum revoltijum*, como dirian mis condiscípulos del Colegio de Las Vegas. Pero antes de hacerlo, pidámosle mil perdones á Don José Segura por haber dilatado por tan largo tiempo nuestra carta. Ya se prometería él al juzgar por nuestro silencio, que en esta vez le íbamos á mandar un articulazo de política como los que engalanan las columnas de *La Voz del Pueblo*; ya se sospecharía acaso que le íbamos a dar para mi muy reverendo y señor mio una disertacion sobre Nuevo México y su pueblo, como lo viene haciendo *El Independiente*; ya esperaría tal vez un espectáculo pirotécnico de muchas flores y retóricas, de muchos versos y chascarillos, mezclados de un poquillo de *consejos* a los *agricultores* como suele hacer el *Nuevo Mundo*.
>
> No, Señor Segura: nada de esas grandezas podemos prometerle. En su veloz carrera por la via de zodiaco, el sol de Julio no ha visto al rabioso can, y por un descuido, sus endemoniados caballos han pisoteado el rabo al animal. Y en punto allí me tiene Vd. al can ahullando tan desaforadamente que los caballos del sol se han espantado, y ese bendito Astro nos tiene á todos postrados con sus rayos.
>
> Desde que nos despertamos hasta volvernos á entregar á las blandas sábanas, las horas se nos pasan en sudar gotas gruesas como cuentas de rosario conquistador. Y hé aquí la verdad del caso, Señor Segura: esta pobre Adelfa se ha visto a punto de tener un sunstroke, y por tanto ni de chanza se ha atrevido á escribirle una jota. Y así las cosas, ¿cómo puede Vd. esperar que le cantemos con plectro arrebatador como lo hacen los colegas citados? ("Correspondencia de Trinidad: Calor insufrible—Explicación—El cuatro de Julio—Juventud y amor," *El Boletín Popular*, Santa Fe, New Mexico, July 15, 1897)

62. "Cualquier observador medianamente curioso no puede menos que notar el cambio que ha ocurrido en Santa Fe y en algunas otras plazas del Territorio de algunos años a esta parte, cambio que claramente indica que poco á poco nos vamos 'americanizando.' Muchos son los indicios que ponen esto de manifiesto y hacen conocer que las costumbres y usos anteriores van lentamente desapareciendo y cediendo á prácticas nuevas á imitación de los que están en boga en los estados. Casi todos los jóvenes de veinte años abajo hablan el idioma inglés con más o menos perfección, y se han olvidado o no hacen aprecio de los juegos y diversiones que eran regla en años anteriores, y hasta los más pretenciosos imitan el tono y maneras de los recien venidos mostrandose más turcos que Mahoma en esto de parlar el inglés á todas horas del dia y de la noche, teniendo casi por mengua hablar su propia [sic] idioma." ("De la Capital: Correspondencia Particular á *El Independiente*," *El Independiente*, Las Vegas, New Mexico, October 5, 1895)

63. "Espiridión no solo amagaste e insultaste a tu futura, hiciste algo más grave, pisoteaste la gramática, las reglas métricas y el sentido común, no lo vuelvas hacer. . . .

—Pero señor, le repliqué, casi nadie estudia esas cosas y, sin embargo, todos hacemos versos. . .

—No son versos, hijo, no son versos!"

Son burradas,
que escriben entusiasmadas
ciertas gentes obsecadas

que se juzgan inspiradas
y que deberían ser aplacadas."
("Mis últimos versos, [Para *La Voz del Pueblo*] *La Voz del Pueblo*, Las Vegas, New Mexico, March 4, 1907)

Chapter 6

1. "El leer o comparar periódicos en español, no quiere decir que el idioma oficial de este gran país vaya a lesionarse en lo más mínimo." ("Un atento llamado a los hispano-americanos: Manifesto," *Revista Ilustrada*, Santa Fe, New Mexico, June, 1928)

2. In truth Aurora Lucero-White's essay forms part of a discourse of contestation that originates in earlier decades. The question of competency in English had been used time and again in the territorial period to impute the worth of *Neo-Mexicano* citizenship. Victor Ochoa, editor of *El Hispano-Americano* of Las Vegas, reported the following item in September, 1892:

> Bueno es saberlo.
> Un anglo-saxon que publica un periodico en Deming y que se llama "The New Mexico Potpourri" publica en uno de sus últimos números un extenso artículo en el que apela al pueblo americano para que no permita ningún hispano-americano ocupar puesto político alguno, apoyandose en que estos (los hispano-americanos) son ignorantes e incapaces de entender el idioma. Por demas son comentarios.
>
> [Something to Keep in Mind
> An Anglo-Saxon who publishes a paper in Deming called "The New Mexico Potpourri" prints a long article in one of his last issues in which he appeals to the *Americano* community to not permit an Hispano to occupy any public post, he supports his position (by saying) that these (the Hispanos) are ignorant and are not capable of understanding the language. No further commentaries are necessary.] ("Bueno es saberlo," *El Hispano-Americano*, Las Vegas, New Mexico, September, 7, 1892.)

3. "Somos ciudadanos americanos, es cierto, y nuestra conducta levanta nuestra lealtad y patriotismo sobre de todo reproche. Necesitamos aprender el idioma de nuestra patria y eso estamos haciendo; pero no necesitamos con tal motivo, negar nuestro origen, ni nuestra raza, ni nuestra lengua, ni nuestras tradiciones, ni nuestra historia, ni nuestro pasado ancestral, porque no nos avergonzamos de ellos, ni jamás nos avergonzaremos; lo contrario, nos enorgullecen." ("Defensa de nuestro idioma" *El Mensajero*, March 3, 1911, Mora, New Mexico)

4. A comprehensive survey of Spanish-language newspapers with the intent of listing gender-identified works by *Nuevomexicanas* would reveal both the abundance and quality of that work. José Escobar was obviously aware that many talented *Nuevomexicanas* made submissions to the newspapers. He notes in his 1896 survey of the progress of the press in New Mexico that the work of women writers often appeared anonymously: "Sino también algunos brillantes talentos de señoritas nativas que usan el pseudónimo para dar a la prensa sus composiciones poéticas en las que resaltan la pureza de los sentimientos y sus almas [But also some brilliant talents among the

young New Mexican ladies who use pseudonyms so as to give to the press their poetic compositions in which (are found) the essence of their feelings and their souls]." ("Progreso Literario de Nuevo México," *Las Dos Repúblicas*, July 11, 1896, Denver, Colorado)

5. "A mi Madre," *El Hispano Americano*, Las Vegas, New Mexico, October 15, 1892.

6. "Al poeta de LA AURORA, tan joven, tan gallardo, tan gentil mancebo, le recomiendo que abra y desenvuelva sus alas y conduzca su imaginacion, mas y mas al mundo ideal, fértil en fantasias en que el poeta olvida el mundo de la realidad, el de hoy, el mañana, el futuro, todo. Le ruego no que abandone á sus sueños que encantan, ensanchan, halagan y consuelan el corazon. Como prueba de mi cariño le dejo mi arco y flechas (no las envenenadas) para que pueda acabar de conquistar á la que hoy es la aurora de sus pensamientos." ("El testamento del Redactor-en-Gefe [sic]," *La Aurora*, August 9, 1884, Santa Fe, New Mexico)

7. Read notes in the introduction to *Prosa y Poesía*: "Escribió también versos de carácter político, cuando sólo tenía 14 años de edad, los cuales a la sazón fueron extensamente celebrados en Nuevo México [He also wrote poetry of a political nature when he was but fourteen, these in time where widely celebrated in New Mexico]." (Chacón 1924, 10)

8. Felipe Maximiliano's work first came to light in 1976 by way of research conducted by Anselmo Arellano of Las Vegas. Arellano samples Felipe Maximiliano's poetry and provides a brief biography of Chacón in *Los pobladores nuevomexicanos y su poesía: 1889–1950*. In 1978, Doris Meyer of Brooklyn College published an article outlining the importance of Chacón's 1924 collection *Poesía y Prosa*. In more recent years scholars have begun to provide a critical analysis of its content. See, for example, Gonzales-Berry, 1989.

9. In a recent interview Herminia Chacón González, Chacón's daughter, estimated that the number of copies to be around three hundred.

10. The language-shift in education was clearly in evidence by this time and *Neo-Mexicano* editors regularly noted its detrimental effect to *nativos*. *El Independiente*, for example, ran the following commentary in March 1908:

> Cuando por primera vez se abrió en Santa Fe, N.M. en Nov.—Dic. 1859 la escuela de Inglés Español de los hermanos cristianos, había en dicho plantel un profesor para cada uno de los idiomas Inglés y Español y los mismos eran enseñados propiamente según conviene á cada uno de dichos idiomas; lo cual hoy día no es así en ninguna institución priviada en Nuevo México, sino que dicho idioma español se ha creado una clase separada é independiente de enseñanza por la cual el padre—madre de tal niño—niña queriendo que se le enseñe, ha tenido que pagar aparte; . . . quedando a cargo del padre—de la madre (que así hablan) la enseñanza del idioma Español.—¿Qué castellano podemos enseñar los padres de familia cuando necesitamos que se nos enseñe? ¿ Acaso no merece dicho idioma que se enseñe propiamente?

> [When the Christian Brothers' Spanish-English school first opened its doors in Santa Fe in November or December 1859 there was in the building an instructor for each language: English and Spanish; and both were taught properly as each language requires. Today this is not the case in any private school in New Mexico, rather it is the case that the teaching of Spanish has become a separate and independent course; such that when a mother or father wish to have their son or

daughter taught in Spanish, they must pay separately for this. . . . instruction in Spanish then becomes the charge of the mother or father. What Spanish can we parents possible teach our families when it is we also who are in need of instruction. Is it not the case that this language merits being taught like any other language?] ("Comunicado," *El Independiente*, Las Vegas, New Mexico, March 4, 1909)

11. "Una prueba de lo bien que nuestro poeta ha sabido aprovechar su tiempo, es la manera en que ha alcanzado aprender y cultivar la lengua castellana, sin ninguna ayuda superior, en un pais cuyo idioma es el inglés, y donde hay pocas o ningunas oportunidades de aprender el castellano con propiedad." (ibid., 7)

12. The disparagement of *Neo-Mexicano* patriotism and loyalty often brought strong reaction from *los periodiqueros*. Nestor Montoya of *La Bandera Americana* wrote the following at the time his son Teodoro was serving in the military in Europe:

> Nuevo Mexico ha dado una prueba más de su lealtad con la sangre de sus hijos en los campos de batalla en el servicio de nuestro gobierno. . . . Y todavía no faltarán Judas que en algún tiempo quiera mancharnos—criticarnos. A esta ralea, á estos bribones, les daremos con nuestra historia en su maldita cara.
>
> [New Mexico has given yet further proof of its loyalty with the blood of its sons on the battlefields in the service of our government. . . . And yet there will not doubt be a Judas who at some time will want to besmirch or criticize us. To those of this ilk, to these rascals, we shall take our history and shove it in their damned faces]. ("Que más se le pide a Nuevo México?" *La Bandera Americana*, Albuquerque, New Mexico, December 27, 1918)

13. "Cuando iban a casarse supieron que eran hermanos," *La Estrella*, Las Cruces, New Mexico, April 26, 1924.

14. For a reading of "Eustacio and Carlota" as social allegory, see Gonzales-Berry's article "Vicente Bernal and Felipe Maximiliano Chacón: Bridging Two Cultures."

15. "Como dijimos en una de nuestras ediciones pasadas, en cada hogar Hispanoamericano debería de haber una de las obras poeticas del Sr. Chacón; ésto debería ser así por varias importantes razones. Una de ellas, que es una obra inspiradora é instructiva; la otra, que la misma nos hará conscientes del valer intelectual de nuestra raza, y creará entre nosotros un nuevo ánimo que nos hará aspirar a la norma respetable de vida que los pueblos blancos deben ocupar, en vez de seguirnos gradualmente resbalando al nivel de peonaje y la esclavitud al cual nuestro pueblo lenta pero seguramente ha ido caminando en los últimos años. ("Nuestro Ilustre Poeta" [reprint from *La Victoria*, Raton, New Mexico] *La Bandera Americana*, June 5, 1925, Albuquerque, New Mexico)

16. The title of Padilla's magazine may have been inspired by the work of publisher N. Pérez Bolet who had begun the publication of *La Revista Ilustrada de Nueva York* [The New York Illustrated Review] in 1895. See Veron A. Chamberlin, & Ivan A. Schulman. *La Revista Ilustrada de Nueva York: History, Anthology and Index of Literary Selections.* Colombia, Missouri: University of Missouri Press, 1976.

17. "Camilo Padilla Dies After Long Fight," *Santa Fe New Mexican*, Santa Fe, November 23, 1933.

18. "El objeto principal del dicho Centro será apoyar y criar interés por el idioma de nuestros mayores y la literatura española; dar conferencias sobre asuntos de interés

general, historia, etc., y tener veladas literario-musicales cada mes y establecer salones de lectura donde nuestro pueblo encuentre periodicos, magazines y libros en español y, si posible, tener una biblioteca de obras en español para uso de los socios." ("Centro de Cultura," *Revista Ilustrada,* Santa Fe, New Mexico, January, 1926 p. 6)

19. "He leído esta carta varias veces; me hé dado pellizcos por desengañarme de no estar soñando. . . . Ah, sí, soñando uno de esos sueños color de rosa de mi amigo Padilla, que con tanto heroísmo se dedica al periodismo elegante y culto en Nuevo México, como quien dice, sacrificando su vida en 'arrojar margaritas' . . . a un pueblo que no aprecia como debería tales sacrificios." ("Cosas raras de la historia de Nuevo México," *Revista Ilustrada,* Santa Fe, New Mexico, October 15, 1914)

20. "Camilo Padilla Dies After Long Fight," *Santa Fe New Mexican,* Santa Fe, November 23, 1933.

21. Genaro Padilla provides a detailed and exhaustive interpretation on the discursive practices of *Neo-Mexicana* writers of the period in his chapter "Lies, Secrets and Silence: Cultural Autobiography as Resistance in Cleofas Jaramillo's *Romance of a Little Village Girl,*" in *My History, Not Yours.*

22. Oral histories with former students who studied with Lucero at Highlands University most often reveal a familiarity with the "classic" works of Spanish Golden Age and Borroque Literature. The names of Golden Age writers such as Calderón, Cervantes, Lope de Vega, and the like punctuate their recollections of study with Lucero.

23. "Tanto periódico bueno, de gran circulación; tanto escritor español de esclarecido talento y hábil pluma que podía presentar claramente la situación en que se halla el pueblo pobre que poseé algunas varas de tierra. La unión y armonía entre los editores es deseable; ahora más que nunca, por la situación crítica en que se ve el pueblo en Nuevo México. ¿Después de despojado de sus tierras y sus casas, que pueden hacer? Obligados a enlosar pavimientos, hasta en los caminos públicos para tráfico de otros; pues jamás lo usan ellos, sino es que los pobres pasan con un triste jumento cargado de leña algunas veces. El dueño del automóvil y el estranjero "turista" esperan que les costeén esos caminos. ¡Emigrar a otros lugares? ¿Porqué y a dónde? Dejarle al estranjero por injustos medios adquirir los terrenos que por doscientos años y más han pertenecido a sus antepasados, que con espada en mano abrieron veredas por montes, selvas y entre salvajes.

Señores editiores, el trabajo no consiste en empezar la defensa; sino en parar la pluma una vez comenzada. La causa en que se dedicaran es grande, sagrada y magnífica. Vivid entre ellos, como yo lo he hecho, en pequeñas poblaciones. Tratad con la gente humilde, como se llama en este mundo. Hablad con "los ignorantes" como los clasifican los ilustres del oriente. Servid de guía, y enseñad a sus hijos." ("El Humilde Hogar," *La Revista Ilustrada,* Santa Fe, New Mexico, November, 1922)

24. "Á alentar en cuanto sea posible, á según alcanzen nuestras débiles fuerzas, la educación de las masas del pueblo." ("Salutoria," *La Bandera Americana,* Albuquerque, New Mexico, August 3, 1901)

25. "Para asi preparar á nuestros futuros ciudadanos á empuñar con firmeza las riendas y soberanía de Estado de la Unión Americana y á desempenar y gozar de nuestros privilegios como ciudadanos de esta gran República." (ibid.)

26. "Pues este particular merece la más delicada atención en vista de nuestra nacionalidad Americana." (ibid.)

27. "Creemos que no habrá un solo hombre en el Territorio que oponga nuestro aserto en generalizar tal idioma." (ibid.)

28. "Nuestras riquezas en todos los tres ramos aludidos son incalculables y solo se necesita inducir la capital para explotrarlos para cambiar la faz y porvenir de nuestro suelo y hacer la felicidad de nuestros habitantes." (ibid.)

29. "La Union de la Prensa Hispana," *La Bandera Americana*, Albuquerque, New Mexico, February 24, 1928.

30. "He visto con tristeza que muchos de los hispano-americanos, por razones que no quiero investigar, pero que nadie ignora tienen predilección por los periódicos escritos en inglés, seguramente por llevar "la corriente" como se dice vulgarmente o porque de hecho no se han percatado de la necesidad de conservar el idioma de nuestros padres, nuestras costumbres y tradiciones, que por ser muy nuestras deberíamos jamás echarlas al olvido." ("Un atento llamado a los Hispano-americanos: Manifiesto," *Revista Ilustrada*, Santa Fe, New Mexico, June, 1928)

31. "Es de parecer que el periodismo hispano es un medio para explotar bobos, pues se conforman con utilizar sus columnas para hacer juego de política de barrio, y por desgracia, fuera de la 'olla' esto es, fuera de tiempo." ("La prensa hispana se hace valer o desaparece," *La Bàndera Americana*, Albuquerque, New Mexico, August 15, 1929)

32. "[La Voz de Pueblo] está en manos de un tejano que apenas puede escribir el idioma nacional que ni por cortesía se interesa en masticar el idioma hispano, pero sí publica unas cuantas columnas en español a los "mexicans" que por desgracia reciben su pasquín." (ibid.)

33. "Que puede beneficiar á la raza latina más que ningún otro, esto es, la asociación de la prensa española en Nuevo México, Arizona, California, Texas y parte de México." ("La Prensa Asociada Hispano-Americana," *La Voz del Pueblo*, Las Vegas, New Mexico, March 5, 1892)

34. "Ahora en 1958 cuando los jefes de familia de 'la santa raza,' son usualmente tan proficientes tanto en inglés como en español, pero como las generaciones jóvenes pueden leer solamente el inglés, ha habido 'movimientos de mayoría,' en muchos hogares de recibir el periódico en inglés en lugar del español. Por esta razón, esta primavera, *El Nuevo Mexicano* se convierte en la novia del *New Mexican* y hasta toma su apellido." ("El fin de una época," *El Nuevo Mexicano*, Santa Fe, New Mexico, April 30, 1958)

Epilogue

1. Herminia Chacón González letter, October 7, 1995, El Paso, Texas.

2. (ibid.)

3. The statement in the orignial Spanish is: "Vieniron a El Paso porque Felix Martínez se trajo a un grupo de personas de Nuevo México para establecer negocios aqui." Herminia Chacón González interview, November 24, 1995, El Paso, Texas.

4. López completed a master's thesis at the University of Denver in 1942 with the title "The Spanish Heritage in the San Luis Valley," and which was later published. Lorin Brown was well known among folklorists for her involvement in the Federal Writers' Project of the W.P.A. in New Mexico.

5. "Teníamos que reportar propaganda Nazi y opiniones de los periódicos mexicanos encontra o *pro* los Estados Unidos." (ibid.)

6. "Pues, era una persona muy independiente. Era White entonces. Y tenía una hija. Se vinieron para acá, y no se cómo decirle . . . no era pretenciosa, y le importaba poco de lo que dijera la gente. Ella hacía lo que le daba la gana." (ibid.)

7. "Al fin se acaba la guerra y nosotros aquí escribiendo papelitos que no valen la pena." (ibid.)

8. "Pues, de vez en cuando se me ocurrían cosas." (ibid.)

9. The three preceding quotes are transcribed as recorded since by this point the interview was being conducted in English. (ibid.)

10. Pedro Ribera-Ortega interview, December 6, 1995

11. "Fin de una época," *El Nuevo Mexicano,* Santa Fe, New Mexico, April 30, 1958.

12. Herminia Chacón Gonzales interview, November 24, 1995, El Paso, Texas.

Sources Cited

Primary sources

Newspapers

El Amigo del Pueblo, Raton, New Mexico; weekly, Spanish; January 8, 1896.

El Anunciador de Nuevo Méjico, Las Vegas, New Mexico; weekly, Spanish; January 12, 1878.

La Aurora, Revista Semanal Independiente, Santa Fe, New Mexico; weekly, Spanish; June 14–November 8, 1884.

La Bandera Americana, Semanario Dedicado a los intereses y Progreso del Pueblo Neo-Mexicano, Albuquerque, New Mexico; weekly; English and Spanish; May 6, 1895–c. December 3, 1938.

Boletín de Anuncios, [Advertisement] Las Vegas, New Mexico; Spanish; 1877.

El Boletín Popular, Periódico Político, Literario y de Anuncios, Santa Fe, New Mexico; weekly, Spanish; 1893; c. October 21, 1885–c. 1910.

La Chachiporra, Las Vegas, New Mexico; weekly, Spanish; October 19, 1888–December 28, 1890.

El Combate, Mora, New Mexico; weekly, Spanish; March 1902–1910; 1914–September 15, 1917.

La Crónica de Mora, Mora, New Mexico; weekly, English and Spanish, Spanish; June 1889–January, 1890; 1894–1896.

El Defensor del Pueblo, Albuquerque, New Mexico; weekly, Spanish; June 27, 1891–May 28, 1892.

Las Dos Américas, El Paso, Texas; weekly, Spanish; March 7–March 21, 1898; June 11–June 18, 1898; July 25, 1898.

Las Dos Repúblicas, Denver, Colorado, and Trinidad, Colorado; weekly, Spanish; January 11, 1896–March 13, 1897.

El Eco de Norte, Mora, New Mexico; weekly, Spanish; August 31, 1908–1922.

El Eco del Valle, Las Cruces, New Mexico; weekly, Spanish; November 18, 1905–October 13, 1917.

La Estrella, Las Cruces, New Mexico; weekly, Spanish; February 6, 1910–December 26, 1931.

La Estrella de Nuevo México, Socorro, New Mexico; weekly, Spanish; March 26, 1897.

La Gaceta de Mora and *Mora Gazetta,* Mora, New Mexico; weekly, English and Spanish; March 27–November 22, 1890; January 1891.

El Gato, Santa Fe, New Mexico; weekly, Spanish; May 25, 1894; June 1–June 29, 1894; July 20–July 27, 1894; August 24, 1894.

El Hispano-Americano, Organo de la Orden de los Caballeros de Mutua Proteccion, Las Vegas, New Mexico; weekly, Spanish; April 7, 1892–November 1, 1920.

La Hormiga de Oro, Albuquerque, New Mexico; weekly; Spanish, November 7, 1903.

El Independiente, Dedicado a los mejores intereses del estado de Nuevo Mexico y en particular del condado de San Miguel, Las Vegas, New Mexico; weekly, Spanish; March 24, 1894–c. August 24, 1928.

El Indito, Albuquerque, New Mexico; weekly, Spanish; November 24–December 8, 1900; April 4, 1901.

El Mensajero, Periodico Politico, de Variedades y Anuncios. Mora, New Mexico; weekly, Spanish; June 10, 1910–1912.

El Mosquito, Mora, New Mexico; weekly, English and Spanish; November 1891–June 30, 1892.

El Nuevo Mexicano, Santa Fe, New Mexico; weekly, Spanish; August 2, 1890–April 30, 1958.

El Nuevo Mundo, Albuquerque, New Mexico; weekly, Spanish; May 1– December 25, 1897; January 1, 1898; May 18–December 7, 1899; January 4–September 20, 1900.

La Opinión Pública, Albuquerque, New Mexico; weekly, Spanish; July 2, 1892–October 2, 1892.

El Progreso, Trinidad, Colorado; weekly, Spanish, 1891–1944.

El Sol de Mayo, Periodico Independiente, de Noticias, Variedades y Anuncios, Las Vegas, New Mexico; weekly, English and Spanish; January 18, 1894–November 22, 1894.

La Revista Católica, Las Vegas, New Mexico and El Paso, Texas; weekly, Spanish; January 2, 1875–September 16, 1962.

La Revista de Taos, Periódico Liberal e Independiente, del pueblo, para el pueblo y por el pueblo, Taos, New Mexico; weekly, Spanish; September 24, 1909–1911.

La Revista de Taos, Ilustrada, Taos, New Mexico; monthly, Spanish; June 1919.

La Revista Ilustrada, Santa Fe, New Mexico; monthly, English and Spanish; November 1907–May 1931.

El Tiempo, Las Cruces, New Mexico; weekly, Spanish, October 5, 1882–July 8, 1911.

La Voz del Pueblo, Santa Fe, New Mexico, weekly, Spanish, August 11, 1888–December, 1888; February 2, 1889.

La Voz del Pueblo, Semanario Dedicado a los Intereses y Progreso Del Pueblo Hispano-Americano, Las Vegas, New Mexico; weekly, English and Spanish; June 14, 1890–February 10, 1927.

Manuscript and Document Sources

Arellano, Anselmo, F. "Through Thick and Thin: Evolutionary Transition of Las Vegas Grandes and its *Pobladores.*" Ph. D. Diss., University of New Mexico, 1990.

The Golden Jubilee, University of St. Louis Yearbook, 1872 (St. Louis, Mo: St. Louis University, 1872) (Courtesy of Mrs. Lucy M. Lucero).

Lucero-White Lea, Aurora. "Kearny Takes New Mexico." Unpublished one-act play. Donnelly Library, New Mexico Highlands University.

———. "Folk Dance Book" (chapbook, 1936).

———. "Los Pastores" (bilingual English/Spanish, 1940).

Vollmar, Edward, R. "History of the Jesuit Colleges of New Mexico and Colorado, 1867–1919." M.A. Thesis, Saint Louis University, 1939.

Walter, Paul, Jr. "The Press as a Source in the Study of Social Problems." M.A. Thesis, University of New Mexico, 1933.

Who's Who in New Mexico (1937)

Interviews

Arellano, Anselmo. Interview with the author. Las Vegas, New Mexico, July 7, 1991; August 6, 1991; November 9, 1991; January 10, 1992.

C. de Baca, Elba. Interview with the author. San Gerónimo, New Mexico, July 15, 1987.

Chacón González, Herminia. Interview with the author. El Paso, Texas, November 24, 1995.

Lucero, Mrs. Lucy M. Interview with the author. Albuquerque, New Mexico, October 24, 1991.

Ribera-Ortega, Pedro. Interview with the author. Santa Fe, New Mexico, December 6, 1995; telephone interview, April 17, 1996.

Sosa, John. Interview with the author. Santa Fe, New Mexico, February, 8, 1992.

Broadsides, Circulars, Documents, Newspaper Articles

Baca, Eleuterio. Letter to Benito. St. Louis Missouri, September 23, 1871 (courtesy of Lucy M. Lucero).

"Colorful Victor Ochoa Still Lives: Scholarly Essay on El Tambor Mineral is Evidence," *El Paso Times*, El Paso, Texas, July 15, 1940.

Escobar, José. Letter of reference for Jesús Enrique Sosa. June 1, 1899 (courtesy of John Phillip Sosa).

Office of State Records and Archives. Santa Fe, New Mexico. Prince papers, Contemporary New Mexicans. "Latest, Up-to-Date History of New Mexico." New Mexican Publishing Company circular, June 1911.

———. Santa Fe, New Mexico. Benjamín M. Read Series II, "Rafael Chacón, 1911." Rafael Chacón, correspondence to Benjamín M. Read. June 9, 1911; June 22, 1911; July 1, 1911; December 18, 1911, and December 21, 1911.

———. Santa Fe, New Mexico. Benjamín M. Read Series II, "Rafael Chacón, 1911." Benjamín M. Read, correspondence to Rafael Chacón. June 20, 1911; June 23, 1911 and July 3, 1911.

Ribera-Ortega, Pedro. "*El Nuevo Mexicano" del pasado en Santa Fe.*" monograph. Santa Fe, New Mexico, 1992.

Sosa, Jesús Enrique. "Instruccion Primaria Para Niños de Villa Lerdo, Diciembre de 1885." Circular (courtesy of John Phillip Sosa).

———. Personal letter to Lucita A. de Sosa. San Juan, New Mexico, May 20, 1904 (courtesy of John Phillip Sosa).

Territorial Archives of New Mexico, Roll 103, FR 998. Camilo Padilla, letter to L. Bradford Prince. New York, June 6, 1889,

Trinidad Public Library, vertical files. "Cuarenta Años de Legislador, ó la biografía del Senador Casimiro Barela." El Progreso Publishing Company circular, August 1911.

Secondary Sources

Books

Acuña, Rodolfo. *Occupied America, A History of Chicanos.* 2d ed. New York: Harper and Row, 1981.

Anderson, George, B. *Illustrated History of New Mexico: Its Resources and its People.* Chicago: Pacific States Publishing, 1907.

Arellano, Anselmo. *Los pobladores nuevomexicanos y su poesía: 1889– 1950.* Albuquerque: Pajarito, 1976.

———. *Las Vegas Grandes on the Gallinas: 1835–1985.* Las Vegas: Telaraña, 1985.

Bakhtin, M. M. *Art and Answerability: Early Philosophical Essays by M. M. Bakhtin.* Translation and notes by Vadim Liapunov. Austin: University of Texas Press, 1990.

Bancroft, Hubert Howe. *The Works of Hubert Howe Bancroft: History of New Mexico and Arizona.* San Francisco: The History Company, 1889.

Bruce-Novoa, Juan. *Retrospace: Collected Essays on Chicano Literature.* Houston: Arte Público Press, 1990.

Cabeza de Baca, Fabiola. *We Fed Them Cactus.* Albuquerque: University of New Mexico Press, [1954] 1994.

Campa, Arthur León. *Spanish Folk Poetry in New Mexico.* Albuquerque: University of New Mexico Press, 1946.

Coan, Charles. *A History of New Mexico.* Chicago: American Historical Society, 1925.

Chacón, Eusebio. *El hijo de la tempestad y Tras la tormenta, la calma.* Santa Fe: Tipografía del Boletín Popular, 1892.

Chacón Felipe, Maximiliano. *Obras de Felipe Maximiliano Chacón, El Cantor Nuevomexicano: Poesía y Prosa,* Albuquerque: New Mexico: Tipografía de La Bandera Americana, 1924.

Chamberlin, Vernon, A., and Ivan A. Schulman. *La Revista Ilustrada de Nueva York: History, Anthology and Index of Literary Selections.* Colombia, Missouri: University of Missouri Press, 1976.

Chávez, John. *The Lost Land: A Chicano Image of the Southwest.* Albuquerque: University of New Mexico Press, 1989.

Davidson, Cathy N.; ed. *Reading in America, Literature and History.* Baltimore: John Hopkins University Press, 1989.

Davis, W. W. H. *El Gringo, New Mexico and Her People.* New York: Harper, 1857; reprint, Lincoln: University of Nebraska Press, 1982.

Deutsch, Sarah. *Not Separate Refuge: Culture, Class, and Gender on an Anglo-Hispanic Frontier in the American Southwest, 1880–1940.* Oxford: Oxford University Press, 1987.

Fernández, Emilio, E. *Cuarenta años de legislador, o la vida de don Casimiro Barela.* Trinidad: Compañía Publicista de El Progreso, 1915.

Gonzales-Berry, Erlinda, ed. *Pasó por aquí: Critical essays on the New Mexican Literary Tradition 1542–1988.* Albuquerque: University of New Mexico Press, 1989.

Goody, Jack. *Literacy in Traditional Societies.* London: Cambridge University Press, 1968.

Grove, Pearce S. et. al., eds. *New Mexico Newspapers: A Comprehensive Guide to Bibliographical Entries and Locations.* Albuquerque: University of New Mexico and Eastern New Mexico University Press, 1975.

Gutiérrez, Ramón, and Genaro Padilla, eds. *Recovering the U.S. Hispanic Literary Heritage Project.* Houston: Arte Público Press, 1993.

Hall, David D., et. al., eds. *Printing and Society in Early America.* Worcester: American Antiquarian Society, 1983.

Harwood, Thomas, Rev. *History of New Mexico Spanish and English Mission of the Methodist Episcopal Church from 1850 to 1910.* Vol. 1. Albuquerque: El Abogado Press, 1908; reprint, Albuquerque: Newly Edited, 1983.

Henríquez Ureña, Pedro. *Las corrientes literarias en la América Hispana.* México: Fondo de Cultura Económica, 1949.

An Illustrated History of New Mexico. Chicago: Lewis Publishing, 1895.

Lucero-White Lea, Aurora. *The Folklore of New Mexico.* Santa Fe: Seton Village Press, 1941.

———. *Los Hispanos.* Sage Books: Denver, 1947.

———. *Literary Folklore of the Hispanic Southwest.* Santa Fe: Seton Village Press, 1948.

———. *Juan Bobo, Adapted from the Spanish Folktale Bertoldo.* New York: Vantage Press, 1962.

McWilliams, Carey. *North From Mexico: The Spanish-Speaking People of the United States.* New York: Greenwood Press, 1970.

Martínez, José Luis. *La expresión nacional.* México: Cien de México, 1993.

Meketa, Jacqueline, Dorgan. *Legacy of Honor: The Life of Rafael Chacón, A Nineteeth Century New Mexican.* Albuquerque: University of New Mexico Press, 1986.

Montejano, David. *Anglos and Mexicans in the Making of Texas, 1836 1986.* Austin: University of Texas Press, 1987.

Navarro Tomás, T. *Arte del Verso.* México: Colección Málaga, 1968.

Noticias Históricas y estadísticas de la antigua provincia del Nuevo México presentadas por sus diputados en cortes D. Pedro Bautista Pino, en Cadiz en el año de 1812, anotadas por el Lic. D. Antonio Barriero en 1839 y ultimamente por el Lic. José Agustín de Escudero. Mexico: Imprenta de Lara, 1849.

Ong, Walter. *Orality and Literacy: The Technologizing of the Word.* New York: Matheun, 1988.

Padilla, Genaro. *My History, Not Yours: The Formation of Mexican American Autobiography.* Madison: University of Wisconsin Press, 1993.

Padre Martínez: New Perspectives From Taos. Taos: Milicent Rodgers Museum, 1988.

Patterson, C. S. *Representative New Mexicans.* Denver, Colorado, 1912.

Paz, Octavio, ed. *Anthology of Mexican Poetry.* Translated by Samuel Beckett. Bloomington: Indiana University Press, 1973.

Prince, L. Bradford. *A Concise History of New Mexico.* Cedar Rapids, Iowa: The Torch Press, 1912.

Read, Benjamín M. *Guerra México-Americana.* Santa Fe: Compañía Impresora del Nuevo Mexicano, 1910.

———. *Historia Ilustrada de Nuevo México.* Santa Fe: New Mexican Publishing, 1911.

———. *Ilustrated History of New Mexico.* Translated to English by Eleuterio Baca, Santa Fe: New Mexican Publishing, 1911.

Rebolledo, Diana, et. al., eds. *Nuestras mujeres: Hispanas of New Mexico, 1582–1992.* Albuquerque: El Norte Publications, 1992.

Rosenbaum, Robert, J. *Mexicano Resistance in the Southwest.* Austin: University of Texas Press, 1981.

Saldívar, Ramón, *Chicano Narrative: The Dialectics of Difference.* Madison: University of Wisconsin Press, 1990.

Salpointe, Jean Bautiste, *Soldiers of the Cross.* Banning, CA: St. Boniface Industrial School, 1898; reprint, Albuquerque: Calvin Horn, 1967.

Sánchez, Pedro. *Memorias sobre la vida del presbítero don Antonio José Martínez.* Translated by Ray John de Aragón. Santa Fe: The Lightning Tree Press, 1978.

Stanley, F. *Ciudad de Santa Fe: Territorial Days, 1846–1912.* Pampa, Texas: Pampa Print Shop, 1965.

Steele, Thomas, J. *Folk and Church.* Colorado Springs, Col.: Hulbert Center Press of Colorado College, 1993.

The Southwestern Journals of Adolph F. Bandelier, 1880–1882. Edited and annotated by Charles H. Lange and Carroll L. Riley. Albuquerque, University of New Mexico Press, 1966.

The Southwestern Journals of Adolph F. Bandelier, 1889–1892. Edited and annotated by Charles H. Lange, Carroll L. Riley and Elizabeth Lange. Albuquerque, University of New Mexico Press, 1984.

Stratton, Porter A. *The Territorial Press of New Mexico, 1834–1912.* Albuquerque: The University of New Mexico Press, 1969.

Twitchell, Ralph, Emerson. *The Leading Facts of New Mexican History.* Ceder Rapids, Iowa: The Torch Press, 1917.

Varela, Félix. *Jicoténcatl.* Edited by Luis Leal and Rodolfo J. Cortina. Houston: Arte Público Press, 1995.

Weber, David, J. *Foreigners in Their Native Land: The Historical Roots of Mexican Americans.* Albuquerque, University of New Mexico Press, 1973.

Whaley, Charolette. *Nina Otero-Warren of Santa Fe.* Albuquerque: University of New Mexico Press, 1994.

White, Hayden. *Tropics of Discourse, Essays in Cultural Criticism.* Baltimore, John Hopkins, 1979.

Articles

"Aurora Lucero-White Lea." *Santa Fe Mirror,* 1961, 209–12.

Bloom, Lansing. "Barreiro's Ojeada Sobre Nuevo México." *New Mexico Historical Review* 3 (1928): 73–96, 145–78.

Campa, Arthur León. "A Bibliography of Spanish Folk-Lore in New Mexico." *University of New Mexico Bulletin* 2, no. 3 (September, 1930): 1–4.

———. "Today's Troubadors." *New Mexico Magazine*, September 1936, 16–17, 49–50.

Castillo, Lupe, and Hermanio Ríos. "Towards a True Chicano Bibliography: Mexican American Newspapers 1848–1942." *El Grito* 3, no. 4 (Summer 1970): 17–24.

———. Part II: "Towards a True Chicano Bibliography: Mexican American Newspapers 1848–1942." *El Grito* 5, no. 4 (Summer, 1972): 40–47.

Cortes, Carlos, E. "The Mexican American Press." In *The Ethnic Press in the United States: A Historical Analysis and Handbook*, edited by Sally M. Miller, 247–60. New York: Greenwood Press, 1987.

Darnton, Robert. "What is the History of Books." In *Reading in America*, edited by Cathy N. Davidson, 27–52. Baltimore: John Hopkins University, 1989.

Gonzales, Juan. "Forgotten Pages: Spanish Language Newspapers in the Southwest." *Journalism History* 4, no. 2 (1977): 50–52.

Gonzales, Phillip B. "The Political Construction of Latino Nomenclatures in Twentieth-Century New Mexico." *Journal of the Southwest* 35, no. 2 (Summer 1993): 158–85.

"The Greaser." *The Atlantic Monthly* 83 (June 1899): 750–60.

Gutiérrez, Felix. "Reporting for La Raza: The History of Latino Journalism in America." *The Media* (July/August, 1978): 29–35.

Gutiérrez, Ramón A. "Aztlán, Montezuma and New Mexico: The Political Uses of American Indian Mythology." In *Aztlan: Essays on the Chicano Homeland*, edited by Rudolfo A. Anaya and Francisco Lomelí, 172–87. Albuquerque: El Norte/Academia Publications, 1989.

Issac, Rhys. "Books and the Social Authority of Learning: The Case of Mid-Eighteenth Century Virginia." In *Printing and Society in Early America*, edited by David Hall et. al., 228–49. Worcester, N.Y.: American Antiquarian Society, 1983.

Kanellos, Nicolás. "A Socio-Historic Study of Hispanic Newspapers in the United States." In *Recovering the U.S. Hispanic Literary Heritage*, edited by Ramón Gutiérrez and Genaro Padilla, 107–28. Houston: Arte Público Press, 1993.

Leal, Luis. "*La Gaceta* (1879–1881) de Santa Bárbara: su contenido literario," unpublished manuscript, 1994.

Lomelí, Francisco. "Eusebio Chacón: An Early Pioneer of the New Mexican Novel." In *Pasó por Aquí, Essays on the New Mexican Hispanic Literary Tradition 1542–1988*, edited by Erlinda Gonzales-Berry, 149–66. Albuquerque: University of New Mexico Press, 1989.

———. "A Literary Portrait of New Mexico: Dialectics of Perspective." In *Pasó por Aquí, Essays on the New Mexican Hispanic Literary Tradition 1542–1988*, edited by Erlinda Gonzales-Berry, 131–48. Albuquerque: University of New Mexico Press, 1989.

Lucero, Antonio. "Homely Virtues of the Spanish Americans." *Old Santa Fe Magazine* 1, no. 4 (1913–1914): 442–46.

———. "Early School Days in New Mexico." *Old Santa Fe Magazine* 2 (1914–1915): 200–205.

Lucero, Aurora. "Shall the Spanish Language be Taught in the Public Schools of New Mexico?" In *Normal University Bulletin* 23 (January 1911): no pagination.

McMurtrie, Douglas C. "The History of Early Printing in New Mexico: With a Bibliography of the Known Issues of the New Mexican Press, 1834–1860." *New Mexico Historical Review* 4 (1929): 372–410.

———. "El Payo de Nuevo Méjico." *New Mexico Historical Review* 8 (1933): 130–38.

Mares, E. A. "The Wraggle-Taggle Outlaws: Vicente Silva and Billy the Kid as Seen in Two Nineteenth-Century Hispanic Documents." In *Pasó por aquí: Critical essays on the New Mexican Literary Tradition 1542-1988,* edited by Erlinda Gonzales-Berry, 167–82. Albuquerque: University of New Mexico Press, 1989.

Meyer, Doris, L. "Anonymous Poetry in Spanish-Language New Mexico Newspapers, 1880-1900." *The Bilingual Review/La Revista Bilingüe* 2 (1975): 75–91.

———. "The Language Issue in New Mexico, 1880–1900: Mexican-American Resistance Against Cultural Erosion." *The Bilingual Review/La revista bilingüe* 2, no. 3 (1977): 99–106.

———. "Early Mexican American Response to Negative Stereotyping." *The New Mexico Historical Review* 53, no. 1 (1978): 75–91.

———. "Felipe Maximiliano Chacón: A Forgotten Mexican-American Author." In *New Directions in Chicano Scholarship,* edited by Ricardo Romo and Raymund Paredes, 111–26. San Diego, University of California at San Diego, 1978.

———. "The Poetry of José Escobar: Mexican Emigre in New Mexico." *Hispania* 61 (1978): 24–34.

"Necrology (Benjamín M. Read)," *Old Santa Fe Magazine* 3, no. 10 (July 1916): 291–96.

Oczon, Annabelle, M. "Bilingual Spanish Language Newspapers in Territorial New Mexico." *New Mexico Historical Review* 54, no. 1 (1979): 45–52.

Salvino, Dana Nelson. "The Word in Black and White: Ideologies of Race and Literature in Antebellum America." In *Reading in America,* edited by Cathy N. Davidson, 140–56. Baltimore: John Hopkins University Press, 1989.

Smith, Patricia Clark. "Acheans, Americanos, Prelates and Monsters in Willa Cather's *Death Comes for the Archbishop* As New World Odyssey." In *Padre Martínez: New Perspectives from Taos,* 101–24, Taos, New Mexico: Millicent Rogers Museum, 1988.

Steele, Thomas J. "The Poet, the Archbishop and the Heavenly Jerusalem: Romanticizing Lamy's 1851 Arrival in Santa Fe." In *Folk and Church,* 104–17. Colorado Springs, Col.: Hulbert Center Press of Colorado College, 1993.

Wagner, Henry R. "New Mexico Spanish Press." *New Mexico Historical Review* 12 (1937): 1–40.

Zobray, Ronald, J. "The Railroad, the Community, and the Book." *Southwest Review* 71 (1986): 474–87.

Index

About the Author

A. Gabriel Meléndez is Professor and Chair of American Studies and a faculty associate of the Southwest Hispanic Research Institute at the University of New Mexico. He is coeditor of *The Multicultural Southwest: A Reader* (University of Arizona Press, 2001). His other works include *Reflexiones del Corazón* (1993) and *Recovering Nuevomexicano Life-Narratives: The Biography of Casimiro Barela* (2003).